GIAMBATTISTA VICO
(See Note 212)

The Autobiography of
GIAMBATTISTA VICO

Translated from the Italian by

MAX HAROLD FISCH

and

THOMAS GODDARD BERGIN

Cornell Paperbacks

CORNELL UNIVERSITY PRESS

ITHACA AND LONDON

First printing, April 1944, by Cornell University Press
Second printing, November 1944
First printing for Great Seal Books 1963
First printing, Cornell Paperbacks, 1975
Second printing 1983

Published in the United Kingdom by Cornell University Press Ltd., London.

International Standard Book Number 0-8014-9088-X
Printed in the United States of America

PREFACE

Vɪᴄᴏ has long been regarded as the greatest of Italian philosophers. Two centuries have passed since his death and the definitive edition of his major work, the *Scienza nuova*. Only small parts of that work, and a few passages quoted from his other writings, have so far appeared in English translation.

The first complete English version of any of his writings is that here offered of his autobiography, with which students of his thought have generally found it advisable to begin. Aside from the light it sheds on his other works, and the interest it has in common with every other intellectual autobiography, Vico's has the unique interest of being the first application of the genetic method by an original thinker to his own writings.

Vico's Italian bristles with difficulties even for Italians, and it is not likely that we have resolved them all. To preserve something of the flavor of the original, we have translated literally wherever a literal rendering seemed readily intelligible; but we have broken up most of his longer periods, and have resorted to paraphrase and bracketed insertions wherever we saw no other way to achieve clarity.

The text we have followed is that of the Laterza edition of Vico's works, Volume V, Bari, 1929, edited by Croce and Nicolini; and many of the notes to our translation have been adapted from those in that edition, to which the reader is referred for further details.

The translation is a work of collaboration. For the introduction, notes and chronological table I alone am responsible. In Major Bergin's absence overseas, the book has gone to press without the benefit of his proofreading.

G. H. Sabine made helpful comments on an early draft of the introduction. James Hutton shed light on some difficult passages in the translation. Giuseppe Cherubini listened to a reading of the translation with the original in hand and improved the rendering at several points.

If the introduction seems disproportionately long, that is because it is intended to serve also for the translation of the *Scienza nuova* which we hope shortly to publish.

April 1944   **M. H. F.**

For the second printing a few slight changes have been made in the introduction, and the translation has been extensively revised, with the help of Elio Gianturco and other friendly critics. To section IV E of the introduction there should now be added a reference to the penetrating, though admittedly one-sided, interpretation of Vico in Laurence Stapleton's *Justice and World Society*.

September 1944   **M. H. F.**

For the Great Seal Books printing, a few further corrections have been made in the introduction and translation, and some supplementary notes have been added on pages 222–222B.

                                                           M. H. F.
                                                           T. G. B.
June 1962

CONTENTS

INTRODUCTION

I. Porcía's "Proposal" and Vico's Autobiography

IN 1728 there appeared at Venice a pocket-size book of about five hundred pages, announcing itself as volume one of a quarterly *Raccolta d' Opusculi Scientifici e Filologici.* It proposed to include articles in theology, ethics, sacred and profane history, "erudition," mathematics, physics, "and even poetry, but only if the compositions be original and distinguished, so that our readers will perhaps encounter few contributions in this field."

Its editor was a young Camaldolite monk, Don Angelo Calogerà; its patroness was the Duchess of Parma and Piacenza, Countess Palatine, sister of the late Empress Eleanor, and mother of the Queen of Spain. Calogerà owed her patronage, and several of the articles in this first volume, to the kind offices of Count Antonio Vallisnieri, Professor of Medicine at Padua and member of the Royal Society of London.

The volume opens with a letter to Vallisnieri from a physician of Rome, describing a birth of vipers through the mouth of their mother; a long and learned reply by Vallisnieri showing that this is anatomically possible and under what conditions it may occur; and an appendix rejecting the suggestion of William Derham that this was no birth, but that the frightened mother had taken her offspring into her mouth and then released them when the danger was past. There follows a description, introduced by Vallisnieri, of a "planisferologium" invented and executed for the Duchess by one Bernardo Facino. This is "a little machine employing numerous inventions to represent, on a vertical plane thirteen inches in diameter, all that goes on from moment to moment within the *primum mobile*—the courses of the brightest stars of the firmament, the sun, the moon, its epicycle and dragon's head; that is to say, the essentials of astronomy according to the most accurate ephemerides." And in the latter part of the volume there is a history of the city of Prato, a life of the sixteenth-century historian Gualdo, a review of a recent edition of the *Decameron,* and a "defense of the promiscuous use of 'your excellency' and 'you.' "

Between these two groups of articles there is "A Proposal to the Scholars of Italy" to write their autobiographies for the edification of young students and with a view to the reform of school curricula and methods. This proposal, animated by a desire "for the advancement of learning in Italy our illustrious fatherland," is followed by much the longest article in the volume, the autobiography of Giambattista Vico, which is offered as a model. The prospective contributor is asked to relate the time and place of his birth, his parentage, and all the episodes of his life which make it remarkable or curious, so far as they can without shame be published to the world and to posterity. He is asked to weave into his narrative an exact and detailed account of all his studies. Beginning with grammar, let him say how it was taught him, whether by the methods in common use, or by some novel one; if the latter, whether it merits approval or not, and why. Proceeding thus from art to art, from science to science, let him point out the abuses and prejudices of schools and teachers, or praise their orderly curricula and sound methods, as the case may be. Let him say not only what is well and what is ill taught in the schools, but what is not taught that should be. Let him then pass on to the particular art or science to which he has devoted himself; the authors he has followed or shunned, and why; the works he has published or is preparing; how they have been criticized, what he has said or might say in defense of them, and what he would now retract. Let him candidly confess his errors, and defend only what seems defensible after due consideration, "with generous neutrality."

Finally, it is emphasized that the proposal is addressed only to creative scholars. "Those who have published nothing but sonnets or the like slender poems, or legal books, or treatises on moral theology, or other things of that sort, will find no place among our men of letters."

About two hundred years later the members of the American Philosophical Association, by a referendum vote, chose certain of their number to write brief intellectual autobiographies, which were published in two volumes in 1930 under the title *Contemporary American Philosophy: Personal Statements.* Each contributor was asked to state his principal philosophic beliefs, the reasons supporting them, and the manner in which he had reached them. It was hoped that the publication of these philosophic autobiographies would serve the purpose of clarifying the minds of the writers and of helping their students to a better understanding of their specific doctrines. This venture was inspired by a similar one in England, and that in turn by a much more ambitious German series going back to 1920: *Die Philosophie der Gegenwart in Selbstdarstellungen,* whose editor took as his motto Fichte's saying that "the kind of philosophy a man chooses depends upon the kind of man he is." In the same decade there were similar collections for various sciences and professions, and the practice became so familiar that it is difficult now to realize the novelty of the Venetian proposal in its own time, or to do justice to the features that distinguish it from any later venture of the same general kind. The novelty is apparent from the fact that autobiography as a literary form was as yet without a name, and the model was called simply "Life of Giambattista Vico written by himself." The distinctive features of the project were these: (a) its primarily pedagogical intent; (b) the representation of all the arts and sciences; (c) a uniform plan for all the autobiographies; and (d) a comprehensive critical supplement to the entire collection.

The proposal bore the name of Count Gian Artico di Porcía, but it was no private crotchet or sudden craze; its sponsors included such recognized scholars as Vallisnieri, Muratori, Scipione Maffei, Apostolo Zeno, and Count Pier Jacopo Martelli; and it had been under discussion at Venice for many years. Father Carlo Lodoli, censor of publications, for instance, had given much thought to the art of writing one's own life, and had coined a Greek name for it. He called it periautography, and its practitioners periautographers. He had collected materials for a treatise expounding and illustrating the art, and had addressed an outline of it to Count Porcía. He had hoped to associate himself with the Count in promoting his enterprise, but his more pressing duties had obliged him to deny himself that pleasure.

Count Porcía himself had made some progress, he said, in the years before 1720, when the death of his chief collaborator had led him to set the project aside for a time. It seems highly probable, indeed, that the initial impetus came as early as 1714, and from the greatest philosopher then living. Louis Bourguet was at that time in Venice, and was in frequent correspondence with Leibniz. On March 22, 1714, Leibniz wrote him from Vienna as follows:

Others besides yourself have expressed to me their esteem for Abbé Conti. . . . Provided one day he gives us something handsome in his own right, we must not begrudge him the glory-spur of wishing to be thought original. Descartes would have had us believe that he had read scarcely anything. That was a bit too much. Yet it is good to study the discoveries of others in a way that discloses to us the source of the inventions and renders them in a sort our own. *And I wish that authors would give us the history of their discoveries and the steps by which they have arrived at them.* When they neglect to do so, we must try to divine these steps, in order to profit the more from their works. If the critics would do this for us in reviewing books, they would render a great service to the public.[1]

Though Conti had recently begun a long sojourn in France and England and did not return until 1726,[2] Leibniz's suggestion was certainly passed on to him, and perhaps by him to his friend Porcía. In any case Bourguet was in touch with the other scholars of Venice and Padua, and we may be sure that Leibniz's letter became a matter of discussion among them, in the course of which Porcía's project gradually took shape.

After the lapse of a few years following 1720 (during which he composed two mediocre tragedies), Porcía had revived his enterprise, and a number of autobiographies had been collected by individual solicitation, not only at Venice and Padua and other northern cities, but also at Rome and Naples. Among these was Vico's. The time was now ripe for an appeal to the learned public at large. From those which had been and should yet be submitted, a careful selection would be made, so as to represent all the arts and sciences by autobiographies of the living Italians who had attained the greatest distinction in them. These would be published in a single volume, which would provide a measure of the proficience and advancement of learning, not by an idle onlooker but by those who had done the work, and at the same time a sure guide for the studies of young men ambitious to contribute to its further advancement. This would be guaranteed not merely by the emphasis on studies and methods in the autobiographies themselves, but also by a critical appendix in which the work of all the contributors would be submitted to an impartial and dispassionate examination, and whatever conclusions seemed warranted would be drawn.

Such was the scope of Porcía's ambitious project. But, as he put it in his "Proposal,"

Since we are not yet in position to publish the entire work, we content ourselves with offering a model in the autobiography [3] of Signor Don Giovanni Battista Vico, the celebrated Neapolitan scholar, which better than any other so far received conforms to the plan we have in mind. This autobiography will serve as a norm for anyone who, by imitating both Signor Vico's generosity and his manner of laying before the public the detail of his studies, will lend a hand to the completion of this useful enterprise.

Unfortunately, the enterprise was never completed, and its sole surviving monument is the autobiography of Vico, which is here for the first time translated into English. In the two centuries that have intervened, the art of periautography or autobiography, like that of biography generally, has flourished beyond all expectation; and we are tempted to judge his performance by standards that are alien alike to the pedagogical undertaking that elicited it, and to Vico's own intentions. When he wrote, there were few models by which he could have been guided, and of these he seems to have had only one consciously in mind. This was Descartes's *Discourse on Method,* and he thought of it not as a model to be followed, but as an example of the faults to be avoided. The very choice of the third person is a reaction from the ubiquitous "I" of the *Discourse*.

Early in the original autobiography of 1725 Vico announced his intention in these words:

We shall not here feign what René Descartes craftily feigned as to the method of his studies simply in order to exalt his own philosophy and mathematics and degrade all the other studies included in divine and human learning. Rather, *with the candor proper to a historian*, we shall narrate plainly and step by step the entire series of Vico's studies, in order that the proper and natural causes of his particular development as a man of letters may be known.

And looking back after six years on his actual performance, he was able to say in his continuation of 1731:

As may be seen, *he wrote it as a philosopher,* meditating the causes, natural and moral, and the occasions of fortune; why even from childhood he had felt an inclination for certain studies and an aversion from others; what opportunities and obstacles had advanced or retarded his progress; and lastly the effect of his own exertions in right directions, which were destined later to bear fruit in those reflections on which he built his final work, the *New Science,* which was to demonstrate that his intellectual life was bound to have been such as it was and not otherwise.[4]

Descartes's *Discourse,* it will be remembered, was published as a preface to his three essays, *Geometry, Meteorics,* and *Dioptrics,* and professed to describe the method by which he had arrived at the discoveries contained therein. But Vico's autobiography was not merely an account of the steps by which he had reached the *New Science;* it was also, as Croce has remarked, "the application of the *New Science* to the life of its author."[5]

How it came to be so, and in what other ways the two were related, we shall now try to indicate.

II. The Autobiography and the New Science

THE decisive event in Vico's life was his failure in the academic "concourse" or competition of 1723. He was then fifty-five years of age, and had lingered for nearly a quarter of a century in the propaedeutic chair of rhetoric, whose chief function was to prepare students for admission to the law course. It paid a miserable hundred ducats a year. In 1717 the "first morning chair of law," which paid six hundred ducats, was vacated by Capasso's promotion to the first "afternoon" chair, which paid eleven hundred. Up to that time all Vico's writings had been occasional or commissioned. He had written out his lectures on rhetoric, and his inaugural orations. One of the latter, *On the Method of the Studies of Our Time,* had been published. He had two works of considerable historical value to his credit. He had been commissioned by the state to write the history of the conspiracy of Macchia, but the essay of another had been published in its stead. He had been commissioned by a nephew of Marshal Carafa to write his uncle's life, and this was published in 1716. And he had composed and published epithalamia, panegyrics, funeral orations and inscriptions, and other occasional pieces. His only significant work not inspired by an occasion or commission was *The Most Ancient Wisdom of the Italians,* adumbrating an original epistemology and metaphysics in which Jacobi later saw an anticipation of Kant's doctrine of the *a priori* element in perception and natural science. But Vico contrived, by extracting his epis-

8

temology from the meaning of certain Latin words, to disguise even this as a routine exercise emanating with all propriety from the chair of Latin eloquence.

When Capasso's chair of civil law was vacated in 1717, Vico set about preparing himself for the future concourse. With the innocence of a scholar who had never learned to play the game of academic politics, he could think of nothing better than to write a legal treatise that could be laid before the commission of judges in evidence of his attainments. Unfortunately, he was constitutionally incapable of a treatise of the traditional sort. But in working on his life of Marshal Carafa he had had to consider questions of international law, and had taken the occasion to study Grotius *De jure belli ac pacis,* which he had since been annotating for a new edition. All his studies, linguistic, philological, literary, legal and historical, were insensibly converging upon a philosophy of human society. With an eye to the chair of civil law, but in perfect good faith, he now composed a first draft of that philosophy under the disguise of a treatise on *Universal Law,* taking its motto from a famous passage in Cicero *De legibus:* "In your opinion, then, the science of law is to be derived not from the praetor's edict, as the majority think now, nor from the Twelve Tables, as they used to think, but *from the very depths of philosophy?"* With the scholar's instinct for presenting everything as a commentary on something else, he designed this treatise as an application to law of the argument of his inaugural oration of 1719, which in turn had applied to the sciences generally the theological formula *de origine, de circulo, et de constantia.* The first volume (1720) corresponded to the first and second parts of the oration, the second volume (1721) to the third. These were followed by another volume (1722) of notes and excursuses. Of the three volumes thus embraced under the general title *Universal Law,* the second had less to do with law than the first, and the third less than the second. Like his inaugural orations, this treatise was composed in Latin, the language alike of the chair he held and of that he hoped to win.

Vico sent copies to Jean Le Clerc, editor of the *Bibliothèque ancienne et moderne,* a learned review of European circulation. Le Clerc's complimentary letter of acknowledgment, and his generous reviews of the first two volumes, were assiduously circulated in Naples by Vico. But they betrayed no real understanding of what he had done, and in any case the praise of a Protestant was calculated to do his cause more harm than good.

The concourse for Capasso's chair and others vacated in the meantime was finally announced in January, 1723. Vico promptly entered his name. He delivered his concourse lecture on a fragment of the *Digest* on April 10, blissfully unaware that the commission of judges was already divided into two factions, both committed to other candidates. Of the twenty-nine votes, fifteen were cast for one of these and fourteen for the other. The winner, Domenico Gentile, a notorious seducer of servant girls (he later committed suicide over one of them) was so incapable of writing a book of any sort that his one attempt was withdrawn from the press after being exposed as a plagiarism.

After this blow, "giving up all hope of ever holding a worthier position in his native city," Vico was freed at last from any temptation to write with an eye to professional advancement. One of the chapters of his *Universal Law* had been timidly entitled "Nova Scientia Tentatur." The title was "invidious," Gentile and others had said, and the treatise unintelligible. Perhaps it could not be made otherwise to them; but at any rate the new science there broached as an adjunct to jurisprudence could now be developed on its own account. Its depths could be sounded and its further reaches explored. He need no longer repeat the merely juridical and not always novel observations that had bulked so large in the first volume of the *Universal Law,* but could devote himself to working out what was really original in the second and third volumes. He could abandon Latin, the language of the academic world that would have none of him, and write henceforth in the language of his country and people. Was it not for this that Providence had thwarted his ambitions? Suppose he had succeeded. He would have spent the rest of his days expounding the *Pandects,* staggering on under the very encumbrance which had prevented the free unfolding of his thought in the *Universal Law.* Did not his own experience, in fact, exhibit in microcosm that action of Providence which his new science sought to trace in the macrocosm of human history?

Vico was now at the height of his creative powers. Driven in upon himself by his great disappointment, and working at high tension, by the end of 1724 he had composed in Italian the greater part of what he later called "the new science in negative form"; in the form, that is, of a destructive criticism of existing theories. These were the natural-law systems of Grotius, Selden and Pufendorf; the utilitarian doctrines of the Stoics and Epicureans, of Hobbes, Spinoza, Bayle and Locke; and the views of such scholars as Casaubon, Saumaise, Voss and Bochart. In December Cardinal Lorenzo Corsini gave Vico permission to dedicate this massive work to him, thereby promising, according to the custom of the time, to assume the whole or a substantial part of the cost of publication; and Vico pressed on in the spring of 1725 to complete the manuscript for the printer.

While he was so engaged, Abbé Lorenzo Ciccarelli (who had just published in Naples the famous first edition of Boccaccio's commentary on Dante) conveyed Porcía's request for his autobiography. Vico "refused several times to write it, but the repeated and courteous pleading of Ciccarelli finally won his consent." Porcía's enterprise was one with which so pedagogical a mind as Vico's could not but sympathize; and as he neared the end of his thousand closely written pages of "the new science in negative form," he was increasingly attracted by the possibility of interpreting his own life as a positive illustration and confirmation of it. Finally the manuscript was completed, and on May 8 he composed his dedicatory epistle to Cardinal Corsini. While he was waiting for the Cardinal to fulfil his implied promise so that the work could go to press, he composed Part A of his autobiography and sent it to Porcía's Roman agent Abbé Esperti, who forwarded it to Porcía on June 23. It gives every sign of having been written with great rapidity, for the most part from memory and without consulting records or documents. But Porcía wrote to Esperti in September that Vico had grasped his idea better than anyone else, and carried it out to perfection.

In the meantime "the new science in negative form" had received its imprimatur on July 15; but on July 20 Corsini wrote from Rome withdrawing his promise because of "many exorbitant expenses" incurred on a recent visit to his diocese of Frascati. This was a blow second only to the defeat of two years before. Vico's friend and ecclesiastical censor, Giulio Torno, suggested that he finance the publication by soliciting subscriptions; but Vico, a bookseller's son who had lived among booksellers for the first thirty-one years of his life, had just enough practical sense to know how impossible it was to find the necessary two hundred subscribers in the Naples of that day. Yet he felt himself committed to publish. His only recourse was to do so at his own expense. He had a ring. It would cover scarcely a fourth of the cost of the two large quarto volumes to which his manuscript would run. Within a few days it came to him with the force of inspiration that his "negative" method had been a mistake; that by the employment of a "positive" method the work could be reduced to a fourth of its compass; that it would not lose but greatly gain thereby; and that the breaking of Corsini's promise was but one more dispensation of Providence.

Thereupon he spent August and part of September composing what he later called "the first *New Science*." Printing began in September and the book came from the press in October, with the same dedicatory epistle to Corsini which Vico had written for the larger work in May; and Vico sent him a handsomely bound copy on fine paper with wide margins, accompanied by an apology that from another's hand would have been charged with irony: "I ought to have sent it to your eminence printed in large and magnificent format, above all in the splendid types of the present age; but my slender means did not permit me to do so." There was perhaps a trace of bitterness there, but no irony. He had published a work of genius, and Corsini was in large part responsible for its clarity of expression and perfection of form.

It must have been late in December that Vico composed Part B of the autobiography, suppressing Corsini's default and concluding with his acknowledgment of the *New Science*. As a matter of fact, the Cardinal had not read it. After glancing at it, he had given it to Marquis Alessandro Gregorio Capponi for an opinion as to the terms in which he should acknowledge it, and had later told him to keep it. At his death Capponi left it with the rest of his books to the Vatican Library, where it is still preserved, with this inscription on the recto of the first page: "Given to me A. G. C. by his eminence Corsini, first to examine and later in gift, December 1725."

Vico's original autobiography is thus to be read as the expression of his state of mind at the end of his two greatest creative efforts: Part A after completing "the new science in negative form," and Part B after publishing "the first *New Science.*" Among the letters that he sent with copies of the book there is one, however, in which he speaks his mind more freely than anywhere in the autobiography. It is worth translating here in full, both for that reason and as an example of his epistolary style. It was sent on October 25, 1725, to his Capuchin friend Father Bernardo Maria Giacco, on whom the allusions to Gentile's venery and the Cardinal's scarlets would not be lost. It reads as follows:

With the great love I bear you and the high respect that is your due, I send your reverence the promised work on *The Principles of Humanity.* In your solitude its reputation will be as much enhanced as in the most famous of the universities of Europe to which it is addressed. In this city I account it as fallen on barren ground. I avoid all public places, so as not to meet the persons to whom I have sent it; and if I cannot avoid them, I greet them without stopping; for when I pause they give me not the faintest sign that they have received it, and thus they confirm my belief that it has gone forth into a desert.

All the other poor works of my mind I owe to myself, because they were devised for my own ends, with a view to winning an honorable station in my native city; but since our university has

considered me unworthy of one, I assuredly owe this work entirely
to it, for its unwillingness to have me occupied in expounding
paragraphs [from the *Pandects*] has left me the leisure to compose
it. Could I owe it a greater debt than this? I am sorry not to be
able to avow it save in your solitude, but I there proclaim that I
begrudge the labor of all the other poor works of my mind, and
would like only this to survive me. For the others were devised to
win me one of the higher chairs in our university, which, by
judging me unworthy of it, has tacitly commanded me to labor at
this work alone, to which all those of my previous life were destined to lead me.

Forever praised be Providence, which, when the weak sight of
mortals sees in it nothing but stern justice, then most of all is at
work on a crowning mercy! For by this work I feel myself clothed
upon with a new man; I no longer wince at the things that once
goaded me to bewail my hard lot and to denounce the corruption of
letters that has caused that lot; for this corruption and this lot have
strengthened me and enabled me to perfect this work. Moreover
(if it be not true, I like to think it is) this work has filled me with
a certain heroic spirit, so that I am no longer troubled by any fear
of death, nor have I any mind to speak of rivals. Finally the judgment of God has set me as on a rock of adamant, for He renders
justice to works of the mind by the esteem of the wise, who are
always and everywhere few. Not men who crib from others' books;
not those who waste their nights in venery and wine, or sweating
out schemes to hoodwink truth and virtue and hide the follies and
ribaldries of the day before so as to pass for wise and good in the
day ahead; nor lastly the indolent who, standing secure in the
shade of their sloth, or roaming about unnoticed in the dense night
of their anonymity, rob the valiant of the honor that is their due,
and make bold at any chance to slash at the fair name of others,
although, in the darkness of their black passion of envy, their poi-
sonous strokes glance and sink into their own entrails. No, but men
of the loftiest intellect, of a learning all their own, generous and
great-hearted, whose only labor is to enrich with deathless works
the commonwealth of letters.

The first of these, or among the foremost, is your reverence,

whom I now devoutly pray to accept, with the magnanimity you
have shown toward the others, this perhaps last but assuredly most
cherished of my offspring, which by your good grace will be more
at home with your coarse woollens than with the scarlets and fine
silks of the great.

With humble respect, believe me, etc.

It was not until March 10, 1728, that Vico sent Porcía Part
B of the autobiography, along with corrections and additions
to the first draft of Part A, and a catalogue of his writings.
By that time Abbé Conti had returned from France and settled again in Venice. He had sensed the greatness of the
New Science and was disposed to use his considerable influence in France and England to win a wider audience for it;
but the original edition in miserable format and brevier
type, even if there had been enough copies left of the thousand printed, would simply not do. So he joined with Porcía
and Lodoli in urging upon Vico a new edition at Venice in
larger type and handsomer format, with further elucidations
and a preface giving a conspectus of the system. Vico worked
for a year and a half on a plan which left the original text
intact, save for corrections, but loaded it with annotations and
appendices. He sent the manuscript to Venice in October,
1729. The printer, probably through Lodoli, raised some objections to its excessive length, disjointed repetitiousness, and
typographical difficulty. Vico had already been angered by
the printing of his autobiography, not as one among many
in Porcía's completed work, but (over his repeated protests)
as a model accompanying the "Proposal," and also by the
printer's scheme for a collected edition of his works. Before
that, his nerves had been racked by the unhappy controversy
with "the Leipzig reviewers" of the first *New Science*. He
was now in ill health, and there were distressing troubles at

home. This was the last straw. He broke off relations with the Venetian printers and demanded the return of his manuscript. Confronted now by the same problem that had beset him when Corsini withdrew his promise, he set to work on a complete rewriting of the work on a new plan embodying his latest views in the text itself. This "second *New Science*" went to press at Naples in July, 1730, and was published in December, in brevier type, forty lines to the small page, as painful to read as the first, and for the same reason: the poverty of its author.

But the work had gained in substance and structure as much as it had lost in physical dress, and in this Vico saw once more the hand of Providence. Cardinal Corsini, to whom the first edition had been dedicated, and who had become for Vico a symbol of such dispensations, was elected Pope Clement XII on July 12, 1730, about the time this second edition went to press; and Vico composed for it this dedicatory inscription:

TO/CLEMENT XII/BEST OF PONTIFFS/FOR THAT/INFINITE PROVI-
DENCE/WITH ONE AND THE SAME/SIMPLE AND ETERNAL COUNSEL/
ORDERING ALWAYS FOR GOOD/THE GREATEST THINGS/AND THE LEAST
ALIKE/WHILE/FOR THE SPLENDOR/OF THE HOLY SEE/AND FOR THE
FELICITY/OF THE CATHOLIC WORLD/IT WAS CONDUCTING YOUR
GRACE/TO THE SUPREME PONTIFICATE/ORDAINED/AT THE SAME
TIME/THAT THESE PRINCIPLES/OF THE NEW SCIENCE/CONCERNING/
THE COMMON NATURE/OF THE NATIONS/DEDICATED/TO YOUR
HOLINESS/WHEN CARDINAL BISHOP/BY VARIOUS AND DIVERS/
SEEMING ADVERSITIES/THAT IN FACT WERE OPPORTUNITIES/SHOULD
BE RECONCEIVED/IN MORE APPROPRIATE FORM/AND ENRICHED/
WITH GREATER DISCOVERIES/TO THE END THAT/IMPROVED AND
AUGMENTED/THEY MIGHT AGAIN TAKE THEIR PLACE/IN THE SACRED
SHADOW/OF YOUR VENERABLE/PROTECTION/GIAMBATTISTA VICO/
PROSTRATE/AT YOUR MOST HOLY FEET/WHICH HE HUMBLY KISSES/
CONSECRATES THEM ANEW

Meanwhile, at the instance of Muratori, Vico was elected on May 17, 1730, to the Academy of the Assorditi of Urbino, and was asked for material to be used in a volume of biographies of its members. In a letter to Muratori on June 5 he courteously declined. He had protested Porcía's use of his autobiography, and could not in decency put out another, however brief. But if the Assorditi wished to reprint that one with his corrections, they might do so. Muratori must have renewed his request, for in a breathing spell in the spring of 1731, with the second *New Science* now off his hands, Vico wrote out a corrected copy of the original autobiography, and in April or May composed a continuation down to the first months of 1731. The continuation therefore had the same relation to the second *New Science* which the original autobiography had had to the first.

The Assorditi volume was never published, but copies of the corrected autobiography and the continuation were found among Vico's papers after his death. The former of these was later lost, but sometime before his son Gennaro died in 1806, he turned over the continuation to the Marquis of Villarosa. It was printed for the first time, along with the original autobiography and a further continuation and extensive notes by Villarosa, in the first volume of his edition of Vico's *Opuscoli* in 1818. Villarosa's continuation, drawing heavily on the oral Vico tradition, has a gossipy character, but remains the chief single source for Vico's later years.

This first complete edition of the autobiography followed upon a succession of editions of the *New Science,* beginning with one at Milan in 1801, which was the first since that which Vico prepared in 1743 and was seeing through the press when he died in January, 1744. Thus Vico's autobiography and its two continuations are intimately connected with the publication of the successive editions of the major work in which his life found its fruition. We pass now to a review of the leading ideas of that work in relation to those of its time and place.

III. The New Science

THE title of Vico's major work was obviously inspired by Bacon's *Novum Organum,* and still more by Galileo's *Dialoghi delle Nuove Scienze,* which, as Hobbes had said, "first opened to us the gate of natural philosophy universal, which is the knowledge of the nature of motion." It was also, perhaps (though this is less clear), a challenge to Hobbes's claim that civil philosophy was founded by his own *De cive.*[6] At any rate, it is in Vico's *New Science,* the *novum organum* of history, and not in Hobbes's *De cive,* that the germs of all the sciences of social change are to be found.

The transition from pre-Galilean to Galilean and Newtonian physics is now a familiar tale, but the complementary transition from pre-Vichian to Vichian history has not yet been fairly told, or even adequately explored.[7] The following paragraphs are therefore but tentative outline heads for some parts of a story which has yet to be written. If (as will appear in Section IV) Vico's influence was not as immediate and palpable in the one case as Galileo's in the other, that was not because his break with the past was less decisive, but because the prestige of Italian culture had sharply declined in the intervening century, and the lead had passed to France and England.

The chief impetus to modern critical and interpretative historiography came from the Reformation. The view gained currency that the weakness of scholasticism was ignorance of history. As Bacon put it: "This kind of degenerate learning did chiefly reign amongst the schoolmen: who having

sharp and strong wits, and abundance of leisure, and small
variety of reading . . . and knowing little history, either of
nature or time, did out of no great quantity of matter and
infinite agitation of wit spin out unto us those laborious webs
of learning which are extant in their books." On the other
hand, what Bacon said of Luther was true in some degree
of all the reformers: "finding what a province he had undertaken against the bishop of Rome and the degenerate
traditions of the church," he "was enforced to awake all antiquity, and to call former times to his succours to make a
party against the present time: so that the ancient authors,
both in divinity and in humanity, which had long time slept
in libraries, began generally to be read and revolved." [8]
The wars of the Reformation era facilitated the process by
dissolution of monasteries and pillage of their libraries,
throwing onto the market vast quantities of manuscripts and
documents, which were acquired by scholars and collectors,
and by the libraries of the new Protestant universities in Germany.

The Counter Reformation was eventually obliged to fight
history with history, and the counter attack had not yet abated
in Vico's day. Indeed its finest fruits matured within his own
lifetime in the collections of the Bollandist Fathers and the
Congregation of St. Maur. Mabillon's *De re diplomatica,*
which founded the discipline of diplomatics and Latin
paleography, was published in 1681. Four years later, when
Vico was a lad of seventeen, Mabillon was in Naples in
search of books and manuscripts. Montfaucon was there in
1698, and his *Palaeographia Graeca* appeared in 1708. But
the great and indispensable work of Reformation and Counter Reformation alike was but the preparation of materials
and tools for history, and not yet history in the modern sense.

A similar and eventually more powerful impetus was afforded by the rise of national states. The work it led to was often done by the same men; Mabillon and Montfaucon, for instance, made notable contributions to French history. Here again the work done during Vico's lifetime surpassed anything before it in thoroughness and accuracy. The greatest philosopher of the age, Leibniz, established new standards in these respects. For forty years historian of the House of Brunswick, he made the history of the dynasty reflect that of nations and of the world, and became himself, in Gibbon's phrase, "a master of the history of the middle ages." [9] In pursuit of his genealogical studies, he made a learned pilgrimage through Germany and Italy, reaching Naples in November of 1689. His inquiries roused the Duke of Modena to appoint Muratori to put the ducal archives in order and prepare a similar history of the House of Este, which Leibniz had traced to a common origin with that of Brunswick. This was only the first of many monumental enterprises performed by Muratori in the fifty years of his librarianship (1700–1750). Among them was the great *Rerum Italicarum Scriptores,* corresponding to Leibniz's *Scriptores Rerum Brunsvicensium.* Gibbon availed himself of the work of both in his *Decline and Fall,* and again in his *Antiquities of the House of Brunswick.*

Leibniz sought also to organize a German historical society to secure the cooperation of local historians, collect provincial sources, and lay the foundation for a universal history. If we examine what he says about history, however, we find much good sense in it, but no trace of the genius that appears in his other work.

Men who pride themselves on philosophy and ratiocination have a way of disparaging the study of antiquity, and the antiquarians in turn make fun of what they call the reveries of philosophers. But we should rather seek to render justice to the services of both. . . .

The use of history consists principally in the pleasure there is in knowing origins, in the justice rendered to the men who have deserved well of other men, in the establishment of historical criticism, especially of sacred history, which supports the foundations of revelation; and (putting aside the genealogies and laws of princes and powers) in the useful teachings which the examples furnish us. . . .

I wish there might be some persons who would devote themselves to drawing from history that which is most useful, as the extraordinary examples of virtue, remarks upon the conveniences of life, stratagems of politics and war. And I wish that a kind of universal history were written which should indicate only such things. . . .

The chief end of history, like that of poetry, is to teach prudence and virtue by examples, and to exhibit vice in such a way as to arouse aversion and lead to its avoidance.[10]

The words are Leibniz's, but the ideas are largely those of the Renaissance humanists, who had provided a third impetus. The "humane letters" which they made the staple of education included history along with grammar, poetry and rhetoric; editions of the Greek and Latin historians became a major occupation of scholars; and the Latin historians particularly—Caesar, Sallust, Livy, Tacitus, Curtius, Justin—were widely read in schools. The relation between history and philosophy became a common topic of educational theory. On the whole, in spite of revivals of Stoicism and Epicureanism, the moral philosophy of Aristotle retained its authority long after the eclipse of his work in other fields. But it was conceived and taught primarily as a body of precepts, and precept was less effective than example. As Thomas Blundeville phrased it in his *True order and Methode of wryting and reading Histories,* morality "is partly taught by

the philosophers in generall precepts and rules, but the his-
toriographers doe teach it much more plainlye by particular
examples and experiences." [11] And Amyot remarked in the
preface to his translation of Plutarch that historical examples
"are of more force to move and instruct, then are the arguments and proofes of reason . . . because examples be the
verie formes of our deedes, and accompanied by all circumstances . . . they do not onely declare what is to be done,
but also worke a desire to do it. . . ." [12] For humanist ethics
was essentially aristocratic, and tended to make honor and
glory the motive to virtue, and thus to enhance still further
the pedagogical value of history. The aristocrat, moved by
the prospect of the survival of his own deeds in history, would
find in those of Alexander, Scipio, Hannibal and Caesar as
handed down by the historians, an added appeal which they
could scarcely have for the common man.

This shift of interest from precept to application, from
theory to practice, from philosophy to history, found its
fullest and most systematic expression in Bacon's *Advancement of Learning*. The moral philosophers had been too exclusively concerned with defining "the exemplar or platform
of good," and not enough with "the regiment or culture of
the mind . . . prescribing rules how to subdue, apply, and
accommodate the will of man thereunto." "Now the wisdom
of application resteth principally in the exact and distinct
knowledge of the precedent state or disposition, unto which
we do apply." We must therefore study "the several characters and tempers of men's natures and dispositions"; "those
impressions of nature, which are imposed upon the mind by
the sex, by the age, by the region, by health and sickness . . .
by extern fortune. . . ." These matters "are touched a little
by Aristotle as in passage in his Rhetorics . . . but they were

never incorporate into moral philosophy, to which they do essentially appertain." [13]

"History, poesy, and daily experience are as goodly fields where these observations grow." "But the poets and writers of histories are the best doctors of this knowledge; where we may find painted forth with great life, how affections are kindled and incited; and how pacified and refrained . . . and how they do fight and encounter one with another. . . . Amongst the which this last is of special use in moral and civil matters; how, I say, to set affection against affection, and to master one by another." "And therefore the form of writing which of all others is fittest . . . is that which Machiavel chose . . . namely, discourse upon histories or examples. For knowledge drawn freshly and in our view out of particulars, knoweth the way best to particulars again." The same interest in application, which makes history the auxiliary of moral philosophy, appears in Bacon's supreme desideratum, "a just story of learning" designed to "make learned men wise in the use and administration of learning. For it is not Saint Augustine's nor Saint Ambrose' works that will make so wise a divine, as ecclesiastical history, thoroughly read and observed; and the same reason is of learning." [14]

Though Bacon said that "knowledges are as pyramides, whereof history is the basis," [15] he looked to historical induction not for the principles of moral philosophy, but only for techniques of application. Before him, however, Bodin had taken the more extreme position that history should teach the ends as well as the means. He was moved to write his *Methodus ad facilem historiarum cognitionem*,[16] he says, by "the incredible usefulness of this science," by which "we are thoroughly instructed, not only what arts are necessary for the maintenance of life, but also in general what things are to be sought and what to be shunned, what is base and what honorable, what constitution and laws are best, and what is the happy life." But Bodin's "method" was directed to the ease and profit of the study of history; like Bacon later, he was preoccupied with its uses, not with the prior question how it could be made scientific. Commentators on older histories and writers of new ones (Machiavelli for an instance of both) who were bent on drawing morals tended to be careless of the facts. In proportion as physics set new standards of precision and it came to be seen how difficult it was to achieve truth and certainty in history, there was less praise of its usefulness.

This change, though not without complications, may be traced in the case of Hobbes. He was taught Greek and Latin at home. At Oxford he sought relief from the scholastic curriculum in continued private study of the classics, and resumed it in the course of his twenty years as tutor and secretary to William Cavendish. Blackbourne says in his supplement to Hobbes's Life that "he came to feel a great distaste for academic learning. . . . Determined therefore to try another method of philosophizing, he diligently pored over the ancient philosophers, poets and historians, both Greek and Latin, and carefully culled from their treasures whatever he could turn to his use." [17] Of the philosophers the chief was Aristotle—certainly the Rhetoric (of which he published an English digest in 1637) and probably the Ethics and Politics —the Aristotle, that is, of the humanists, not of the scholastics. Of the poets, the chief was Homer, to whom he returned in his old age. Of the historians, the chief was Thucydides, "the most politic historiographer that ever writ," [18] and the crown and end of Hobbes's humanist period was the translation of the great historian which he undertook, it has been said,[19] as a sort of philosophic reconnaissance comparable to Machiavelli's *Discourses on Livy*.

For in history, actions of honour and dishonour do appear plainly and distinctly, which are which; but in the present age they are so disguised, that few there be, and those very careful, that be not grossly mistaken in them. . . . For the principal and proper work of history being to instruct and enable men, by the knowledge of actions past, to bear themselves prudently in the present and providently towards the future: there is not extant any other . . . that doth more naturally and fully perform it, than this of my author. . . . For he setteth his reader in the assemblies of the people and in the senate, at their debating; in the streets, at their seditions; and in the field, at their battles. So that look how much a man of understanding might have added to his experience, if he had then lived a beholder of their proceedings, and familiar with the men and business of the time: so much almost may he profit now, by attentive reading of the same here written. . . . Digressions for instruction's cause, and other such open conveyances of precepts, (which is the philosopher's part), he never useth; as having so clearly set before men's eyes the ways and events of good and evil counsels, that the narration itself doth secretly instruct the reader, and more effectually than can possibly be done by precept.[20]

Hobbes was then forty. Shortly thereafter he discovered Euclid and Galileo and developed an epistemology in which science as "knowledge of consequences" or "conditional knowledge" is contrasted with absolute knowledge or knowledge of fact, whose register is history. His own political philosophy claimed of course to be science, but there was no immediate change in his view of the credibility and value of history. A decade later he could still say in his *Elements of Law* (1640), perhaps with a glance at Descartes:

Now there be many things which we receive from report of others, of which it is impossible to imagine any cause of doubt: for what can be opposed against the consent of all men, in things they can know, and have no cause to report otherwise than they are (such as is a great part of our histories), unless a man would say that all the world had conspired to deceive him.

But this acknowledgment of the authenticity of history was omitted from the corresponding section of the *Leviathan* (1651), which emphasized rather the dubious character of all political doctrine grounded on history, the invalidity of criticism based on historic practice, the purely rhetorical value of historical allusions, and the harm that has been done by reading history, so that "there was never any thing so dearly bought, as these Western parts have bought the learning of the Greek and Latin tongues." In his *De corpore* (1655) he wrote more calmly of philosophy in general that it "excludes history, as well natural as political, though most useful (nay necessary) to philosophy; because such knowledge is but experience, or authority, and not ratiocination." But in the Latin version of the *Leviathan* (1668), the definitive statement of his political theory, he is ready to say curtly that "history is divided into natural and civil, neither of which pertains to our subject." [21]

Hobbes thus reached late in life a view not unlike that with which Descartes began. After the usual training in "humane letters," mathematics and philosophy at La Flèche, and in law and medicine at Poitiers, Descartes at the age of twenty "entirely abandoned the study of letters," including history and law. He recognized that "the memorable actions of history elevate the mind, and if read with discretion help to form the judgment"; and that some reading of history, by acquainting us like travel with the manners of other nations, may disabuse us of the notion that there is anything peculiarly rational about our own.

But he who spends too much time in traveling becomes a stranger in his own country, and he who is too curious about the customs of the past is generally quite ignorant of those of the present. Besides . . . even the most faithful histories, if they do not alter or enhance the value of things to make them more readable, at least nearly always omit from them the baser and less notable circumstances; whence it comes that the rest does not appear as it really is, and that those who regulate their conduct by examples drawn therefrom are apt to fall into the extravagances of the knight-errants of romance, and to conceive projects which exceed their powers.

This early anti-historical bent appears most clearly in Descartes's remarks on the necessary imperfection of whatever has been a slow growth: buildings, cities, laws, religions, sciences, even the mind of an adult!

I imagined that those peoples who were once half-savage and have become civilized only by slow degrees, forming their laws only as the damage suffered from crimes and quarrels has constrained them, could not be so well governed as those who, from the time they first came together, have observed the constitution of some wise lawgiver. . . . Again, I thought that since we have all passed through childhood to manhood, and had long to be governed by our desires and our preceptors (in frequent conflict with each other, and neither perhaps counseling always for the best), it is almost impossible that our judgments should be as clear and firm as they would have been had we enjoyed the full use of our reason from birth and been always guided by it alone.

Only later, when Descartes had elaborated his conception of science as rational knowledge of the mathematical type, did his critique of humanism assume definitive form.

That you may more distinctly conceive the nature of the knowledge of which I shall treat, I beg you to observe the difference which separates the sciences from the simple knowledge-by-acquaintance [*connaissances*] which is acquired without any discourse of reason, such as languages, history, geography, and in general whatever depends on experience alone. I readily grant that the life of a man is too short for him to acquaint himself with all that the world contains; but I am also persuaded that only a fool would wish to if he could, and that an honest man is no more obliged to know Greek or Latin than Swiss or Low-Breton, the history of the Empire than that of the least state of Europe; and that he should devote his leisure to something honest and useful, and burden his memory only with what is most necessary.[22]

Though this anti-historical bias was carried to further extremes by Malebranche, it may fairly be argued that it was an easy and inevitable step from criticism of history to historical criticism, and that the latter was in fact a later phase of the same movement. Spinoza and Bayle treated documents and their accepted interpretations as standing between the mind and the past it sought to recover, in precisely the same way that Descartes had treated the constructions of the imagination as standing between the mind and the reality it sought to know. Bayle's "historical Pyrrhonism" was simply an extension of Descartes's methodical doubt, and as the *cogito ergo sum* had been the residuum left by doubt, so, in history, there remained as certain fact whatever criticism was unable to demolish. The difference was that whereas the *cogito* had opened the way to a vast and imposing system, historical criticism, as represented by Bayle's *Dictionnaire historique et critique* (1697), contented itself with, and even gloried in, the systematic juxtaposition of unrelated facts, and perversely dwelt with greatest detail on those that were least significant.

In summary, it may be said that historical research and publication were immensely accelerated by the Reformation and Counter Reformation, and by the rise of national states; that there were many collections and compilations, but almost no histories proper, of permanent value; that the study of ancient history, or at any rate the editing and reading of the ancient historians, was fostered by the humanists; that they made much of the uses of history, but that historians who wrote in this tradition had little conscience about the facts; that the Maurists especially developed techniques for dating documents and determining their authenticity; that the rationalists cast piecemeal doubt on the credibility even of duly authenticated primary sources; that great progress was thus made in lower criticism, not much in higher, and almost none in the invention and testing of explanatory hypotheses; in short, that there was an increasing concern to find out *wie es eigentlich gewesen,* but scarcely any to find out *wie es eigentlich geworden.* Perhaps the only grand-scale work before 1725 that displays both, and certainly the only general history that takes adequate account of law and institutions, is the *Civil History of the Kingdom of Naples,* which Pietro Giannone published in Naples in 1723 after twenty years of intensive labor. It was promptly put on the Index and translated into English. In its pages Gibbon "observed with a critical eye the progress and abuse of Sacerdotal power, and the Revolutions of Italy in the darker ages," and learned "the use of irony and criticism on subjects of Ecclesiastical gravity." [23]

THE society that nourished Giannone was the same that nourished his slightly older contemporary Vico, and in their youth it was the freest-thinking society in Italy. Its eclectic interests and enthusiasms included atomism and Epicureanism, which have always had for free minds at Naples an appeal enhanced by local patriotism. For Naples was the Italian seat of Epicureanism in Roman times; it was there that Siro and Philodemus taught and Virgil and perhaps Lucretius studied. In the Renaissance, Giovanni Pontano, founder of its Accademia Pontaniana, was the first serious critic of the text of Lucretius. And now in Vico's boyhood a fresh impetus to Epicurean studies had been given by the writings of Pierre Gassendi. Marchetti's Italian translation of Lucretius, though not printed until 1717, was widely circulated in manuscript in the 1680's and 1690's. The new eclecticism also included the Renaissance forerunners of modern naturalism, Telesio, Bruno, and Campanella, who had all three taught at Naples. More prominent, however, were the experimentalism of Galileo, Bacon and Boyle, and the rationalism of Descartes and Hobbes. The dominant elements were Gassendist and Cartesian, and there was a gradual shift from the former to the latter. What united them all was opposition to Aristotle, Galen, and the scholastics. The exponents of the new philosophy were denounced as atheists by the clerical party, and the more reckless of them were prosecuted by the Inquisition.

The centers of these new studies were of course not in the monasteries nor in the University, but in the Academy of the *Investiganti* and its various successors, in two or three of the bookstores, and in an incredible number of literary salons, most of them with libraries attached. The pioneers of the awakening were Tommaso Cornelio (1614–84), Lionardo di Capua (1617–95), and the slightly younger Francesco d'Andrea (1625–98). In imitation of the French Academy of Sciences and the Royal Society of London, they founded the Academy of the *Investiganti*. It had "for its devise a setting dog, with a motto out of Lucretius: *Vestigia lustrat.*" So we are told by Giannone, who gives us an account of its more famous members, "besides many others of great parts, who made it their whole study to shake off the heavy yoke which the philosophy of the cloisters had put upon the necks of the Neapolitans." [24] Their influence spread through the city and raised the average level of its culture to a height unequalled before or since. There were forty-odd bookstores along the short Via di San Biagio dei Librai. That of Vico's father was one of the smallest. Among the more famous of the salons in Vico's youth were those of Nicola Caravita (1647–1717) and Giuseppe Valletta (1636–1714). That of the latter was the most distinctively philosophical, and his library was much the best in the city. Giannone made good use of it. The bulk of it was bought by the Fathers of the Oratory in 1726, at Vico's appraisal of fourteen thousand ducats. "Thirty years ago," he wrote, "it was worth thirty thousand, but I had to go by the current market price, which in the case of Greek and Latin books (even the most elegant and accurate first editions) is now less than half what it was then, and the greater body of it consisted of such books."

During the same years in which the new philosophy spread, Naples was also a chief center of the quietism of Molinos, with its emphasis on silent or "mental prayer" and "living in tranquillity of spirit." [25] Gaspar Muñoz, who translated the works of Molinos into Italian, was an influential Franciscan at Naples from 1664 to 1693. The most popular quietist preacher was Father Antonio Torres, whom Vico praises in his funeral oration for Angiola Cimmino. There were others among the Fathers of the Oratory, whose church Vico attended. The Jesuits aroused popular prejudice against quietism by charging it with asserting the uselessness of confession, oral prayer, and the cult of the saints. By pressure exerted through Louis XIV and his ambassador at Rome, they had Molinos denounced by the Inquisition as a heretic, though Pope Innocent XI (who had no love for Jesuits) thought him a saint and sought to save him. The way was thus opened for prosecution of the quietists at Naples, of whom Burnet says there were still twenty thousand some six months after the arrest of Molinos at Rome. Two of the leading Fathers of the Oratory were involved; one of them seems to have died in prison. Torres was forbidden to preach or hear confession, but the ban was removed in 1692; and about the turn of the century Giannone was a member of a congregation of lawyers to which he preached Sunday morning sermons "so learned, fervent and serious that many came to hear him." "It was my good fortune," Giannone says, "to have as my spiritual father this same Torres, who instructed me in the true and solid Christian morality, and warned me to put no faith in vain superstitions and outward shows, which ought to be deemed pharisaic and pagan rather than evangelical and Christian." [26]

Vico says nothing of the Inquisition in his autobiography, but his writings are not fully intelligible to one who does not bear in mind that it was active in Naples throughout his lifetime.[27] The city had been torn by a century of strife between the Spanish and Roman Holy Offices, both vigorously resisted by the citizens, who based their protests on a proclamation of 1510 exempting that notoriously pious city and kingdom from the Inquisition. They consistently demanded that alleged heretics be tried by the "via ordinaria," that is by the local episcopal courts following the usual procedure for criminal trials, as distinguished from the secret procedure of the Inquisition, which denied the accused almost every means of defense, and confiscated his property. But even after temporary victories against both Holy Offices, the episcopal courts themselves often employed inquisitorial methods under pretense of adhering to the via ordinaria. Before Vico's birth the

Spanish Inquisition had withdrawn from the field, but the Papal persisted until long after his death. When he was a lad of fifteen, a priest employed in teaching philosophy was imprisoned and compelled to abjure the two propositions that "The definition of man is not that he is a reasoning animal" and that "Brutes have a kind of imperfect reason." That was in 1683. In 1688 the Holy Office moved simultaneously against the quietists and the "Epicureans and atheists." Of the latter, the three most deeply compromised, and one of their witnesses, were Vico's closest friends. (Two of them he later honored as prompters of his *Ancient Wisdom of the Italians,* and one of these he still later chose as secular censor of his *Universal Law* and *New Science.*) Their foremost protectors, moreover, were Vico's chief patrons, Valletta and Caravita. After the imprisonments of 1692 and the sentence of 1693, envoys were sent to Rome with a memorial of protest to the Pope by Valletta. Meantime Carlos II had prohibited all further residence in Naples of papal delegates or commissioners; but trials for heresy continued by inquisitorial methods in the archiepiscopal court; and in 1695 an Edict of Denunciation renewed the hold of the Inquisition. The Deputies of the people appealed to Charles of Austria in 1709, and in 1711 they employed Capasso to draw up a comprehensive report on inquisitional methods. Even after the accession of Carlo VII in 1734, when Naples had such protection as a resident king could afford, there were fresh outrages in 1738 and 1739, and again in 1743, the last year of Vico's life.

Now the chief defect of detail in Vico's autobiography is that it not only exaggerates his isolation from the new philosophy during his Vatolla years (1686–95), but represents him as having taken up a position against it when he did become acquainted with it, a position which in fact he did not approach until about 1708, and did not fully reach before 1720. Actually the Rocca family divided the year between its residences at Vatolla, Portici and Naples, and there was probably no year in which its tutor did not spend some weeks or months in Naples. He was therefore in nearly continuous touch with the new eclecticism throughout his youth, and all its elements were represented in his early thought. The shift from Gassendi (that is from Democritus, Epicurus and Lucretius) to Descartes took place in his own mind as well as in Neapolitan culture. His most inspired poem, "Affetti di un disperato," [28] reflects Lucretian moods and studies in the critical year 1692; it could not have been written by a devout Christian. In 1731, after publishing the second *New Science,* which expounded his fully developed aesthetic theory based on imagination and excluding science and all didacticism from poetry, he was prepared to say of Lucretius that "except for the poetic proems to his six books, and except for a few digressions, like the inimitably delicate description of the young heifer that has lost its mother, and the incomparably grand description of the plague at Athens, in the remainder he treats of physics in a style indistinguishable from that in which it would have been taught in a Latin course in natural philosophy." [29] But that was a libel against the most stupendous of Latin poems, penned by a poet who still loved it in spite of himself, and who had just published what is like nothing so much as a prose poem *De rerum humanarum natura.*

Actually, moreover, Vico became a Cartesian and remained so until his own original doctrine began to emerge; that is, until about the age of forty.[30] Indeed, the greatest critic of Descartes was himself the greatest Cartesian of Italy. The very device by which he contrived in retrospect to give himself a seeming isolation from the movement—the alleged solitude of his nine Vatolla years—was itself a Cartesian touch inspired, perhaps unconsciously, by the retreat to Holland in the ninth year of which Descartes wrote the *Discourse,* far from all encounter with Parisian friends, "as solitary and retired as in the remotest deserts." So near is philosophy to fiction.

The teaching of Vico's first six inaugural orations (1699–1706) is largely Cartesian. In the third he seems even to share the contempt of Descartes and Malebranche for history. "You, philologist, boast of knowing everything about the furniture and clothing of the Romans and of being more intimate with the quarters, tribes and streets of Rome than with those of your own city. Why this pride? You know no more than did the potter, the cook, the cobbler, the summoner, the auctioneer of Rome." [31] A decade later, though still acknowledging the great service of Descartes in freeing us from the authority of Aristotle and the method of the scholastics, he regrets that "the study of languages is today considered useless, thanks to the authority of Descartes, who says that to know Latin is to know no more than Cicero's servant girl did." [32] In the chapter "Nova scientia tentatur" of his *Universal Law* (1721) he recalls his former anti-historical Cartesianism: "All my life I had delighted in the use of reason more than in memory, and the more I knew in philology the more ignorant I saw myself to be. Descartes and Malebranche were not far wrong, it seemed, when they said it was alien to the philosopher to work long and hard at philology." But if that view were pushed too far it would be the death of jurisprudence and theology, and thereby of Christian states. "So that these most eminent philosophers, if they had been zealous for the common glory of Christendom, not for the private glory of philosophers, ought to have pressed forward the study of philology far enough for philosophers to see whether it could be reduced to philosophic principles" [33] and thereby made a new science.

Vico's own approach to this new science was by way of a new theory of knowledge. The first clear trace of this appears in his inaugural oration of 1708 comparing the ancient and modern methods of study. The moderns have instituted great improvements in the physical sciences, but have unduly depreciated those studies whose matter depends on the human will and therefore involves vicissitude and probability—languages, poetry, eloquence, history, jurisprudence, politics. Moreover, the moderns have extended the geometrical method to sciences where it can only yield a misleading appearance of demonstration without its real force. "In geometry we demonstrate because we create; before we demonstrate in physics, we must be able to create there also." [34]

This germ was developed into a full-blown theory of knowledge in the *Ancient Wisdom of the Italians* in 1710. There is now a frontal attack on Descartes. The *cogito ergo sum* is no refutation of scepticism, no basis for science; the sceptic is certain enough of his thinking and of his existence alike, but the certainty is that of simple consciousness (*conscientia*), not of science (*scientia*), and the *cogito* leaves it so. "The rule and criterion of truth is to have made it. Hence the clear and distinct idea of the mind not only cannot be the criterion of other truths, but it cannot be the criterion of that of the mind itself; for while the mind apprehends itself, it does not make itself, and because it does not make itself it is ignorant of the form or mode by which it apprehends itself." [35] Still less have we scientific or demonstrative knowledge of God's existence and nature. "Those who try to prove God *a priori* are guilty of impious curiosity; for to do that amounts to making oneself the god of God, and thereby denying the God one seeks." [36] God knows all things, because He is their creator. In mathematics man counterfeits God's creation by abstraction and definition, and thereby achieves science; but this science is not knowledge of realities like God's knowledge of the created universe, but of man-created fictions. Its certainty is not a matter of Cartesian self-evidence, but arises from the fact that it is a constructive science, not only in its problems but even in its theorems, though the latter have commonly been supposed to be objects of contemplation only. In proportion as human knowledge contains anything more than such abstractions or unreal entities, it is less certain: mechanics less certain than geometry and arithmetic, the rest of physics less certain than mechanics, psychology and history less certain than physics. Physics is made to approximate true science, not by the application of the geometric method after the fashion of Descartes, but by the employment of the experimental method of Bacon and Galileo, for the reason that he who performs an experiment creates the conditions under which he makes his observations. "The things which are proved in physics are those to which we can perform something similar, and the ideas as to natural things which are thought to have the most perfect clarity and on which there is the completest consensus, are those to the support of which we can bring experiments by which we so far imitate nature." [37] Vico here, as in his basic principle itself, anticipates Kant, who says that Bacon and Galileo saw that "reason has insight only into that which it produces after a plan of its own"; "holding in one hand its principles . . . and in the other the experiment . . . it must adopt as its guide . . . that which it has itself put into nature. It is thus that the study of nature has entered on the secure path of a science, after having for so many centuries done nothing but grope in the dark." [38]

Vico thus emancipated himself from the metaphysics, theology and physics of Descartes by reducing those favored sciences to a level with the studies Descartes had despised: history, observation of nature, empirical knowledge of man and society, eloquence and poetry. But this was scarcely a vindication of his own cherished pursuits with which Vico could long remain satisfied.

While working on his life of Antonio Carafa, he read or reread Grotius *On the Law of War and Peace* to orient himself in questions of international law on which he was obliged to touch; and in Grotius he saw for the first time how philosophy and philology, the science of universals and the research into every sort of particular fact, need not remain two separate forms of knowledge merely juxtaposed or opposed, but might be united to constitute "a system of universal law." Grotius led him on to other natural-law theorists, such as Selden and Pufendorf, and Pufendorf's critique of Hobbes led him to inform himself also of the works of that greatest system-builder of a nation not given to building systems. In Hobbes he found the clue for a further and decisive extension of his own theory of knowledge. For Hobbes, who allowed that geometry had been handed down to us by the Greeks, and that Galileo had laid the foundations of natural philosophy, but asserted that civil philosophy was no older than his own *De cive* (1642), had later said:

Of arts, some are demonstrable, others indemonstrable; and demonstrable are those the construction of the subject whereof is in the power of the artist himself, who, in his demonstration, does no more but deduce the consequences of his own operation. The reason whereof is this, that the science of every subject is derived from a precognition of the causes, generation, and construction of the same; and consequently where the causes are known, there is place for demonstration, but not where the causes are to seek for. Geometry therefore is demonstrable, for the lines and figures from which we reason are drawn and described by ourselves; *and civil philosophy is demonstrable, because we make the commonwealth ourselves.* But because of natural bodies we know not the construction, but seek it from the effects, there lies no demonstration of what the causes be we seek for, but only of what they may be.[39]

Grotius, Pufendorf, and above all Hobbes taught Vico further that the first founders of civil society were not philosophers filled with "recondite wisdom" as he had hitherto thought, but man-beasts devoid of culture or humanity, yet guided by an obscure instinct of self-preservation that in time would draw them into social compact and thus lay the foundation-stone of civilization. It needed only the hint to revive in Vico memories of his youth, when, reading for the first time the marvelous fifth book of Lucretius, he had encountered a similar hypothesis, Epicurean but seductive: the great forest of the earth primordially rich in life-giving juices, nourishing gigantic members in men and beasts;—the first men devoid of religion, language or law; living alone in caves beside the streams; feeding on acorns, arbute-berries and other wild fruits; hunting the beasts with stones and clubs; promiscuously copulating on sight and impulse;—the first construction of huts and other rude shelters; the wearing of skins of slain beasts to ward off the cold; the gradual turning to monogamy and recognized paternity;—the theory of the spontaneous origin of speech, the comparison with the gestures of children, and the polemic against the conventionalist theory of language;—the first acquaintance with fire brought by the first stroke of lightning (or by the friction of trees in a storm), and its application to the cooking of food and the fashioning of tools and weapons;—the founding of cities and citadels; the origin of laws; the origin of religion in the awe and fear inspired by thunder and lightning, earthquakes, cataclysms, the motions of the planets, comets, meteors;—and the other details of that vast vision of the rise of man.[40]

There sounded again in Vico's ears the conversations he had heard thirty years before, in which his friends who were soon thereafter haled before the Inquisition had said that "before Adam there were men in the world, who were composed of atoms, as all the animals were; and the shrewder among them began to build houses, farms, forts and cities; and formed unions among themselves, some here, some there; and the shrewdest made themselves out to be sons of Saturn, Jupiter or some other god . . . in order to be honored and venerated by the people; and later, when Christ our Lord came into the world, he also was ambitious to rule, and had himself declared the son of God, though he was not, and promulgated laws and got himself disciples and followers; and because the Hebrews knew he was an impostor, they had him taken and killed." [41]

He also recalled certain suggestions on the origin of speech and writing, which he had read in Bacon without sensing at the time that they had potentially an importance far beyond that which their author claimed for them. Somewhat in the vein of Lucretius, Bacon had spoken of the spontaneous origin of speech, of gestures preceding words, of ideographic or hieroglyphic writing arising by spontaneous analogy, before the invention of alphabets.[42]

Thus from Lucretius, Bacon and the natural-law theorists Vico derived suggestions which had an irresistible appeal to a mind struggling to free itself from the last remaining shackles of intellectualism. Certainly to posit as the founders of civilization not sages but brutes; to posit as the primitive and therefore basic forms of apprehension not reason but instinct, feeling, intuition, manipulatory inventiveness (that is, the apprehension not of the universal but of the particular); and to posit as the primitive and basic modes of generalization not the universals of science and philosophy but those of poetry ("poetic characters" as Vico came to call them)— was to emancipate oneself at last from Descartes and give a new dignity to those philological and historical disciplines which he had despised as resting on inferior cognitive faculties.

In the seething ferment of these new ideas in which Vico was immersed from his fiftieth to his sixty-fifth year (1717–1732), it could not fail to give him repeated pause that the initial suggestions, the points of departure, were all in pagan or Protestant authors; that in Lucretius and his master Epicurus they were accompanied by explicit denials of divine providence, and in all the rest, in spite of prudential professions of faith, by an implicit denial; and that earlier and cruder expressions of partly similar ideas had subjected the dearest friends of his youth to imprisonment and condemnation by the Inquisition. It was not worldly caution that moved him, but pious scruple; for whatever his youthful vagaries had been, he was now a devout Catholic, on terms of intimacy with monks and priests whose sympathy he cherished and whose praise he coveted in his increasing alienation from the Cartesian intellectual atmosphere about him. Yet worldly caution would not have been pointless, as shortly appeared from the response to the first expression of his new ideas in the *Universal Law*. Its critics were anticurialists in constant opposition to the clerics with whom Vico was now on such friendly terms, and especially to the ultracurialist Torno, whom he had chosen for his ecclesiastical censor. "Under color of a simulated piety," as he wrote to his friend Father Giacco, they not only charged his *Universal Law* with irreligion, but also revived against him the memory of his youthful "weaknesses and errors, which, as I have gravely noted them in others, remain deeply etched in my memory." [43]

It is not possible to trace with any assurance the precise steps by which Vico moved toward a resolution of the conflict between his Catholic piety and his eminently secular if not heretical philosophy. But he attributes the immediate inspiration of his *Universal Law* to a passage of St. Augustine,[44] and it seems likely that in rereading the *City of God* while meditating his new philosophy of history, he came gradually to see how a reinterpretation of the action of providence in history would not only put his scruples at rest, but also supply a radical philosophic deficiency in all the authors from Epicurus to Hobbes whose lead he was following, and substitute a "rational *civil* theology of divine providence" for the specious *natural* theology which was riding in the wake of physical science. For this purpose, the essential distinction was that between the general providence which extended to all the gentile peoples, and the special grace which in antiquity was confined to the Hebrews. The latter was direct and transcendent, the former indirect and immanent, operating through nature and second causes, leaving individual freedom of choice intact, yet effecting a regular evolution in the aggregate toward society and civilization. The immanent logic of this process of development was uniform for all peoples in its general outline, and "providence" was the obvious formula for it.

The crux of the matter was the problem of origins, the

historian's problem par excellence, which Bacon, in his inventory of histories, had cavalierly dismissed as insoluble.

As to the heathen antiquities of the world, it is in vain to note them for deficient. Deficient they are no doubt, consisting most of fables and fragments; but the deficience cannot be holpen; for antiquity is like fame, *caput inter nubila condit,* her head is muffled from our sight. For the history of the exemplar states [of Greece and Rome] it is extant in good perfection.[45]

Vico was both more sceptical and more hopeful. Under his scrutiny the extant history of the exemplar states themselves dissolved into fables and fragments as far as the Peloponnesian and the Second Punic War. But he undertook to reconstruct their history and that of heathen antiquity as well, by applying to these very fables and fragments a new exegesis, based on comparative mythology and a new genetic psychology ("a metaphysic of the human mind" he called it) in place of the meager and rationalistic psychology of the natural-law theorists.

Hobbes had said that civil philosophy was demonstrable because we make the commonwealth ourselves. Certainly Leviathan was not begotten by any such contract as he defined; yet the clue was there, needing only to be rightly understood. The commonwealth was made by man, but not by such men as we now are, at the conscious, rational, intellectualist level on which we elaborate definitions of the social contract. Yet the first makers of it may be discovered by probing the depths of our own minds, and applying that depth psychology to Bacon's fables and fragments. At the end of his long search, when the *New Science* has fully matured, Vico is able to sing this song of triumph:

In the night of thick darkness which envelops the earliest antiquity, so remote from ourselves, there shines the eternal and never failing light of a truth beyond all question: that the world of human society has certainly been made by men, and its principles are therefore to be found within the modifications of our own human mind. Whoever reflects on this cannot but marvel that the philosophers should have bent all their energies to the study of the world of nature, which, since God made it, He alone truly knows; and that they should have neglected the study of the world of nations, which, since men have made it, man can truly know. This aberration was a consequence of that infirmity of the human mind, by which, immersed and buried in the body, it naturally inclines to take notice of bodily things, and finds the effort to attend to itself too laborious.[46]

C. THE PRINCIPLES OF THE NEW SCIENCE[47]

MODERN historiography, so far as it differs from ancient and medieval in principle and not merely in technical proficiency, range and quantity of output, rests on the discovery of man as a peculiarly historical being, subject to a development transcending the life of any individual, nation or race. It is by virtue of this discovery that modern history has been the complement and polar opposite of modern physics in the making of the modern mind.

Wherever the impact of this discovery is felt, the interest in history shifts from personal feats and exploits, wars, treaties, alliances, and dynastic successions, to customs, laws, institutions, forms of economic and social organization, languages, arts, religions, sciences, climates of opinion. History ceases to be Cicero's "storehouse of the countless lessons of the past," Augustine's mixed career of the two cities, the medieval roll call of saints and sinners, heroes and villains, Machiavelli's repertory of models for a wise prince's imitation, Bossuet's epiphany of a kind of celestial Louis XIV, Bayle's register of atomic doubt-resistant fact, or Bolingbroke's "philosophy teaching by examples." It is not embarrassed by the failure of peoples and governments to learn anything from it, since it has nothing to teach but history. It has acquired an end of its own, which emancipates it from theology, morals and politics. In pursuit of that end, it calls into being a corps of auxiliary disciplines: anthropology, genetic and social psychology, sociology, comparative mythology, comparative law, philosophy of history.

So far as this discovery and the adumbration of these auxiliary disciplines can be ascribed to a single man or book, the man is Vico and the book is the *New Science*. The discovery and the adumbration were in the first place outgrowths of the attempt to solve a problem inherited from the natural-law theorists, but in the successive versions of Vico's major work from the *Universal Law* to the third *New Science* (1720–1744) the problem was increasingly overshadowed by the new historiography brought to bear upon it.

The problem as Vico found it was the construction of civil society out of individual units. In that form the problem was insoluble; but specious solutions had been proposed in terms of an abstract natural law deduced from the assumed nature of these individual units: a law *quod semper, ubique, et ab omnibus*. This law supposed to transcend history was in reality only "the natural law of the philosophers" of the seventeenth century, a rationalization of the demands of the rising middle class, representing therefore a stage of culture remote from the beginnings of civil society. To ascribe universality to this law was in effect to extend indefinitely backwards the psychology of a developed civilization. To this and every similar "vanity of the scholars" and "vanity of the nations," Vico opposed his fundamental axiom that "every theory must start from the point where the matter of which it treats first began to take shape." [48] The problem of the construction of civil society must accordingly be reformulated as the problem of its historical origins.

The "natural law of the philosophers" was conceived in terms of the distinction drawn by the later Roman jurists between civil law, natural law, and "law of nations" (*ius civile, naturale, gentium*). This distinction was a late product of philosophic reflection and analysis; even then, there were not three distinct bodies of law corresponding thereto; still less was this the case in the beginnings of law and society. For the concrete reality in which all three were merged without distinction, Vico therefore employed the portmanteau phrase "natural law of the peoples" (*ius naturale gentium, diritto naturale delle genti*), which he contrasted with the "natural law of the philosophers," the abstractions, that is, of Grotius, Pufendorf and Hobbes. This one law was natural, as growing naturally with the growth of society; it was civil, as being for each society *its* law, the changing measure of *its* changing civilization; and it was *ius gentium* in the double sense of (*a*) law of the peoples, as being the work not of the "recondite wisdom" of mythical founding sages, but of the "vulgar wisdom" of the peoples themselves, and (*b*) universal law, as having beneath superficial differences of form a substance which at a given stage of a society's development was identical with that of any other at the corresponding stage of its development. In this pregnant sense of the phrase, the problem inherited by Vico was reformulated as that of "the natural law of the peoples."

To the first *New Science* Vico prefixed a synopsis beginning as follows:

IDEA OF THE WORK

in which is meditated a Science concerning the nature [= genesis] of the nations, from which [nature] has issued their humanity [= civilization], which in every case began with religion and was completed by sciences, disciplines, and arts.

BOOK ONE

"We wander ignorant of the men and the places": VIRGIL.—Necessity of the end and difficulty of the means of finding this Science within the ferine wandering of Hobbes's licentious and violent men, of Grotius's solitary, weak and needy simpletons, of Pufendorf's vagrants cast into this world without divine care or help, from which the gentile nations have arisen.[49]

His starting point was therefore roughly the state of nature of the natural-law theories. In order to reach it from *Genesis,* as his scruples required, he imagined the descendants of Ham and Japheth, and those of Shem except the Hebraic line, as dispersed after the flood, wandering in "the vast forest of the earth," forgetting the speech and customs of their ancestors, and descending to the level of beasts.

During the two centuries Vico allowed for this process of bestialization, the earth slowly dried, until the first thunder-claps caused by its exhalations startled these brutish men here and there in the act of shameless canine copulation with captured women, and terrified them into the shelter and secrecy of caves for their intercourse. Out of these retreats of fear and shame the first families arose, with a settled life apart in the caves of the earth, sanctioned by "the frightful religions" started in their minds by the thunderbolts of the sky god. With settled habitations came clearing and tilling of the soil, ownership, property, morality, and burial of the dead. Marriage, childbirth, burial, the sowing and reaping of crops, were surrounded with religious ceremonial. The family-father was its king, priest and prophet, sacrificing to the gods to win their favor, and taking auspices to declare their will. He was the arbiter of right and wrong, rewarding the good and punishing the wrongdoer. This "state of the families," "monastic, Cyclopean, monarchic," and not the antecedent chaos, with its "bestial communism of women" and "confusion of human seeds," was the true state of nature from which the civil state emerged; and the three pre-political institutions of religion, marriage, and burial of the dead were the first principles of the new science. This primitive stage of social evolution Vico called "the age of the gods."

The state of nature was one not of static equality, but of differentiation, inequality, and dialectical change. There was inequality between the organized family and the "lawless vagrants" still living in that chaos out of which the family grew; inequality within the family, inequality between family and family, inequality among the vagrants themselves. The more violent and enterprising of the latter raided the homesteads of the settlers and burned or carried off their crops; but they preyed also on the weaker and more helpless of their own kind, who were thereby driven to throw themselves on the mercy of the settlers. "Grotius's simpletons and Pufendorf's waifs, to save themselves from Hobbes's men of violence, fled to the altars of the strong." These refugees were received as dependents, "clients," serfs, tillers of the soil, "hewers of wood and drawers of water." The family unit was thus enlarged and still further differentiated, and the tension between its elements was heightened. To the distinctions of sex and generation there was added a distinction of blood and class.

The serfs of a family had less in common with its blood members than with the serfs of another; the father of a family had more in common with the father of another than with his own serfs. To secure themselves against mutinies of their serfs as well as against outlaw invasions, the fathers formed mutual alliances, patrician orders, "heroic states," with the fathers as citizens and the serfs as plebs. The heroic state was not a monarchy like the earlier family state, for its king was simply one of the fathers, the magistrate of the order; often, in fact, there were two or more such magistrates. It was not a democracy, for the "people" was simply the patrician order, exclusive of the plebs; the only freedom, the only rights, were those of the patricians; the fatherland was the land of the fathers. It was in fact a feudal aristocracy. This second stage of social evolution Vico called "the age of the heroes."

The whole life of these heroic states centered in the conflict between patricians and plebeians. The two classes, as Vico put it, had two eternal contrary properties, the plebeians wishing always to change the state, and the nobles to preserve it as it was. The patricians were better organized; they owned the land; they had the arms and the military discipline; they had a monopoly of public office and knowledge of law; they alone knew how to ascertain the will and win the favor of the gods; the solemn rites of marriage and burial were theirs alone; and they were bound by oath to keep the plebs in subjection. But it was inevitable that the plebs should press successively for land tenure, legal marriage, legitimate children, testamentary succession, citizenship, eligibility to office, and the sharing of the auspices, the key to all the rest. And it was inevitable that the ruling class should be compelled to admit the plebs to one after another of the rights which it had at first so jealously guarded. The heroic states were transformed into democratic or "free popular republics," and the third stage of social evolution, the historical age, "the age of men," began.

It was their economic and social position in relation to each other, and not a difference of mentality, which determined that in the long unfolding of legal change the plebeians should represent reason and the patricians authority. The approximation of law to equity, the gradual establishment of equal rights, was brought about by the struggle of the plebeians to acquire full *humanitas*. The vindication of the rational nature of man as man was an historical process, the same process by which the rationality was achieved; and the main spring of the process was the dialectical opposition of the classes.

But the age of men ran its course too. The discipline, respect for law, and social solidarity of the patrician orders gave way to a humane and easy tolerance. Philosophy took the place of religion. Equality led to license. There was dispersion of private interests and decline of public spirit. Birth was first displaced by wealth as the sign of fitness to rule, since to acquire or retain it implied industry, thrift, and foresight. But in time even the property qualification was swept away, and political power was extended to those who lacked the leisure or the will to exercise it wisely. The meanest citizen could press the public force into the service of his appetites and whims, or sell his vote to the highest bidder among faction leaders and demagogues. The external symptoms of the process of disintegration were abated by the rise of bureaucratic monarchies, for the most part even more "humane" than the democracies, yet relieving nobles and plebeians alike of public responsibility. In this last phase of "the age of men," the humanization and softening of customs and laws continued, until breakdown within or conquest from without brought on a reversion to barbarism, and a new cycle of the three ages began. In Europe Christianity now took the place of the "frightful religions" of the first "age of the gods"; the later middle age revived the feudal institutions of the "age of the heroes"; and "the natural law of the philosophers" of the seventeenth century was a product of the second "age of men."

We are now in position to discern what was involved in Vico's reformulation of the problem of the construction of civil society as that of its historical development, and in his solution of it by working his way back from "the natural law of the philosophers" to "the natural law of the peoples." The problem could not be solved by the analytic device of starting with the human beings of the second "age of men," stripping them of the utilitarian advantages they owed to the politically organized societies in which they lived, yet leaving them in full possession of the rational faculties required to appreciate those advantages and to contract at the lowest terms for their recovery. For these men and these faculties were the men and the faculties of these societies at this stage of their development, two cycles removed from the origins of civil society. They had become what they were by the same historical process by which the societies themselves had evolved. In fashioning this world of nations, man had fashioned himself. The fully developed rationality, the planning intelligence of his mature humanity, was the outcome of that process; and it was a fatal error to read it back into the initial steps, which were taken by brutish men who did not so much as know the meaning of a promise.

The only approach to a social contract in the age-long process was the alliance of the fathers which marked the transition from the family state to the heroic state. But this was no single act of prudent foresight, the work of a constitutional assembly drawing up articles of federation. It was itself a long process in which larger and more permanent unions grew insensibly out of smaller and more temporary ones, each improvised under the stress of a particular occasion and having no aim beyond it. Far from intending the national states and cultures which later eventuated, the fathers did not consciously plan even the heroic states which were the immediate outcome of their spontaneously acquired habits of cooperation. Instead, *rebus ipsis dictantibus,* the heroic states were called into being and gradually strengthened by repeated mutinies of serfs and raids of outlaws, who least of all had any such design.

Here as throughout the development of man and society there was thus an inherent logic transcending the conscious intentions of individual agents. For this immanent logic, which Hegel was later to call "the cunning of reason" deploying the passions of men, which Wundt was to call "the heterogony of ends" and Bosanquet "a teleology above the level of finite consciousness," Vico sought no other formula than that of providence acting not by force of laws imposed from without but "making use of the customs of men, which are as free of all force as the spontaneous expressions of their own nature."

Men have themselves made this world of nations . . . but this world has evidently issued from a mind often diverse, at times quite contrary, and always superior to the particular ends that men have proposed to themselves; which narrow ends, made means to serve wider ends, it has always employed to preserve the human race upon the earth. Men who meant to gratify their bestial lust and abandon their offspring, founded instead the chastity of marriage from which the families arose. The fathers meant to exercise without restraint their paternal power over their serfs, and they subjected them to the civil power from which the cities arose. The ruling class of nobles meant to abuse their lordly freedom over the plebeians, and they had to submit to the laws which established popular freedom. The free peoples meant to shake off the yoke of their laws, and they became subject to monarchs. The monarchs meant to strengthen their own positions by debasing their subjects with all the vices of dissoluteness, and they disposed them to endure slavery at the hands of stronger nations. The nations meant to dissolve themselves, and their remnants fled for safety to the wilderness, whence, like the phoenix, they rose again. That which did all this was mind, because men did it with intelligence; it was not fate, because they did it by choice; not chance, because the results of their always so acting are perpetually the same.[50]

Under the spell of the tremendous advance of physical science in the seventeenth century, the thinkers of Vico's time had come to regard it as having a certainty far superior to that of history, and to regard the laws of physical nature as constituting a revelation of God superior to any revelation of Himself in history; indeed, as being the only revelation above suspicion. Not content to raise history again to an equal status in these respects, Vico's theory of knowledge claimed for it a higher evidence, and his new science became in one of its aspects "a rational civil theology of divine providence" claiming precedence over the "natural theology" which contemplated that attribute of God in the physical order.[51] For though Vico dwelt by preference on Bacon's "exemplar states" of Greece and Rome, what he sought and found in them was "an ideal eternal history, traversed in time by the history of every nation in its origin, growth, acme, decline and fall." [52] The ideal eternal state was thus not the abstract state of Plato, nor some particular state at some past or future stage of its development, but "the great city of the nations founded and governed by God," [53] or, more simply, history itself.

Vico's reconstruction of the development of society and civilization, by which his problem was solved, was made possible by a discovery which he calls "the master key" of his new science; namely that "the first gentile peoples were poets . . . who spoke in poetic characters." [54] This discovery had cost him, he says, the laborious researches of twenty years, groping his way back "from these humane and refined natures of ours to those wild and savage natures which we cannot really imagine and can only apprehend with great toil." [55] It is at this point that we can observe most clearly that transition from rationalism to historicism in Vico's own mind, which took place in the thought of Europe generally in the century after his death. For he himself had begun with most of the prejudices which it was the burden of his new science to undermine. As Bacon had assumed in his *Wisdom of the Ancients* that the fables and myths preserved in Homer and Hesiod were relics from wiser and better times, so Vico, in his *Ancient Wisdom of the Italians,* had assumed that the Latin language had early been made by disciples of Etruscan and Greek teachers a repository of profound philosophy, and especially of that of Zeno of Elea. On this assumption, he had proceeded to read his own metaphysics and epistemology into certain Latin roots and phrases. One is tempted to say that if he had begun with no such assumption, he would have found the way less toilsome to his mature view that the wisdom of the ancients was popular, not recondite or profound; poetic, not philosophical; practical, not theoretical. But it is more likely that he would not have found the way at all; that if he had not looked for abstruse and speculative ideas in the roots of speech, he would never have discovered the true character of the fantastic thought in which language began.

The primary importance of this discovery for Vico arose from the fact that when he had turned the problem of the construction of society into that of its historical origin and development, he was at once confronted by traditions assigning the founding of states and their constitutional changes to sages, lawgivers and poets. To take these traditions at face value was to land in a rationalism nearly as preposterous as that of the social contract from which he was struggling to escape. On the other hand, to interpret them as noble lies of Plato's kind, pedagogical impostures invented for reasons of state, was not only a worse rationalism, but deprived of evidential value the only materials available for early history. Just as the "frightful religions" of primitive men were not contrived by clever impostors but sprang directly from the fear and credulity of the people themselves, so the mythical stories of the origins of society were not artful allegorical renderings of antecedent ratiocination, but spontaneous expressions of the folk mind of the ages preceding the rise of reflective thinking. As yet incapable of logical abstraction and generalization, primitive man thought in terms of "fantastic universals" or "poetic characters," particular men (real or imagined) and particular acts or gestures magnified into types of social classes and institutions. Romulus, for example, was such a poetic character or type of the fathers founding Rome on feudal clientships, and dividing it into patrician and plebeian orders. To him were ascribed on the one hand all "the properties of the founders of the first cities of Latium," and on the other all the laws, developed over centuries, "concerning the orders." Numa was a type of the religiosity of the fathers in their priestly rôles; to him were assigned all the laws "concerning sacred things and divine ceremonies," even those which arose "in the most pompous period of Roman religion." Tarquinius Priscus was a similar type of the fathers surrounding their political power with the trappings of majesty; Tullus Hostilius of the organization of their military system; and Servius Tullius of their concession to the plebs of bonitary ownership of land. These and the other so-called kings of Rome were of a piece with Minos and Cadmus, Draco and Lycurgus among the Greeks. But historians in the age of men, who had lost the key to primitive psychology and supposed that men had always thought like themselves, took these popular traditions for literal history and invented chronological systems which they could be trimmed to fit. Until their work was dissolved again into the elements from which they had composed it, and until these mythical elements were interpreted by the new science, there could be no credible history of Greece and Rome before the Peloponnesian and the Second Punic War.

Vico not only tracks the evolution of civil society into the subtlest nuances of its subordinate phases, but sketches in the parallel development of the other elements of culture, as if to reinforce his main thesis that the state exists by nature and history and not by convention, by showing that this is true of human culture as a whole. Corresponding to the three stages of the political cycle are three kinds of "natures" (ways of apprehending the nature of the world and of man)—animistic, mythopœic, scientific; three kinds of customs—religious, punctilious, humane; three kinds of natural law; three kinds of language expressed in three kinds of characters; three kinds of jurisprudence employing three kinds of authority and as many of "reasons"—divination, reason of state, natural equity—in as many of judgments. Vico has a sharp eye for organic relations among the aspects of a single culture, as in his fine pages deriving the Socratic and post-Socratic logic, metaphysics and moral philosophy from the disputations of the Athenian assembly and courts.[56] But it is "one of the constant labors" of the new science to show that "the natural law of the peoples" had an independent origin and development among each people, and only later, "as a result of wars, embassies, alliances and commerce, came to be recognized as common to the entire human race." [57] And not the least of Vico's achievements was his brilliant critique of "the fiction that the law of the Twelve Tables came to Rome from Greece." His other chef-d'œuvre of criticism was his "discovery of the true Homer" as the Greek people of the heroic or poetic age, mythological in thought, barbaric in manners, and ignorant of the "recondite wisdom" of the philosophers. The two critiques had a precisely parallel development in Vico's thinking, and played parallel rôles in his reconstructions of Greek and Roman history. And just as the permanent value of his Homeric theory lay not in the denial of a personal Homer but in the recovery of the modes of thought and feeling of the age reflected in the Homeric poems, so that of his demonstration of the essentially archaic and genuinely Roman character of the Twelve Tables lay in his showing how "the ancient Roman law was a serious poem, and the ancient jurisprudence a severe kind of poetry, within which are found the first rough outlines of legal metaphysic." [58]

One of the principal aspects of the new science is "a history of human ideas," the first important step toward the realization of Bacon's great desideratum of "a just story" of "the general state of learning . . . from age to age." Here as elsewhere Vico concentrates by preference on the origins and early stages. The second book of the second *New Science,* much the longest of the five, is called "Of Poetic Wisdom" (the vulgar wisdom of the age of heroes) and has for its main divisions poetic metaphysics, logic, morals, economics, politics, physics, cosmography, astronomy, chronology and geography. Whereas Bacon's *Novum Organum* had shown "how the sciences as they now stand may be further perfected," Vico's *novum organum* of history disclosed "the ancient world of the sciences, how crude they were in their origins, and how they were gradually refined until they reached the form in which we have received them." [59] Here is one more expression of Vico's reaction against the rationalism which exalted natural science and disparaged history. He puts the sciences in their place by swallowing them up in history, and anticipates the later view that the true philosophy of science is simply its history.

IV. Vico's Reputation and Influence

In the present state of Vico studies, a satisfactory account of his influence is not possible, for the reason that research into the diffusion of his ideas beyond Italy in the eighteenth century has scarcely begun, and that in the nineteenth century, where we are on surer ground, they had already so permeated the thought of Europe that, with few exceptions, those who took the trouble to read him for themselves did not so much learn from him as recognize in him what was already their own, and acknowledge him as the great forerunner of doctrines and causes to which they were already committed. It is not likely that we shall soon be in a better position in this respect, for the diffusion was piecemeal: there was no eighteenth-century thinker who grasped the whole range of Vico's thought; and outside Italy his influence was largely indirect and anonymous. The acknowledgment of intellectual debts was still a rare grace, not yet a canon of literary etiquette. The acknowledgments in respect of Vico lie buried in unpublished letters and in books indexed imperfectly or not at all, and are turned up by chance here and there in the course of other investigations. Many links are still to be discovered, particularly in Great Britain. In the meantime, we can do little more than sketch the history of his reputation, and indicate directions in which further research may establish genuine influence.[60]

A. IN ITALY

THE story of the varying fortunes of Vico's ideas in Italy has often been told, and it will suffice here to mention a few episodes which had repercussions elsewhere. There was a fairly continuous Vico tradition in aesthetics and literary criticism;[61] Conti absorbed some elements, and Pagano more; they are prominent in the dissertations and notes accompanying Cesarotti's translations of Homer and Ossian; they animate the discourses and essays of Foscolo; and eventually inspire the work of such masters of criticism as De Sanctis and Croce. There was also a continuous Vico tradition in jurisprudence, economics, and political theory; his name and ideas are never far to seek in the immensely productive Neapolitan school of law. This tradition goes back to his ablest pupil, Genovesi, who occupied at Naples the first European chair of political economy, and to whom we owe the memory of Vico's pungent comment on people who keep up appearances in public by starving themselves at home: "There are too many whose carriages are drawn by their own guts."[62] More widely known abroad was Ferdinando Galiani, whose education had been directed by his uncle, Vico's friend Celestino Galiani, and who was himself the first publicist in whom Vico's influence bore fruit. Friend and indefatigable correspondent of the leaders of the French enlightenment, he was its shrewd though good-humored critic, and the standpoint of his criticism was Vichian though the shafts of wit and the practical applications in his essays on trade in grain, on money, on the duties of neutral princes, were his own. In the last quarter of the century Filangieri in his *Science of Legislation* (1780–85) attempted a conciliation of Vico's ideas with those of Montesquieu and the Encyclopedists. His work was admired and its circulation promoted by Franklin, and an English translation appeared in 1806. Pagano, mentioned above as a critic, was more famous in Italy and abroad for his works on criminal procedure. "If you would attain

Vico's flights," said Cuoco, "you must begin by walking in Pagano's footsteps." [63]

Two controversies of some proportions kept Vico's name before the educated public in the eighteenth century. The first revolved around his critique of the Law of the Twelve Tables, which was attacked and defended in Italy and France within his lifetime. The second was the famous contest of the *Ferini* and the *Antiferini,* which also began in his lifetime, but culminated between 1760 and 1780. His theory of the ferine origin of gentile humanity was defended by the former party, and attacked by the latter as incompatible with Scripture and with Catholic philosophy. The chief protagonists of the two sects were the Neapolitan Emanuele Duni,[64] professor of jurisprudence at the University of Rome, and the Dominican G. F. Finetti,[65] who saw more clearly than others that the *New Science,* however innocent in intent, was by no means innocuous in effect. To admit the feral state as the starting-point for the rise of humanity, and to make the development of society a matter of internal dialectic, was to put the entire structure of Catholic thought in jeopardy. He saw too that Vico's theory of the origin of religion was Lucretian, not Christian; and that the disintegration of the personality of Homer and of other heroic characters would open the way to the ultimate disintegration of Moses, the patriarchs and prophets. Duni's defense of Vico, on the other hand, was incidental to his application of the principles of the *New Science* to Roman history, and his adaptation and development of Vico's philosophy of law. He has some fine pages on the way in which the class struggle, when apparently resolved in its political guise, openly assumes the economic form.[66] In a dedicatory letter to Tanucci in his *Essay on Universal Jurisprudence,* he has these memorable words, expressing feelings not peculiar to himself, but common to nearly all the Italian epigoni of Vico in the eighteenth century, and to many in the nineteenth:

I must confess to your excellency the sin of having taken Vico's works in my hands a thousand times, and a thousand times turned away from them lest my talent should be taken captive. But then, whether by the exigencies of my profession, or by the surprising pleasure which overcame me whenever I succeeded in penetrating his thought to its depths, or whether by both together, I was led to banish from my sight all books but his, and I determined, in spite of every natural aversion, to drink the bitter draught until it coursed in my veins, and my mind renewed its youth with the joy of being able in good faith to glory in having grasped something of the truth.[67]

But neither Duni nor anyone else who borrowed this or that from Vico in the pre-revolutionary period was able to free himself altogether from the prevailing rationalist temper, to grasp Vico's thought as an integral whole, or even to place himself at its living center. Not until the enlightenment had run its full course, not until a social movement arose for which Vico's historical vision was a vital necessity, was there widespread serious study and adequate comprehension of it. This movement was the post-revolutionary reaction, whose foremost representatives were the Federalists in America, Burke in England, De Maistre in France, and Vincenzo Cuoco in Italy. The transmission lines from Vico to the Federalists and Burke have not been traced; but De Maistre studied him and quoted him in an important passage of his *Considerations on France* (1796) and elsewhere, and it has been shown that his ideas were largely Vichian;[68] and Cuoco's *Historical Essay on the Neapolitan Revolution of 1799* (1800) was consciously thought out from the center of Vico's vision. The Neapolitan republicans, he argued, had acted under the illusion that they could transfer the French Revolution to southern Italy; that a politico-social movement which had grown out of conditions peculiar to a single country could be grafted onto a country where those conditions were absent. This illusion was nourished by that of the French themselves, who "mistook as an effect of philosophy what was really the effect of the political circumstances in which their nation found itself." The philosophy had been imported easily enough, but even it could not really sink its roots into Italian soil, for Italy had already its native political philosophy in Machiavelli and Vico, who had provided in advance the necessary corrective of the abstract formulas of the rationalists and Encyclopedists, from which Montesquieu alone of French thinkers had been relatively free. Italian unity could only be achieved by the Italians themselves attaining a national consciousness reflecting the circumstances and the intellectual traditions of Italy, not those of France. Croce has called this book of Cuoco's "the first vigorous manifestation of Vichian thought, anti-abstract and historical, the beginning of the new historiography founded on the conception of the organic development of peoples, and of the new politics of national liberalism, at once revolutionary and moderate." [69]

Cuoco was the ablest of a group of Neapolitans who became Vico missionaries to northern Italy and France after the failure of the revolution at Naples. Their enthusiasm was communicated to Monti, Foscolo, and Manzoni, and gave the impetus for a series of new editions of Vico's works, beginning with that of the *New Science* at Milan in 1801. One of their number, Francesco Lomonaco, published a short life of Vico. Another, Francesco Salfi, reviewed the new editions in the *Revue Encyclopédique;* and discussed Vico in books and essays in French, one of which contained an analysis of his doctrines which was indirectly (as we shall see) the means of bringing to Jules Michelet his first acquaintance with them. Another, Pietro de Angelis, aroused the interest of Victor Cousin, was introduced by him to Michelet, and put the *New Science* in his hands. De Angelis spent his last years in Buenos Aires, which became the chief American center of interest in Vico. Cuoco himself addressed a letter on Vico's doctrines to De Gérando when he was at work on his *Histoire comparée des systèmes de philosophie;* gave them prominence in a series of articles in the *Giornale italiano* of Milan; and spoke of their significance for Italian culture in his recommendations for the reform of public instruction under Murat's regime.

If Vico's reputation had hitherto been predominantly Neapolitan, it now became Italian and international; and the *New Science* became the book of the Risorgimento. Wherever Italian patriots went—Foscolo, Prati and Mazzini to England, Ferrari and Gioberti to France and Belgium—they carried it in hand or in mind. Each succeeding school of philosophy—the liberal Catholic idealism of Rosmini and Gioberti, the positivism of Ferrari, Cattaneo, Siciliani, Villari and Ardigò, the Hegelian idealism of Spaventa and De Sanctis—had its interpretation of Vico. Ferrari edited his works (1835–37) and made "Vico and Italy" a war cry of nationalism. Prati lent the *New Science* to Coleridge at Highgate. Mazzini wrote Ugoni from London in 1839 that if Ferrari's edition were at hand he would attempt an article in *The British and Foreign Review* on the doctrines of Vico, "unknown or misunderstood here." [70] Spaventa in his *Italian Philosophy in its Relations with European Philosophy* (1862) traced "the circulation of Italian thought" through the two main movements of modern philosophy, the Cartesian of which Bruno and Campanella

were precursors and the Kantian of which Vico was, returning in each case to Italy to complete the cycle. Since Vico
was "the true precursor of all German thought," the Italian
reception of Hegelianism was but its home-coming.[71] Siciliani
devoted the first book of his *Renewal of Positive Philosophy
in Italy* (1871) to a "history of the *New Science* and critique of
the critics, interpreters and expositors of Vico's doctrines."
The unification of Italy once achieved, the interest in Vico
declined for a generation (except among positivists, sociologists and jurists), but was revived and augmented in the first
decade of the present century by Croce, who in his *Aesthetic*
interpreted the *New Science* as "philosophy of the spirit,
with particular amplification given to the philosophy of the
aesthetic spirit," and whose own philosophy has developed
pari passu with continuous reinterpretation of Vico's.[72] More
recently, Vico was restored to good Catholic standing, and
was unhappily again for a time a political symbol; he and
Mazzini were "the two greatest forerunners of Fascism."[73]

B. IN GERMANY

MEANWHILE, by paths that are still but partially known, Vico's
reputation was slowly spreading in Germany, where one
might have looked for the readiest reception and the most
rapid diffusion of his ideas. Hamann, "The Mage of the
North," was engaged on economics in 1777, and in one or
another of the Italian works on the subject he came upon
references to Vico's *New Science*. Supposing that the science
in question was the political economy of the Physiocrats, he
procured a copy from Florence and found in it not economics
but philology. So we learn from a letter [74] briefly describing
it to his disciple Herder, who therefore knew of Vico before
writing his *Ideas toward the Philosophy of the History of*

Mankind (1784–87), though he first discusses him in his *Letters in Furtherance of Humanity* (1797).[75] In the meantime Herder had traveled in Italy in 1789 and gained more for his philosophy of history in his first eight days at Naples than in three or four months at Rome; at Naples he had found "men quite different from those at Rome" and "quite different writings."[76] Perhaps he was prepared for this by Goethe, who had secured his appointment as court preacher at Weimar, for Goethe had visited Naples in March, 1787, and Filangieri had there made him acquainted with the *New Science* of

an old author in whose unfathomable depths these modern law-enthusiasts find the greatest stimulus and edification. His name is Giambattista Vico; they prefer him to Montesquieu. Glancing rapidly through the book which they presented to me as a sacred treasure, I saw that it contained sibylline presentiments of the good and just that would or should hereafter be realized, based on serious contemplation of life and tradition. It is a happy thing for a people to have such a patriarch [*Aeltervater*]. The writings of Hamann will one day appear in this light to the Germans.[77]

Goethe had taken the book back to Germany, and he lent it to Jacobi in 1792. Jacobi was sufficiently interested to secure some of Vico's other writings. In the *Ancient Wisdom of the Italians* he found a passage in which he discerned an anticipation of Kant. In his *On Divine Things and their Revelation* (1811) he called attention for the first time to this relationship, and quoted the passage, somewhat abridged and paraphrased.

The kernel of the Kantian philosophy is the . . . truth that we comprehend an object only so far as we are able to call it into being before us in thought, to create it in understanding. . . . Long before Kant, at the beginning of the eighteenth century, Vico wrote at Naples: "In geometry we demonstrate, because we create; before we demonstrate in physics, we must be able to create there also. Hence those people are to be condemned for impious curiosity who try to prove God *a priori*. The clarity of metaphysical truth is like that of light, which we know only by means of things that are opaque; for we see not light but light-reflecting objects. Physical things are opaque; they have form and boundary, and in them we see the light of metaphysical truth." [78]

(Three years later Coleridge lifted this quotation from Jacobi and adapted its context in his *Theory of Life,* so that the earliest known reference to Vico in English literature arrived via Filangieri, Goethe, and Jacobi.)

When Friedrich August Wolf published his *Prolegomena ad Homerum* in 1795 and gave the impetus to nineteenth-century higher criticism, he had no first-hand knowledge of Vico's more brilliant "discovery of the true Homer" sixty-five years before, though its results may have reached him indirectly through Wood or through Zoega and Heyne. Vico's name first attracted his attention several years later in the dissertations accompanying Cesarotti's translation of the *Iliad*. Wolf made other efforts to find the *New Science* before applying to Cesarotti himself, who sent him a copy in 1802; for Wilhelm von Humboldt wrote him from Berlin in 1801 that the library did not have it, and that Professor Buttmann, the Greek philologist, knew nothing of it or its author. Wolf published in his *Museum der Alterthumswissenschaft* in 1807 an article entitled "G. B. Vico on Homer," grudgingly acknowledging Vico's priority but showing no understanding of the importance of Vico's general theory of poetry, of which his Homeric criticism was only an application.

A long and lively controversy was initiated by the Swiss philologist J. K. Orelli in an article on "Niebuhr and Vico" in 1816, pointing out that the latter had still more wonderfully anticipated the views of Niebuhr than those of Wolf.[79]

From Niebuhr there was no response, but his friends took steps to remove any suspicion of plagiarism. As Savigny put it in his memoirs of Niebuhr in 1839,

Vico, with his profound genius, stood alone among his contemporaries, a stranger in his own country, overlooked or derided, although now the attempt is made to claim him as a national possession. Among such unfavorable circumstances his spirit could not come to full fruition. It is true that one finds in him scattered thoughts on Roman history resembling Niebuhr's. But these ideas are like flashes of lightning in a dark night, by which the traveler is led further astray rather than brought back to his path. *No one could profit from them who had not already found the truth in his own way.* Niebuhr in particular learned to know him only late and through others.[80]

Besides Orelli and Savigny, and perhaps the writings of Duni on Roman history, these others included Leopardi, who was befriended by Niebuhr in Rome in the eighteen-twenties. Leopardi's Neapolitan friend and editor Antonio Ranieri, speaking at the unveiling of a statue of Vico at Naples in 1861, reminded his hearers that in the interpretation of early Roman history Vico had come to be generally called the grandfather and Niebuhr the grandson (the father being Duni), and then related that

Giacomo Leopardi, while still a young man, was living at Rome in modest quarters. Niebuhr discovered and visited him there, and later made him known to the German public. But Giacomo, who had long been vexed by the unhappy silence of his visitor, finally took heart and called Vico his grandfather; and Niebuhr maintained from then on a still more unhappy silence, because his painful feeling of being in this point only a grandson sealed his mouth.

A German translation of the *New Science,* with Vico's autobiography prefixed, was published by W. E. Weber in 1822. In the same year Savigny, discerning the affinity of Vico's historical jurisprudence to his own, gave a copy of the first edition of the *Universal Law* to K. H. Müller, who published a translation in 1854, with notes comparing Vico's doctrines with those of Hegel, Niebuhr, Savigny and other German writers.

When Eduard Gans in 1837 published Hegel's lectures on the philosophy of history, he reviewed in his preface the various attempts at such a philosophy before Hegel, and found only three to be compared with his; namely, those of Vico, Herder, and Friedrich von Schlegel. German scholars continued to interest themselves in Vico at intervals, but neither Mommsen nor any considerable historian save Fridegar Mone acknowledged indebtedness to him; even Windelband's history of modern philosophy barely mentioned his name; and excepting an able monograph by the German Catholic Karl Werner (1881) there was no thoroughgoing study or just appreciation of his works until Croce's Vico revival spread to Germany. Croce dedicated his now classic exposition of Vico's philosophy (1911) to Windelband and sent him a copy along with a set of Vico's works. Windelband promptly added to the fifth edition of his history a long footnote giving a rounded though summary account of Vico's doctrines, which showed that he had read Croce's book but not that he had read Vico. In the first winter of the First World War Windelband lectured at Heidelberg on the philosophy of history, using Herder and Vico as representatives of two conceptions of it, the former that of universal history, the latter that of the laws exemplified by all particular histories. Windelband still referred to Croce for his understanding of Vico.

Especially interesting in Vico [he said] is his cyclical theory of historical process, with its *corsi* and *ricorsi,* and very acute and just is his observation that once a people has risen from barbarism to civilization it falls back into a new barbarism which is worse than the first. We are today in an excellent position to confirm his observation by the comparative method, since we have to do with the first sort of barbarism in our antagonists on the one side [Russia] and with the second in those on the other [France and England].[81]

The gradual recovery of sanity after the war brought a series of sober and valuable contributions to Vico studies by younger German scholars influenced by Croce——until Nazi scholarship followed the Fascist lead in deriving their common philosophy from Vico through Sorel.[82]

C. IN FRANCE [83]

IN 1728 Montesquieu was traveling in Italy, with the *Persian Letters* behind him and the *Greatness and Decline of the Romans* and the *Spirit of the Laws* still ahead. At Venice he met Antonio Conti, who was then in the first flush of his enthusiasm for the *New Science*. He probably showed it to Montesquieu and gave him some account of its leading ideas; and we know he urged him to procure a copy at Naples. Montesquieu may have met the author during his stay there in the following year, and received from his hands the copy of the first edition which was preserved in the library at La Brède until its dispersal a few years ago. The analogies between his principles and Vico's have persuaded some scholars that he studied the book, and an occasional verbal echo suggests that he had at least opened it here and there; but he nowhere refers to it, and until a careful comparative study has been made, a conclusion seems unwarranted.

Rousseau was at Venice for eighteen months in 1743–44 as secretary to the French embassy; and he there conceived the design of a great book on *Political Institutions*. The third and definitive edition of the *New Science* appeared early in 1744; Venice was the greatest book market of Italy, and the propaganda of Conti, Porcía and Lodoli had made it the chief center of interest in Vico's major work. It is probable, therefore, that Rousseau's attention was drawn to it as having a bearing on his own design, and he may have bought a copy of the third edition. As early as 1749 he began work on his *Essay on the Origin of Languages,* in the first six chapters of which he repeated the main points of Vico's theory—mute languages, hieroglyphics, the primacy of poetry over prose, of figurative language over language proper, and so on—and took a view of Homer resembling Vico's.[84] First intended for the *Encyclopedia,* and then as an appendix to his *Discourse on the Origin of Inequality,* it was gradually developed into an essay preparatory to his greater work on *Political Institutions,* and the very idea of using the origin of language as a clue to that of civil society may have come from Vico.

Ferdinando Galiani was secretary to the Neapolitan embassy at Paris for ten years beginning in 1759, and some traces of Vichian ideas in the writings of Diderot and his other Parisian friends are perhaps due to him. He represented Vico as a forerunner of Montesquieu, and said, half in jest, that "Vico dared attempt to ford the quagmire of metaphysics, and although he was bogged down he gave footing to a more fortunate thinker on the spirit of the laws of the nations." When Boulanger's three-volume *L'antiquité devoilée par ses usages* was posthumously published by Holbach in 1766, Galiani wrote to Tanucci: "The Frenchman has plundered Vico without citing him; but there are many here who have learned of the plagiarism and who ask me for the *New Science.*" On his visit to Paris in the same year, Beccaria must have spoken of the *New Science* at Holbach's, for a few months later Morellet, the French translator of his *Treatise on Crimes and Punishments,* wrote to him: "You will remember that you promised a copy of Vico to me, and also to the Baron. Please send them at your first opportunity."

The Marquis of Chastellux published in 1772 a two-volume work *On Public Felicity, or Considerations on the Condition of Humanity in the Various Epochs of History.* Voltaire placed it above the *Spirit of the Laws,* and enriched his copy with notes which were included in a later edition. Chastellux had been in Naples, and an Italian translation of his work was published there in 1782. Though it owed perhaps more to Muratori's book with a similar main title, it followed Vico on the history and primitive government of Rome; and Cuoco later wrote that Chastellux "understood Vico's doctrines better than anyone else." An English translation of this work was published in 1774. As early as 1759 Chastellux had been one of the circle of Hume's French admirers, and Hume established especially cordial relations with him during his stay in France in 1763–65. Although Vico is not mentioned in the published letters of Chastellux to Hume,[85] this may have been one avenue of transmission of Vico's ideas to the Scottish school.

Condillac's aesthetics may have owed something to Vico, directly or through Warburton. Of De Maistre we have already spoken. Fauriel, historian of Provence, friend and mentor of Madame de Staël, of Cabanis, Manzoni, Guizot and Thierry, made a study of the *New Science* in 1799, and his various historical and critical works show its influence. He later discussed Vico and the new aesthetics with Manzoni, who drew a famous comparison between Vico and Muratori in his *Discourse on Lombard History.* Guizot, soliciting an article for the *Archives philosophiques* in 1817, wrote Fauriel: "If you have time to do one on Vico too, that would be splendid." As late as 1838, an article on "Vico and His Times," submitted by Fauriel for a friend, was accepted by the *Revue des deux mondes,* but for some reason was not published. Renan did not greatly exaggerate when he said in 1855 that Fauriel was the man who had put into circulation the greatest number of new ideas in the first half of the century; and his lifelong interest in Vico was the source of no small part of them.

But the decisive event for Vico's European reputation in the nineteenth century was Michelet's discovery of the *New Science* in 1824.[86] It is a curious accident of history that this discovery was indirectly due to a Scottish philosopher who nowhere mentions Vico, though he has been suspected of borrowing from him his theory of the certainty of mathematics as resting not on axioms but on definitions. As early as 1821 Michelet was reading Shaftesbury, Reid and Stewart, all three in English, along with Gibbon and Hallam in French translations. While meditating on Gibbon and Stewart, he conceived the idea of a history of civilization reconstructed from the languages of the various peoples. In January, 1824, in Buchon's terminal notes to his translation of Stewart's *General View of the Progress of Metaphysical, Ethical and Political Philosophy since the Revival of Letters,* he found an account of Vico drawn from Salfi's essay on Filangieri, and a fragment by Cousin on the philosophy of history. These moved him to seek the acquaintance of Salfi and Cousin. Cousin encouraged him to study and translate Vico, and introduced him to De Angelis, who gave him the *New Science* and other works of Vico, and to Quinet, who was translating Herder at Cousin's suggestion. By July of the same year, Michelet had learned enough Italian to read Vico, and begun a translation. In the same months he read Ferguson's *Essay on the Progress of Civil Society* (1767) and Priestley's *Essay on Government* (1768), especially its chapter on "The Progress of Civil Societies to a state of greater perfection." Of this critical year in his intellectual development Michelet later noted: "1824. Vico. Effort, infernal shades, grandeur, the golden bough." "From 1824 on, I was seized by a frenzy caught from Vico, an incredible intoxication with his great historical principle." Three years later he published an abridged translation of the *New Science* under the title *Principes de la philosophie de l'histoire,* and a brilliant sketch of Vico's life and work in the *Biographie Universelle,* concluding with this sentence: "No English or Scottish writer, so far as I know, has mentioned Vico, with the exception of the author of a recent brochure on the state of studies in Germany and Italy."

In the summer of 1828 Victor Cousin returned in triumph to the Sorbonne and delivered before audiences of two thousand a series of lectures on the history of philosophy, with the result that, as Sir William Hamilton observed in the *Edinburgh Review* in the following year, "oral discussion of philosophy awakened in Paris and in France an interest unexampled since the days of Abelard." The eleventh lecture was devoted to "The Historians of Humanity," Bossuet, Vico and Herder. "The fundamental character of the *New Science,*" said Cousin, "is the introduction into history of a point of view purely human."

Religion also forms, according to Vico, a part of the state and of society; while, according to Bossuet, the state forms a part of religion. According to Vico, religion relates to humanity, but according to Bossuet, the services of humanity are entirely at the disposal of religion; the point of view has completely changed, and this was, in my opinion, an immense step in the progress of the science of history, of which the ultimate aim is to cause everything to reenter into humanity. . . . Neither ought we any more to forget that Vico was the first who, instead of suffering himself to be imposed upon by the splendor that encircles certain names, was bold enough to submit them to a strict examination, and who has taken from many illustrious personages in history their personal greatness, in order to give it back to humanity itself, to the time, to the century, in which these persons made their appearance.

After indicating the respects in which Herder marked a further advance, he said: "These are the works that I would recommend to my young hearers. . . . I congratulate myself on having encouraged my two young friends, Michelet and Quinet, to give to France Vico and Herder."

Michelet's abridged translation of the *New Science,* from which Cousin's own knowledge of Vico was derived, was reissued in 1835, accompanied by translations of Vico's autobiography and some of his minor works and letters. Of this translation Robert Flint said in 1884:

Nowhere out of Italy has Vico been studied with so much intelligence and sympathy as in France. What of European reputation he possesses, is very largely due to M. Michelet's "Œuvres Choisies de Vico." Michelet most wisely renounced the idea of a literal rendering, and applied himself to reproduce with faithfulness and vividness the substance and spirit of his author. He so succeeded that the great majority even of persons capable of reading the original will find it much more profitable to read his translation, itself a work of genius.[87]

That, in fact, is what nineteenth-century readers of Vico did. Weber's German translation (1822) and a later French one by the Princess Belgioioso (1844), both more literal than Michelet's, were little read; but even Italians found Michelet's translation more intelligible than the original.

Meanwhile Michelet had published in 1831 a history of the Roman Republic and an introduction to universal history, and begun publication of his monumental history of France. In the preface to the Roman history he paid a tribute to Vico which he repeated in the preface to the *Œuvres choisies*.

In the vast system of the founder of the metaphysics of history, there already exist, at least in germ, all the labors of modern scholarship. Like Wolf, he said that the *Iliad* was the work of a people, its learned work and last expression, after many centuries of inspired poetry. Like Creuzer and Goerres he interpreted the heroic and divine figures of primitive history as ideas and symbols. Before Montesquieu and Gans he showed how law springs from the customs of a people and represents faithfully every step of its history. What Niebuhr was to find by vast research, Vico divined; he restored patrician Rome and made its *curiae* and *gentes* live again. Certainly, if Pythagoras recalled that in a previous life he had fought beneath the walls of Troy, these illustrious Germans might have remembered that they had all formerly lived in Vico. All the giants of criticism are already contained, with room to spare, in the little pandemonium of the *New Science*.

The basic idea of the system is bold; bolder perhaps than the author himself suspected. It touches all the great political and religious questions that agitate the world. The instinct of Vico's adversaries did not fail them here; hate is clairvoyant. Fortunately the book was dedicated to Clement XII. The apocalypse of the New Science was placed upon the altar until time should break open its seven seals.

The text of the New Science is this: *Humanity is its own work.* God acts upon it, but by it. Humanity is divine, but no one man is divine. The heroes of myth—Hercules who thrusts mountains aside, Lycurgus and Romulus, swift legislators who accomplish in a lifetime the long work of centuries—are creations of the people's thought. God alone is great. When man craved god-men, he had to condense generations into an individual person; to combine in a single hero the conceptions of a whole poetic cycle. Thus it was that he fashioned his historical idols—a Romulus, a Numa. Before these gigantic phantoms the people remained prostrate. The philosopher bids them rise. "That which you adore," he says to them, "is yourselves, your own conceptions."

The introduction to universal history was composed at top speed after the revolution of July, 1830; dashed off, he later said, "on the burning pavements of Paris." It opened with these words:

With the world began a war which will end only with the world: the war of man against nature, of spirit against matter, of liberty against fatality. History is nothing other than the record of this interminable struggle.

This view of history as a struggle of liberty against fatality, which Michelet identified with Vico's conception of man making his own history, became the dominant theme of his great history of France, which was inspired by the same July revolution but was forty years in the writing. Looking back on his labors in his preface of 1869, Michelet wrote: "I had no master but Vico. His principle of living force, of humanity creating itself, made both my book and my teaching."

We have seen that there were others working on Vico before Michelet's translation first appeared. Of these perhaps the most enthusiastic was Ballanche, who in his *Essays on Social Palingenesis* (1823-30) adapted Vico's view of the relation of the origin of language to that of society, called him "one of the most penetrating minds that ever existed," and said that if he had been better known in the eighteenth century he would have exercised a moderating and beneficial influence on the subsequent social revolutions. But it was due to Michelet more than anyone else that intellectual France teemed with Vichians, conscious and unconscious, toward the middle of the nineteenth century. Philosophers, historians, jurists, classical scholars and critics did him honor and invoked his name to bless their speculations; poets and novelists found inspiration in him; he fired the imagination of young men with the most varied ambitions. Of all this work influenced by Vico through Michelet perhaps the most permanently valuable was that of Fustel de Coulanges on the ancient city and the origins of feudalism.

Not the least of Michelet's services was his sympathetic interpretation of contemporary German thought. It was his work on Vico that opened the way for him to the study and appreciation of Wolf, Creuzer, Goerres, Niebuhr, Savigny, Gans, and above all of Jakob Grimm. His absorption of Savigny, Gans and Grimm was particularly important for the development of historical jurisprudence in France. By viewing all these German thinkers in a Vichian perspective, by conceiving them as continuers of Vico's work, nursing to maturity the seeds he had sown, giving body to his visions, Michelet was able to discern the relations among them, and to interpret each by the others. Thus Vico served through Michelet as a mediator between German and French culture.[88]

D. IN GREAT BRITAIN AND IRELAND

OUR ignorance is most profound in the case of Great Britain and America. There is a certain irony in this, for Vico obviously hoped for a more favorable reception of his doctrines in England than elsewhere abroad. Of his "four authors," Bacon was the one to whom he owed the stimulus to treat the list of sciences as something incomplete, to be enlarged and supplemented by new sciences. He admired the Baconian method, "so fruitfully employed by the English ever since in experimental philosophy," supposed himself to have "transferred it from the physical to the human and civil order," and hoped on that ground that his *New Science* would recommend itself to English readers. Even the *verum factum* formula of his early theory of knowledge was perhaps suggested by Bacon's doctrine of the relation between knowledge and power. He praised the *De veritate* of Lord Herbert of Cherbury as applying the method of "topics" to metaphysics. Selden was for him one of "the three princes" of the doctrine of natural law. Hobbes helped him to extend his theory of knowledge to history, and set for him the problem of which his new science was the solution. He acknowledged the "magnanimous force" of Hobbes's attempted solution in *De cive,* and liked to quote his saying that if he had read as much as other men he would have known as little. He ranked Newton with Leibniz as "the two foremost geniuses of this age." [89]

A scholar moved to enlighten our ignorance might well begin with an inventory of English visitors to Naples in Vico's lifetime. Gilbert Burnet, for instance, was there in 1685, and his son William (later governor of New York) in the early years of the following century. Vico probably met them both, and seems to have drawn on the former's published letters to Robert Boyle in his history of the conspiracy of Macchia. [90] Addison was there in 1701, and the many editions of his *Remarks on Italy* gave prevalence to a low opinion of contemporary Italian culture, which was not decisively challenged until the heyday of Romanticism, and which effectively discharged borrowers from Vico of the obligation to acknowledge their debts. Shaftesbury spent the last fifteen months of his life at Naples in 1711–13, befriended by Vico's friends Valletta and Doria, on whose behalf he transmitted to Burnet and Newton "some small literary works" [91] which probably included Vico's *Treatise on Method* and *Ancient Wisdom of the Italians.* (Vico later introduced his second *New Science* with an allegorical engraving and commentary thereon, a procedure perhaps suggested by Shaftesbury's in his *Second Characters*.) Berkeley was there for some months in 1717 and 1718,[92] and Vico's friend Doria was among the first serious critics of Berkeley's idealism. When the first *New Science* appeared in 1725, some Englishmen who were in Naples bought up all the copies they could find and sent them to London. "They well understood," says Lomonaco, "the profit that might be drawn from it, both for literature and for philosophy." [93] Vico himself sent a copy to Newton, which may have reached him about a year before his death.[94]

The projected Venetian edition of the *New Science* was intended by Conti (who had been made a member of the Royal Society of London on Newton's motion) to reach a wider public in England as well as on the continent. Whether he took any steps in behalf of the second and third editions published at Naples, we do not yet know. It is scarcely credible that the Vichian ideas scattered through the writings of Blackwell, Ferguson, Hume, Wollaston, Warburton, Hurd, Monboddo, Wood, Blair, Duff, Mason, Brown, Lowth, Warton and Burke, are due solely to their having been in this or that respect *animae naturaliter Vicianae,* or to a gradual unfolding of Shaftesbury's seminal thoughts, or even to an indirect and diluted Vichian influence through Italian and French authors mentioned in previous sections.[95] Hume's natural history of religion, for instance, is up to a point eminently Vichian. So is Blair's view that the "times which we call barbarous" were most "favorable to the poetical spirit," and that "imagination was most glowing and animated in the first ages of society." So is Monboddo's theory of the origin and progress of language. So are many such passages as the following in Ferguson's *Essay on the History of Civil Society,* which had an influence in England and Germany out of all proportion to its merits.

On this scene [the temperate zone], mankind have twice, within the compass of history, ascended from rude beginnings to very high degrees of refinement. . . .

No constitution is formed by concert, no government is copied from a plan. . . . The seeds of every form are lodged in human nature; they spring up and ripen with the season. . . . We are therefore to receive with caution the traditionary histories of ancient legislators, and founders of states. . . .

If nations actually borrow from their neighbours, they probably borrow only what they are nearly in a condition to have invented themselves. . . .

When we attend to the language which savages employ on any solemn occasion, it appears that man is a poet by nature. . . .[96]

Yet no one has so far reported any evidence of direct acquaintance with Vico's writings on the part of any of these men, or indeed so much as a passing allusion to him in any English book, journal or private letter of the eighteenth century. Here, then, is a virgin field for students of the history of ideas.

So far as our own research has disclosed, the earliest avowed English disseminator of Vichian ideas was Samuel Taylor Coleridge.[97] He first quoted Vico in his *Theory of Life* in 1816, but this was not published until 1848, and in any case the quotation was borrowed from Jacobi. But in 1825 an Italian exile, Gioacchino de' Prati, lent him a set of the sixth edition of the *New Science,* printed at Milan in 1816, in three volumes of which the first contained the autobiography in place of an introduction. On May 14 Coleridge wrote to Prati:

I am more and more delighted with G. B. Vico, and if I had (which thank God's good grace I have not) the least drop of *Author's* blood in my veins, I should twenty times successively in the perusal of the first volume (I have not yet begun the second) have exclaimed: *"Pereant qui ante nos nostra dixere."*

He chose a motto from the autobiography for his *Aids to Reflection,* which was passing through the press at the time. He planned a translation of Bacon's *Novum Organum,* to be illustrated by Vichian parallels. He urged Prati to write "a series of Critical and biographical Sketches of the most remarkable revolutionary minds," beginning with "a spirited Sketch of Vico's Life and great Work," and offered to assist him with his English. From 1825 until his death in 1834, his letters and table talk give evidence of further reading and continued interest in Vico. He was impressed by Vico's theory of the origin of language. On one occasion he drew a parallel between the condition of the plebs at Rome as represented by Vico and that of the negroes under the West India planters. But more than anything else it was Vico's "discovery of the true Homer" that he praised and defended, and it was apparently by his instigation that his son-in-law Henry Nelson Coleridge included a translation of that section of the *New Science* in the second edition of his *Introductions to the Study of the Greek Poets* in 1834.

Coleridge's influence, reinforced by Michelet's, was responsible for much of the interest in Vico on the part of English writers in the second and third quarters of the nineteenth century. The two groups to whom he most appealed were the leaders of the Broad Church movement on the one hand, and the positivists and "rationalists" on the other. The former were largely intellectual heirs of Coleridge. His *Confessions of an Inquiring Spirit,* in which he took up the Bible to read it for the first time like any other book, and which laid down the line the Broad Churchmen were to follow in Biblical criticism, was composed about the time that Coleridge was reading Vico, and went some way toward applying to the Bible and to Hebrew religion the principles Vico had applied to gentile literature and religions.

In this first group we may count Thomas Arnold, the first English historian to acknowledge indebtedness to Vico. His famous essay on "The Social Progress of States" was first published as an appendix to his edition of Thucydides in 1830. The thesis of the essay was that "states, like individuals, go through certain changes in a certain order, and are subject at different stages of their course to certain peculiar disorders"; that "the largest portion of that history which we commonly call ancient is practically modern, as it describes society in a state analogous to that in which it now is; while, on the other hand, much of what is called modern history is practically ancient, as it relates to a state of things which has passed away."

Arnold shows "how the popular party of an earlier period becomes the antipopular of a later; because the tendency of society is to become more and more liberal, and as the ascendency of wealth is a more popular principle than the ascendency of nobility, so it is less popular than the ascendency of numbers." There are thus two critical periods, the transitions from aristocracy to plutocracy, and from plutocracy to democracy. In the latter case, the struggle "is between property and numbers, and wherever it has come to a crisis, I know not that it has in any instance terminated favorably. Such was the state of Greece in the time of Thucydides; of Rome during the last century of the commonwealth; and such has been the state of England since the revolution of 1688." "The final struggle here only takes place when the real differences between the contending parties have reached the widest point of separation; when the intermediate gradations of society are absorbed in one or other of the two extremes, and the state is divided only between the two irreconcilable opposites of luxury and beggary."

Arnold in 1830, unlike Marx and Engels in 1848, wanted to avoid such a revolution by purging the existing system of its abuses and preparing the way for a gradual granting of power to the working class in a future comfortably remote. His brilliant essay is, indeed, as has recently been observed,[98] the perfect analysis of English social movement on the eve of the Reform Bill, and there were few men in England who could have made it with so much discernment.

But the whole conception is adapted from Vico, and depends in particular on Vico's insight that "the old Homeric monarchies were in fact an instance of power depending on blood, and therefore of the ascendency of nobility. They were like the feudal monarchies of modern Europe, essentially aristocracies, in which the separation of all the chiefs or nobles from the inferior people was far more strongly marked than the elevation of the king above his nobles."

This ascendency, enjoyed in the earliest state of society by noble birth, has been traced in various countries, and its phenomena most successfully investigated, by Giovanni Battista Vico, in his *Principi di Scienza nuova;* a work disfigured indeed by some strange extravagancies, but in its substance so profound and so striking, that the little celebrity which it has obtained out of Italy is one of the most remarkable facts in literary history. Vico's work was published in 1725, yet I scarcely remember ever to have seen it noticed by any subsequent writers who have touched upon the same subject even down to our own times.

The last sentence contains an implied rebuke of Niebuhr, to whom, after Vico, Arnold was chiefly indebted.

The *Foreign Review* published in the same year (1830) an article on Vico, dwelling on his anticipations of Wolf and Niebuhr and showing that on some points of difference the subsequent discovery of Cicero's *De republica* had vindicated Vico. In the next year Henry Hart Milman made Henry Nelson Coleridge's book the occasion for an extended review of the Homeric controversy in the *Quarterly Review.* Vico's "bold and original conceptions on many subjects connected with the history of mankind are now emerging into light," he said, and the *New Science,* "coinciding in a remarkable manner with the tone of thinking prevalent among the continental writers of the present day, many of whose speculations it had anticipated, is acquiring a tardy fame, and winning its way to something like an European reputation." And in 1833 Coleridge's disciples Hare and Thirlwall, the translators of Niebuhr, published in their *Philological Museum* a long and able article on Vico by John Kenrick, calling attention to his anticipation not merely of Wolf and Niebuhr but also of Warburton's exposure of the widespread notion that hieroglyphics were "an invention of the priests or philosophers of Egypt, to conceal a sublime doctrine from the knowledge of the vulgar, or keep them in subjection by maintaining a monopoly of science." Kenrick leaned somewhat on Michelet, and observed that "whoever is not in love with difficulty for its own sake, will do well to seek his knowledge of Vico's system in M. Michelet's work; for Vico himself is the Heraclitus of modern philosophers." This article contained much the best exposition and criticism of Vico's doctrines in English prior to Flint's book in 1884, and is still useful.

Intimately associated with Arnold, Hare, Thirlwall, and other Broad Church leaders, first in Rome and later in London, was Baron Bunsen, who had married Frances Waddington in 1817. He had been secretary to the Prussian embassy at Rome under Niebuhr, later succeeded him as ambassador, and was Prussian minister to England from 1842 to 1854. In the successive versions of his philosophy of history he did less than justice to Vico because of an exaggerated notion of the originality of the German thinkers, but paid tribute to him as having recognized, especially in the history of legal institutions, "at once a divine order and a process of evolution intelligible to our reason."

From our point of view, the fact is of most decisive significance that while the Romanic prophets, Vico and Montesquieu, in laying the foundations of their theories of the universe, do indeed acknowledge God and Christianity, yet, in raising their superstructure, they take their stand exclusively upon law, and not upon religion. They stand on the defensive against the claims of their Church and Theology. This is the universal and necessary attitude of Romanic philosophers towards the popular religion. As laymen, they have no right to know much about it, still less to enquire for themselves into anything affecting it; and, at all events, must not attempt to discuss it from their philosophical point of view. Hence, they come to find themselves out of harmony with the Semitic element and with dogmatic theology; both which, nevertheless, form the sources of a considerable proportion of the jurisprudence of Christian Europe.[99]

In 1862 Coleridge's disciple Frederick Denison Maurice, influential leader of Broad Church thought and of Christian Socialism, and founder of the Working Men's College and of Queen's College for women, published a history of *Moral and Metaphysical Philosophy,* the first and so far the only English history to give an account of Vico fairly proportioned to that of other philosophers, and to place him in the general movement of modern philosophy.[100] This history was first undertaken in 1835 for the *Encyclopædia Metropolitana,* which Coleridge had designed and for which he wrote in 1817 the "Preliminary Treatise on Method." Maurice's son says that from 1835 onwards "this article, as it gradually developed in future editions into his complete treatise on the subject, occupied him, with short intervals, throughout almost his entire life, either in preparation, study, writing or revision." [101] The first and shortest version, which appeared in the 1845 edition of the *Encyclopædia,* does not include the account of Vico, which made its first appearance in the entirely rewritten and separately published edition of Maurice's history in 1862. He explains Vico's isolation and lack of immediate influence by his increasing absorption in an investigation of the common law of nations which had no point of attachment to the practical concerns of his time and place.

His method of pursuing it has made him of immense use to later times. But he had to make great sacrifices, and not only sacrifices of immediate interest and reputation, that he might engage in the pursuit. . . . We should like to hear the voice of the Neapolitan citizen rising above that of the cosmopolite. . . . That he could be what he was without a country; that he could even claim for Italy something of its old right to speak as a witness for all the nations, not for herself specially; should increase the admiration with which we regard him. But we may partly understand why Montesquieu, who, amidst all his general studies, was essentially the nobleman of the South of France—why Voltaire, who, with all his cosmopolitanism, was the oracle of Paris and the model of its writers, should have necessarily obtained an influence in their day which could not be reached by a more elevated and profound thinker, who only appealed to Europe generally, who spoke of the demands of mankind, without being attached to any definite circle of men.

When Maurice comes to Herder he is in a position to say:

It will strike our readers that Herder had not quite a right to speak of the road which he proposed to travel as one that had never been travelled before. Vico had surely attempted a philosophy or science of humanity as much as any man in later or older days had attempted a philosophy of nature or of mind. He does not bring to that attempt the information . . . which Herder has amassed. . . . But . . . as a compensation for the encyclopedic knowledge of the German, there is in the Neapolitan a penetration into the meaning of signs and symbols, a critical genius, and a profound reverence for the intuitions of different races, which we cannot think has any parallel in his successor. In our day the influence of Vico has been far more felt by other countries, and we should suppose by Germany, than that of the author of the *Ideas*.

Of the second group of English writers interested in Vico, the positivists and rationalists, we may speak more briefly. John Stuart Mill had some acquaintance with Vico's ideas, perhaps through Michelet, and referred to his theory of cycles in his *System of Logic* in 1843; but in the following year he confessed to Comte that he had never read Vico himself. This confession was elicited by a long letter from Comte,[102] who had been reading Vico for the first time and found himself confirmed in a view he had already expressed in his *Positive Philosophy* in connection with Montesquieu and Condorcet, that all such constructions prior to the nineteenth century were bound to be abortive. Yet Comte had seen in some of Vico's axioms "a first step toward the sense of the veritable evolution of society," thought his genius superior to that of Montesquieu, planned to insert a page or two on Vico in the second edition of his major work, and did discuss him briefly in his *Positive Polity*. Vico's chief positive merit, he thought, consisted in "a quite profound and often sound understanding of the historical philosophy of language."

Vico's name was duly entered in the Positivist Calendar, with Herder's as its leap-year substitute; but the *New Science* was not included in the Positivist Library.[103] Yet it was read. John Henry Bridges, for example, in an article in the *Positivist Review* on "Fetichism and Positivism," wrote that

The first to call attention systematically to this [fetichistic] mode of regarding the surrounding world was the Neapolitan thinker Vico, early in the eighteenth century. With Vico, as afterwards with Comte, it formed the basis of his philosophy. Let us recall a few of Vico's words: "Men, ignorant of the causes of things, and unable to explain them even by analogy, endowed surrounding objects with their own nature. So it is that when they see the magnet attracting iron they say the loadstone is enamoured of the metal." "All nature," he goes on to say, "becomes to primitive man a vast animated body capable of passion and affection." "It is noteworthy," he observes, "that in all languages a large number of expressions relating to inanimate things are taken from the human body, or from human feelings and passions. *Head* signifies summit, or beginning; *forehead, shoulders,* front and back; we speak of any kind of opening as a *mouth;* the rim of a vessel is a *lip;* a rake or a comb has *teeth;* so, too, we speak of the *gorge* of a river, of the *flesh* of fruits, of a *vein* of metal. Wine is the *blood* of the grape; in a mine we descend to the *bowels* of the earth; the sky or the sea *smiles;* the wind *whistles,* the waves *murmur;* a table *groans* under the weight of provisions. Innumerable examples may be gathered from all languages." [104]

In the first volume of his *History of Greece* (1846), in the chapter on the "Grecian Mythes, as Understood, Felt and Interpreted by the Greeks Themselves," George Grote devoted a four-page footnote to Vico, with long citations from Ferrari's edition of his works.

The mental analogy between the early stages of human civilisation and the childhood of the individual is forcibly and frequently set forth in the works of Vico. That eminently original thinker dwells

upon the poetical and religious susceptibilities as the first to de-
velope themselves in the human mind, and as furnishing not
merely connecting threads for the explanation of sensible phae-
nomena, but also aliment for the hopes and fears, and means of
socialising influence to men of genius, at a time when reason was
yet asleep. . . . He remarks that in an age of fancy and feeling,
the conceptions and language of poetry coincide with those of
reality and common life, instead of standing apart as a separate
vein. . . .

[The New Science] places these early divine fables and theological
poets . . . in their true point of view, and assigns to them their
proper place in the ascending movement of human society: it refers the mythes to an early religious and poetical age, in which
feeling and fancy composed the whole fund of the human mind,
over and above the powers of sense: the great mental change which
has since taken place has robbed us of the power, not merely of
believing them as they were originally believed, but even of conceiving completely that which their first inventors intended to
express.

The views here given from this distinguished Italian (the precursor of F. A. Wolf in regard to the Homeric poems, as well as of
Niebuhr in regard to the Roman history) appear to me no less
correct than profound; and the obvious inference from them is,
that attempts to *explain* (as it is commonly called) the mythes
(i. e. to translate them into some physical, moral or historical statements, suitable to our order of thought) are, even as guesses, essentially unpromising. Nevertheless Vico, inconsistently with his own
general view, bestows great labour and ingenuity in attempting to
discover internal meaning symbolised under many of the mythes
. . . which he draws out and exhibits under the form of a civil
history of the divine and heroic times. . . .[105]

It is evident that Grote had overlooked or failed to grasp the
"master key" of the New Science, the doctrine of "poetic characters." Perhaps because he sensed its perversity, he omitted

the critical part of the footnote from later editions of his *History*.

Buckle's *Introduction to the History of Civilization in England* (1859–61) referred to Vico several times, though it was taxed with omitting him by critics who consulted only the "List of Authors Quoted" and the index. "Before Montesquieu," Buckle said, "the only two great thinkers who had really studied Roman history were Machiavelli and Vico; but . . . Vico, whose genius was perhaps even more vast than that of Montesquieu, can hardly be considered his rival; for, though his *Scienza Nuova* contains the most profound views on ancient history, they are rather glimpses of truth than a systematic investigation of any one period." And again:

It is this deep conviction that changing phenomena have unchanging laws . . . which, in the seventeenth century, guided in a limited field Bacon, Descartes, and Newton; which in the eighteenth century was applied to every part of the material universe; and which it is the business of the nineteenth century to extend to the history of the human intellect. This last department of inquiry we owe chiefly to Germany; for, with the single exception of Vico, no one even suspected the possibility of arriving at complete generalizations respecting the progress of man, until shortly before the French Revolution, when the great German thinkers began to cultivate this, the highest and most difficult of all studies.

But he charged Vico with the failing common to metaphysicians of regarding their doctrines not as hypotheses to be verified but as theories proved by reason and needing only historical illustration.[106]

Alfred Henry Huth in his *Life* of Buckle (1880) devoted several pages to Vico as the earliest of Buckle's forerunners:

The great skeptic Vico was the first who fairly grasped the view that we must look for the laws of history, not in divine interference, but in natural and earthly circumstances. . . . This view, which his position at Naples made dangerous, and his religion perhaps made him unwilling to express, he concealed under the veil of that very Providence which he denied, saying that man was so constituted by it that he must move in a constant direction. He generalizes history. He saw that the history of the Roman Empire, the only history he knew, was not a solitary and peculiar instance of growth followed by maturity and decay, but the result of general laws. . . . Nay, so bold were his generalizations and so skeptical his mind, that he denied that Zoroaster, Pythagoras, Solon, and Dracon had had any existence, and averred that their codes were first produced by the wants of man, and then ascribed to them, by that tendency in ignorant ages to ascribe everything great to individuals. . . . His method is the same as Comte's. . . .

In an account of the aims of his histories of European morals and of the spirit of rationalism, Lecky wrote in 1870:

Both books belong to a very small school of historical writings which began in the eighteenth century with Vico, was continued by Condorcet, Herder, Hegel, and Comte, and which found its last great representative in Mr. Buckle (from many of whose opinions I widely differ, but from whom I have learnt very much). What characterises these writers is that they try to look at history, not as a series of biographies, or accidents, or pictures, but as a great organic whole; that they consider the social and intellectual condition of the world at any given period as a problem to be explained, the net result of innumerable influences which it is the business of the historian to trace; and that they especially believe that intellectual belief has not been due merely to arguments or other intellectual causes, but has been very profoundly modified in many curious ways by social, political, and industrial influences.[107]

Similar views were later expressed in the histories of rationalism and free thought by Robertson and Benn; by J. B. Bury in his *Idea of Progress;* and by Joseph McCabe in the *Biographical Dictionary of Modern Rationalists.* Bury thought it "obvious how readily [Vico's] doctrine could be

adapted to the conception of Progress as a spiral movement."
Robertson traced "Tylor's outstanding theorem of 'Animism' " to Vico and Hume, who "may have read Vico." [108]
Benn remarked that Carlyle had found no place in his gallery
for the hero as philosopher, and that the character of Vico
"might go far to supply that void." [109]

With few exceptions, the representatives of both the Broad
Church and the positivist and rationalist schools drew their
knowledge of Vico from secondary sources, or at best from
Michelet's translations. The first British philosopher to make
a thorough first-hand study of the whole range of Vico's
writings was Robert Flint. In 1872 he published what was
to have been the first volume of a history of the philosophy of
history in Europe. This first volume was devoted to France
and Germany, and was to have been followed by one on Italy
and England, in which Flint hoped "to trace with fulness and
in detail the effects of Vico's historical speculations on Italian
thought." [110] Twenty years later, instead of this second volume, which was again promised but never appeared, he made
a fresh start by publishing an enlargement and revision of
part of the first, that on France and French Belgium and
Switzerland.[111] In the meantime, however, he had written a
masterly little volume on Vico for Blackwood's series of
Philosophical Classics for English Readers (1884), which remains the standard exposition in English.

The editor of the series, William Knight, read Flint's volume to no purpose if at all, for in his *Philosophy of the Beautiful,* "being outlines of the history of aesthetics," published
five years later (1889), he disposed of Vico in a single and
uninforming sentence. Bosanquet in his *History of Aesthetic*
(1892) did not so much as mention Vico, though he believed
that he had passed over "no writer of the first rank." But

Saintsbury, perhaps because Croce had sent him his essay, "G. B. Vico, First Discoverer of Aesthetic Science," borrowed Flint's set of Ferrari's edition of Vico's works, and included in the third volume of his *History of Criticism* (1904) a fairly proportioned though unsympathetic account of Vico. Of what he conceived to be "purely literary criticism" he found "little or nothing in Vico." "I have not yet found a place where he deals with any author in a purely literary spirit. The zeal of his New Science of Humanity has eaten him up. A poem is a historical document. . . ."

And it would be really "unphilosophical" to leave him without pointing out, what has not, so far as I know, been pointed out before, how noteworthy he is as exemplifying the corruption of a thing accompanying quite early stages of its growth. We have throughout maintained that the Historical method is the salvation of Criticism, and in this very period we are witnessing its late application to that purpose. Vico is the very apostle, nay, more, the prophet, of the Historical method itself. Yet here, as elsewhere, the postern to Hell is hard by the gateway of the Celestial City.

In a footnote, as if to soften the acerbity of his judgment, he added: "To do Vico full justice, we must admit that his object was less to break up Homer, as they break up Caedmon and Isaiah, than to attribute the whole work to the whole early Greek people."

A new era in Vichian studies, in England as elsewhere, was inaugurated in the first decades of the twentieth century by the bibliographical, editorial, historical and critical work of Croce, Gentile, and Nicolini. Croce's *Philosophy of Giambattista Vico* was translated into English in 1913, and after the interruption of scholarly work by the First World War there was a series of illuminating essays and chapters on Vico by C. E. Vaughan, J. G. Robertson, and Thomas Whittaker, and a model of the biographer's art by H. P. Adams. At least one English philosopher-historian, R. G. Collingwood (the translator of Croce's book), has absorbed Vico's thought and made it his own; and suggestive interpretations of Vico's ideas are scattered through his writings. A few critics, such as Herbert Read,[112] have begun to draw upon Vico's ideas, and creative literature itself to show his influence.

The most striking case is James Joyce. Already steeped (like Coleridge before him) in Dante and Bruno, he read and digested Vico in Trieste about 1905, and proceeded to naturalize him in his imagination as an eponymous hero of the rocky road to Dublin—Vico Road in the suburb of Dalkey. There are traces of Vico in *Ulysses,* and its Odyssean parallelism may have been partly inspired by Vico's "discovery of the true Homer." But Vico's cyclical theory of *corso* and *ricorso,* conveniently symbolized by the real Vico Road, is the express theme of *Finnegans Wake.* Freely adapting Vico's three ages (theocratic, heroic, and human) and his three institutions (religion, marriage, and burial), and making a fourth of the recurrence to the first, Joyce divides the book into four parts. The last words of the fourth, "A way a lone a last a loved a long the," begin a sentence which is completed by the opening paragraph of the first: "riverrun, past Eve and Adam's, from swerve of shore to bend of bay, brings us by a commodius vicus of recirculation back to Howth Castle and Environs." (Vicus is the Latin form of Vico's name, which means a street or road with houses on either side.) Thus "The Vico road goes round and round to meet where terms begin" (p. 452). "Teems of times and happy returns. The same anew. Ordovico or viricordo" (p. 215). Vico appears in person as "the producer (Mr. John Baptister Vickar)" (p. 255). On the opening page there is a hundred-lettered clap of Vico's all-initiating thunder, which recurs at intervals. The time machine with which Joyce operates is "Our wholemole mill-wheeling vicociclometer" (p. 614). As Vico reduces gods and heroes to folk characters, the protean initials of Joyce's hero, who "moves in vicous cicles yet remews the same" (p. 134), have by "a pleasant turn of the populace" given rise to the nickname "Here Comes Everybody" (p. 32). The hero's subconscious mind, expatiating in sleep, is the historical consciousness of the race; and the pregnant language of the book is reminted from the much-handled and partially-defaced words of common speech to give vivid reality to Vico's theory of the history embedded in language. In the school-day section of the second part, the book takes the temporary appearance of an annotated schoolbook, and one set of marginalia, in pompous capitals, is a burlesque of Vico's terminology. "PROBAPOSSIBLE PROLEGOMENA TO IDEAREAL HISTORY." "THE LOCALISATION OF LEGEND LEADING TO THE LEGALISATION OF LATIFUNDISM." "PANOPTICAL PURVIEW OF POLITICAL PROGRESS AND THE FUTURE PRESENTATION OF THE PAST." At intervals, all four parts are condensed into a series of four words or phrases: "thunderburst, ravishment, dissolution, and providentiality" (p. 362); "eggburst, eggblend, eggburial, and hatch-as-hatchcan" (p. 614); "sullemn fulminance, sollemn nuptialism, sallemn sepulture and providential divining" (p. 599).

William Butler Yeats had attended the lectures on Croce's *Aesthetic* given in London by Douglas Ainslie, and in 1924 he read and annotated Croce's *Philosophy of Giambattista Vico* in Collingwood's translation. In Italy in 1925 he adopted the Fascist interpretation of Vico advanced by Gentile and other idealists. In the early 1930's, as an introduction to his Swift play, "The Words upon the Window-Pane," he wrote an essay drawing the parallel and contrast between Vico's *New Science* and Swift's *Discourse of the Contests and Dis-*

sentions between the Nobles and the Commons in Athens and Rome. "Had we [Irish] a thinking nation," he wrote in his notebook, "the *Discourse* with its law of nations might be for us what Vico is to the Italians." In the essay itself, expounding Vico's cyclical theory, he said that the social order

was harsh and terrible until the Many prevailed, and its joints cracked and loosened, happiest when some one man, surrounded by able subordinates, dismissed the Many to their private business . . . Students of contemporary Italy, where Vico's thought is current through its influence upon Croce and Gentile, think it created, or in part created, the present government of one man surrounded by just such able assistants as Vico foresaw . . . Pascal thought there was evidence for and against the existence of God, but that if a man kept his mind in suspense about it he could not live a rich and active life, and I suggest to the Cellars and Garrets that though history is too short to change either the idea of progress or the eternal circuit into scientific fact, the eternal circuit may best suit our preoccupation with the soul's salvation, our individualism, our solitude. Besides we love antiquity, and that other idea —progress—the sole religious myth of modern man, is only two hundred years old.

In 1938 Yeats wrote in his *On the Boiler:* "Vico was the first modern philosopher to discover in his own mind, and in the European past, all human destiny. 'We can know nothing,' he said, 'that we have not made.' " This conception, as Louis MacNeice has remarked, is prevalent in Yeats's later poetry.

> Whatever flares upon the night
> Man's own resinous heart has fed.[113]

E. IN THE UNITED STATES

THERE has been as yet no study of Vico's reputation in America, but investigation would probably show that, though his name has been more familiar here than in England, there has been little first-hand study of him until recent years. Perhaps the earliest visitor who knew his writings was Chastellux, who was accompanied by a grandson of Montesquieu on his travels here in 1780–82. Franklin, who might have learned of Vico through Filangieri, as Goethe did, had a cast of mind too alien from Vico's to appreciate him.

Lorenzo da Ponte, friend of Casanova and librettist to Mozart, who had kept an Italian bookstore in London with scholars like Mathias, Roscoe and Walker for patrons, spent the last thirty-three years of his life in this country, chiefly as teacher of Italian language and literature and operatic entrepreneur in New York City. In 1831 he compiled a catalogue of Italian books for sale there, and a copy of the *Scienza nuova* was listed with the following note: "This illustrious Neapolitan has won belated recognition as one of the most sublime philosophers of the Republic of Letters. All the London journals speak of him with enthusiasm." [114]

Cousin's Sorbonne lectures on the history of philosophy were translated here by Linberg (1832) and by O. W. Wright (1852) and both translations were widely read, especially in college courses. From the thirties through the sixties there was a series of articles on the philosophy of history in various journals, nearly all giving some account of Vico, usually based on Cousin's lecture and on Michelet's French paraphrase of the *New Science*.[115] The earliest of these articles, under the title "Progress and Limits of Social Improvement," was contributed to the *North American Review* by Edward Everett's less famous brother, Alexander Hill Everett, during his editorship of that journal. It was ostensibly a review of the sixth edition of the *Scienza nuova,* to which, however, he refers only once, in a long footnote in which he says that "the public attention has lately been attracted" to Vico's work by "the praise which Cousin has bestowed upon it" and by Michelet's translation.

Our libraries are overrun with works upon the manner in which nations *ought* to be governed; but there are scarcely any upon the principles that *in fact* regulate their progress, and determine their condition, including the forms of their governments, at the different periods of their history. The work of Vico, which we have placed at the head of this article, is the only one of much importance upon this subject, and in this the author has done little more than propose the problem,—his own solution being far from complete or satisfactory. The principal merit of his book lies, in fact, in the title, which proves that Vico had distinctly conceived the original and important idea, that the circumstances which regulate the origin, progress and decline of nations are susceptible of generalization, and may be stated and classed as a separate branch of philosophy. In his attempt to do this, Vico failed, and the principles of the *New Science* are still to be discovered.

The sociologist George Frederick Holmes suggested to Comte in 1852 that "Vico, though somewhat of a pedant, appears to present stronger claims to your regard than Condorcet, as your legitimate precursor in historical science." Theodore Parker, reviewing Buckle in 1858, reproached him for ignorance of Vico. But serious study of his writings began with John Fiske. In an essay on Buckle written at the age of nineteen he remarked that "the *Scienza nuova* of Vico contained many new and startling views of history, and the writings of Montesquieu presented a daring attempt to constitute a social science; but both these great thinkers were crippled by a lack of materials. . . ." In November, 1863, while a student at the Harvard Law School, he had an interview with Charles Eliot Norton, who wanted him to be a regular reviewer and contributor to the *North American Review*. They talked of Vico's place in modern thought, and

Norton lent Fiske his copy of the *New Science*. In the course of his study of it Fiske wrote:

It is the driest, obscurest metaphysicalest book I ever got hold of. Confucius is a more lucid writer. "Mortgages" and "Remainders" are pleasanter to peruse. And still it has many capital ideas—some of them quite Maine-y-Cornewall Lewisy—enough to keep me from throwing down the book, even while I curse at its clumsy phraseology.

The results of his study do not appear in any extended discussion of Vico in his published writings; he simply assimilated so much of Vico as he could into his own thinking. In his *Outlines of Cosmic Philosophy* he makes the casual remark in a footnote that "the theory of Vico that social progress takes place in cycles in which history literally repeats itself, is based upon a very inadequate knowledge of the results of the cooperation of many interacting forces"; a remark which betrays a very inadequate comprehension of Vico.[116]

The American Social Science Association, founded just after the Civil War, was hard put to justify its continued existence as history, economics, political science and other disciplines seceded to form associations of their own. Those who sought to keep alive the ideal of an integral science of society harked back to its great forerunners, and Vico's name was often invoked along with Comte's. Frank B. Sanborn, one of the founders of the Association and for many years its general secretary, sketching the history of social science in 1878, found its pioneers in Vico, Adam Smith and Comte, and quoted an Italian corresponding member to the effect that "the *New Science* of Vico is this same new science of our own day, which considers human society as an organic whole, and studies its development and its different aspects through long periods of time." But by 1892 Sanborn was reduced to speaking of it as "this federation of sciences—this syndicate of philosophy, economics, philanthropy, ethics, and natural science," and his trinity was reconstituted thus:

Vico, the Italian, who invented the philosophy of history, Adam Smith, the Scotchman, who invented political economy, as we understand it, and Franklin, the American (greatest of the three), who put social science upon the plainest practical footing.[117]

As in the cases of H. S. Maine, G. C. Lewis, E. B. Tylor and others in England, it appears that Vico was not read by the great American continuer of his work, the anthropologist Lewis Henry Morgan, or even by such historians as Brooks and Henry Adams, for whom the construction of a philosophy of history was a consuming passion. But of late years the sociologists have again become aware of his pioneer efforts, and an American by adoption, Pitirim Sorokin, quotes him often and (unlike Spengler and Toynbee) freely acknowledges his anticipation of the main results of his own more elaborate and methodical investigations. He sees in history a trendless fluctuation or cycle of what he calls ideational, idealistic and sensate cultures, each with its own typical forms of art, science, ethics and law, of social, political and military institutions. He regards these three cultures as roughly parallel to Vico's three ages of gods, heroes and men.

Since the Fascist era, Italian scholars resident in this country have made helpful contributions to American understanding of their compatriot. Noteworthy among these is Elio Gianturco, to whom we owe a doctoral dissertation on *Joseph de Maistre and Giambattista Vico* (1937) and a series of articles and reviews, in one of which he argues that "Vico's most outstanding achievements lie in the history of Roman law, where he is supremely great." [117a]

So FAR we have traced Vico's reputation and influence in the various national cultures, with occasional reference to the way in which episodes in one of these have had repercussions in others. In conclusion, however, we must speak of one movement of international proportions in which his name and ideas have constantly recurred, and which may, more than others, have his future reputation in its hands. After making a careful study of Lassalle's great work on property, the *System of Acquired Rights* (1861), Marx wrote to its author from London: "It surprises me that you seem not to have read Vico's *New Science*—not for anything you would have found in it for your special purpose, but for its philosophic conception of the spirit of Roman law in opposition to the legal Philistines." Because of the difficulty of Vico's Italian style, he advised Lassalle to use the Princess Belgioioso's French translation, from which he quoted several passages "to whet your appetite." "Vico contains in the germ Wolf (on Homer), Niebuhr (on Roman history in the 'regal' period), the foundations of comparative philology (not without caprice), and a great deal else that is original. I have so far never been able to lay my hands on his more strictly juridical writings." [118] On the same day Marx wrote to Engels in lighter vein: "Vico says in his *New Science* that Germany is the only country in Europe where 'an heroic language' is still spoken. If he had ever had the pleasure of acquainting himself with the Vienna *Presse* or the Berlin *Nationalzeitung,* the old Neapolitan would have changed his mind." [119] Five years later he referred to Vico in an important footnote to *Capital:*

A critical history of technology would show how little any of the inventions of the eighteenth century was the work of a single individual. No such book has yet been published. Darwin has aroused our interest in the history of natural technology, that is in the development of the organs of plants and animals as productive instruments sustaining the life of these creatures. Does not the history of the productive organs of man in society, the organs which are the material basis of every kind of social organization, deserve equal attention? Since, as Vico says, the essence of the distinction between human history and natural history is that the former is made by man and the latter is not, would not the history of human technology be easier to write than the history of natural technology? By disclosing man's dealings with nature, the productive activities by which his life is sustained, technology lays bare his social relations and the mental conceptions that flow from them.[120]

In 1896, after four years of work on Vico, Georges Sorel contributed to the Marxist *Devenir Social* [121] a book-length "Étude sur Vico" using this footnote as a touchstone for determining the soundness and importance of the various elements in Vico's thought, and finding in what he called "Vico's ideogenetic law" an anticipation of the Marxist doctrine of ideas as functions of the modes of production. Sorel later applied certain of Vico's ideas, especially that of cyclical recurrence, to the history of primitive Christianity [122] and the theory of the general strike; [123] and Croce observed in retrospect that Marx and Sorel had brought to maturity Vico's "idea of the struggle of classes and the rejuvenation of society by a return to a primitive state of mind and a new barbarism." [124]

Marx and Engels seem to have taken from Vico, perhaps in the first place through Michelet but later at first hand, the formula that "men make their own history," from which their historical materialism was developed. Vico had conceived the whole historical process as an organic growth and dissolution and regrowth in which at any stage each aspect of culture—

custom, morality, law, government, language, art, science, religion, philosophy—has a form and character different from that which it had in the preceding stage. But Marx and Engels made explicit a distinction which remained latent in Vico, between primary and secondary activities. In order to make history, men must live, and in order to live they must eat, drink, clothe and shelter themselves, and reproduce their kind. These primary activities involve a double relationship, physical and social. A certain mode of production, or industrial stage, is implemented by a certain mode of cooperation, or social stage. Because each generation is absorbed into or finds itself in possession of the productive system won by the previous generation, which serves it as the raw material for new production, a connection arises in human history, a history of humanity takes shape.

Men make their own history [says Marx], but they do not make it out of the whole cloth. They make it out of conditions not of their own choosing, but such as lie ready to hand. The traditions of all past generations weigh like an Alp on the brain of the living.[125]

The relations in which men stand in and to the system of production condition all their other relations. These relations, with their strains and stresses and dislocations, are reflected in our consciousness, in our thinking, in our language, in the ideological constructions of our politics, law, morality, religion, metaphysics. These secondary activities have no continuous and independent history of their own, intelligible in abstraction from the primary activities which they reflect, interpret, justify, decently cloak, and often disguise. Thus the essence of historical materialism is that economic history is the deep central channel of the stream of history which must be sounded before its surface currents, eddies, shallows and backwaters can be adequately understood.

Historical materialism in this sense went beyond anything directly asserted by Vico, but, as it seemed to his Marxist interpreters, in a direction in which he himself had gone a long way. The Italian Marxist, Antonio Labriola, a correspondent of Engels, in his *Essays on the Materialist Conception of History,* accordingly recognized Vico as one of its forerunners. These essays were edited by Croce in Italian and by Sorel in French, and made an indelible impression on the young Trotsky in his Odessa prison. Labriola's lectures at Rome on the philosophy of history had taken their start from Vico, and he thought at first of calling the second essay and the volume itself *From Morgan to Vico.*[126] Marx's son-in-law Paul Lafargue in his *Economic Determinism: The Historical Method of Karl Marx* (1907) worked out more fully a similar view of the relations between Vico, Morgan and Marxism; and elsewhere he described Marx's personal grasp of history in terms of Vico's theory of knowledge.[127] It is no accident, therefore, that Vico enjoys high repute in present-day Russia as the progenitor of the theory of the class struggle; [128] or that Trotsky quoted Vico on the first page of his *History of the Russian Revolution;* or that Edmund Wilson started *To the Finland Station* from Michelet's discovery of Vico.

THE LIFE OF
GIAMBATTISTA VICO

WRITTEN BY HIMSELF

THE LIFE
OF GIAMBATTISTA VICO

WRITTEN BY HIMSELF

[PART A, 1725]

GIAMBATTISTA VICO was born in Naples in the year 1670 [129] of
upright parents who left a good name after them. His father
was of a cheerful disposition, his mother of a quite melancholy temper; both contributed to the character of their child.
He was a boy of high spirits and impatient of rest; but at the
age of seven he fell head first from the top of a ladder [130] to
the floor below, and remained a good five hours without
motion or consciousness. The right side of the cranium was
fractured, but the skin was not broken. The fracture gave
rise to a large tumor, and the child suffered much loss of
blood from the many deep lancings. The surgeon, indeed,
observing the broken cranium and considering the long period of unconsciousness, predicted that he would either die
of it or grow up an idiot. However by God's grace neither
part of his prediction came true, but as a result of this mischance he grew up with a melancholy and irritable temperament such as belongs to men of ingenuity and depth, who,
thanks to the one, are quick as lightning in perception, and
thanks to the other, take no pleasure in verbal cleverness or
falsehood.

After a long convalescence of three years or more he returned to the grammar school. [131] Because he performed so
expeditiously at home the tasks his teacher assigned, his father, who thought his expedition was negligence, one day

asked the teacher if his son was performing his duties as a good student. The answer being in the affirmative, he asked that the lessons be doubled. But the teacher protested that he was obliged to regulate his pace by that of the other students; he could not well be in a class by himself and the class ahead was far advanced. Whereupon the boy, who was present at the interview, with great boldness begged the master to permit him to pass to the class above; he would supply by himself the necessary preparation for this level. The teacher, more to find out what a child's intelligence was capable of than with any expectation of his really succeeding, granted him permission and to his great surprise beheld in a few days a pupil acting as his own teacher.

When he had lost this teacher he was taken to another, with whom however he spent but a short time; for his father was advised to send him to the Jesuit fathers, and they entered him in their second grade. Here the teacher, observing how gifted he was, pitted him against his three ablest pupils, one after another. In the "diligences," as these fathers call them, that is to say extraordinary scholastic exercises, he humbled the first of the three; the second fell ill in attempting to emulate him, and the third, because he was favored by the Company, was passed into the third grade by privilege of "proficiency" before the "list," as they call it, was read. Offended by what seemed to him an insult, and learning that in the second semester he would have to repeat what he had done in the first, Giambattista left the school and, withdrawing to his home, learned by himself in Alvarez [132] all that was left for the fathers to teach him in the third grade [of the grammar school] and in the humanity school; and the following October he passed to the study of logic. In this period, during the summer, he would sit down at his desk at nightfall;

and his good mother, after rousing from her first slumber and telling him for pity's sake to go to bed, would often find that he had studied until daybreak. This was a sign that as he grew older in the study of letters he would vigorously maintain his reputation as a scholar.

It was his lot to have for teacher the Jesuit father Antonio del Balzo, a nominalist philosopher; and having heard in the schools that a good summulist was an excellent philosopher and that Petrus Hispanus was the best writer of summulae, he began to study him with great zeal. Later, having learned from his teacher that Paulus Venetus was the most acute of all the summulists, he began also to study him, with a view to further advancement. But his mind, still too weak to stand that kind of Chrysippean logic, was almost lost on it, so that to his great sorrow he had to give it up. His despair made him desert his studies (so dangerous it is to put youths to the study of sciences that are beyond their age!) and he strayed from them for a year and a half. We shall not here feign what René Descartes craftily feigned as to the method of his studies simply in order to exalt his own philosophy and mathematics and degrade all the other studies included in divine and human erudition. Rather, with the candor proper to a historian, we shall narrate plainly and step by step the entire series of Vico's studies, in order that the proper and natural causes of his particular development as a man of letters may be known.

Just as a high-spirited horse, long and well trained in war and long afterwards let out to pasture at will in the fields, if he happens to hear the sound of a trumpet feels again the martial appetite rise in him and is eager to be mounted by the cavalryman and led into battle; so Vico, though he had wandered from the straight course of a well disciplined early youth, was soon spurred by his genius to take up again the abandoned path, and set off again on his way. The occasion was provided by the restoration after many years of the *Infuriati*,[133] a famous academy in San Lorenzo, where prominent men of letters mingled with the principal lawyers, senators and nobles of the city. Illustrious academies yield this most beautiful fruit to their cities: that by them young men, whose age by reason of good blood and little experience is full of trust and of lofty hopes, are fired to study for the sake of praise and glory. Then when the age of discretion arrives with its concern for utilities, they are able to obtain them honestly through worth and merit. So Vico returned to philosophy under Father Giuseppe Ricci, another Jesuit, a man of penetrating insight, a Scotist by sect but at bottom a Zenonist. From him he was greatly pleased to learn that "abstract substances" had more reality than the "modes" of the nominalist Balzo. This was a presage that he in his time would take most pleasure in the Platonic philosophy, to which no scholastic philosophy comes nearer than the Scotist does; and that later he would be led to discuss the "points" of Zeno, as Aristotle had done in his *Metaphysics* but with sentiments far different from his perverse ones. But Ricci seemed to him to linger too long over explanations of being and substance in their distinctions as metaphysical degrees. He was impatient for new knowledge. He had heard that Father Suarez in his *Metaphysics* discussed everything that could be known in philosophy in a distinguished manner such as becomes a metaphysician, and in an extremely clear and easy style, as in fact he stands out by his incomparable eloquence. So again he left school, to better purpose than before, and retired to his home for a year to study Suarez.

Just once in this time he betook himself to the Royal Uni-

versity of Studies, and his good genius led him into the class
of Don Felice Aquadia, the excellent head lecturer on law,
just when he was giving his pupils this judgment of Hermann
Vulteius: that he was the best who had ever written on the
civil institutes. This opinion, stored away in Vico's memory,
was one of the principal causes of all the better ordering of
his studies and his consequent advancement in them. For
later it happened that, being set to the study of law by his
father, he was sent to Don Francesco Verde, partly because of
the nearness but principally because of the great fame of this
lecturer. With him he spent but two months, attending lectures full of cases on the minutiae of the practice of both [civil
and ecclesiastical] courts. The lad could not discern the principles of these cases as befitted one who had already begun to
acquire the universal mind from metaphysics and to reason of
particulars by axioms or maxims. So he told his father that
he wished no longer to study with Verde, for he felt that he
was learning nothing from him. And making use now of
the dictum of Aquadia, he begged his father to borrow a copy
of Hermann Vulteius [134] from a certain doctor of laws named
Nicola Maria Giannettasio,[135] undistinguished in the court
room but very learned in sound jurisprudence, who with time
and great diligence had assembled a very precious library of
learned legal books. With this book he told his father he
would study the civil institutes by himself. His father was
much surprised, for he had been greatly impressed by the
wide popularity of the lecturer Verde; but, since he was a
man of discretion, he was willing to satisfy his son in this
matter. While his son was asking him for the Vulteius, which
was very difficult to obtain in Naples, he had recalled, like
the bookseller he was, that he had some time before given
one to Nicola Maria, so he requested it of him. Nicola Maria

desired to know from the son himself the reason for the request, and the latter told him that in Verde's lessons only the memory was exercised and the intellect suffered from lying idle. His judgment or rather good sense beyond his years so pleased the good man, wise as he was in these matters, that, making to the father a firm prediction of his son's success, he did not lend but gave outright to the youth not only the Vulteius but also the *Canonical Institutes* [136] of Henricus Canisius, who was in Nicola Maria's opinion the best of the canonists who had written on them. And thus the good word of Aquadia and the good deed of Nicola Maria set Vico on the good road to both the laws.

Now in checking particularly the citations from the civil law he found a great pleasure in two things. One was in seeing how, in their summaries of the laws, the scholastic interpreters had abstracted into general maxims of justice the particular considerations of equity which the jurisconsults and emperors had indicated for the just disposition of cases. This attracted him to these medieval interpreters, whom he later perceived and judged to be the philosophers of natural equity. The other was in observing with what great diligence the jurisconsults themselves examined the wording of the laws, senate decrees and praetors' edicts which they interpreted. This won him to the humanist interpreters, whom he later perceived and considered to be pure historians of the Roman civil law. Each of these pleasures was a sign: the one of all the study that he was to give to investigating the principles of universal law, the other of the profit he was to derive from the Latin language, especially from the usages of Roman jurisprudence, the most difficult part of which is knowing how to define the legal terms.

When he had studied both institutes in the texts of civil and canon law alike, without taking any heed of the so-called "materials" to be learned within the five-year period of legal training, he decided to apply for admission to the courts. For his instruction in court practice, Don Carlo Antonio de Rosa, a senator of great probity and the protector of his house, presented him to Fabrizio del Vecchio, a most upright lawyer who afterwards as an old man died in extreme poverty. And for his better acquaintance with legal procedure, chance would have it that a little later a suit entrusted to Don Geronimo Acquaviva was brought against his father before the Sacred Council. Now sixteen, he prepared this case by himself and then defended it before the Rota with the assistance of the said Fabrizio del Vecchio, and carried off the victory. For his argument in this case he earned the praise of Pier Antonio Ciavarri, a most learned jurist and councilor of the Rota, and on leaving he received the congratulations of Francesco Antonio Aquilante, an old advocate before that court, who had been his adversary.

From the sequel, as from many similar cases, it readily appears how men can be well started in some branches of learning while in others they wander about in miserable errors for lack of the guidance afforded by comprehensive knowledge coherent in all its parts. For in Vico's mind there now took shape the argument of his *On the Method of the Studies of Our Time,* later to be rounded out by his work *On the One Principle of Universal Law,* to which his other work *On the Consistency of the Jurisprudent* is an appendix. At the same time, though already possessed of the metaphysical mind whose whole labor is to know the truth throughout by genus and differentia, he abandoned himself to the most corrupt styles of modern poetry, which finds its only pleasure in vagaries and falsehood. In this he was encouraged by Father

Giacomo Lubrano, a Jesuit of infinite erudition and famous, at that time, for sacred eloquence, which almost everywhere had fallen into decay. One day when Vico called upon him for an opinion of his progress in poetry and submitted for his correction a canzone on the rose, the father, a generous and kindly spirit, was so pleased that although he was advanced in years and had attained great fame as a sacred orator, he did not hesitate to recite to this youth he had never seen before an idyll of his own on the same subject. But Vico had taken up this sort of poetry as an exercise of the mind in feats of wit, which affords pleasure only through falsehood so extravagantly presented as to surprise the right expectation of its hearers; wherefore, as it would be displeasing to grave and serious minds, so it delights the still weak minds of youth. And indeed this sort of extravagance may well be considered an almost necessary diversion for the wits of young men, grown over-subtle and stiff in the study of metaphysics. For at this age the mind should be given free rein to keep the fiery spirit of youth from being numbed and dried up, lest from too great severity of judgment, proper to maturity but too early acquired, they should later scarcely dare attempt anything.

At this time his health, already delicate, was endangered by consumption, and the family fortunes had been severely reduced. Yet he had an ardent desire for leisure to continue his studies, and his spirit felt a deep abhorrence for the clamor of the law courts. It was therefore a happy occasion when in a bookstore he had a conversation on the right method of teaching jurisprudence with Monsignor Geronimo Rocca, Bishop of Ischia and a distinguished jurist, as may be seen from his works. For the Monsignor was so well satisfied with his views as to urge him to go as tutor to his nephews in a castle of the

Cilento, beautifully situated and enjoying a perfect climate. It belonged to the Monsignor's brother, Don Domenico Rocca, in whom he was to find a most kindly Maecenas, who shared his taste in poetry. He was assured that he would be treated in every way as a son of the family, and so it proved in fact. The good air would restore his health, and he would have all the leisure he needed for study.

So it happened that living in the castle for nine years [137] he made the greatest progress in his studies, digging into laws and canons, as his duties obliged him to. Led on from canon law to the study of dogmatic theology, he found himself in the very middle of Catholic doctrine in the matter of grace. This came about particularly through the reading of Richardus,[138] the theologian of the Sorbonne (for he had happily brought with him this book from his father's shop). Richardus by a geometrical method shows that the doctrine of St. Augustine is midway between the two extremes of Calvin and Pelagius, and equidistant likewise from the other opinions that approach these two extremes. This disposition enabled him later to meditate a principle of the natural law of the nations, which should both be apt for the explanation of the origins of Roman law and every other gentile civil law in respect of history, and agree with the sound doctrine of grace in respect of moral philosophy. At the same time Lorenzo Valla, by his reprehension of the Roman jurists in point of Latin elegance, led him to cultivate the study of the Latin language, beginning with the works of Cicero.

However, while he was still wedded to the corrupt style of poetry, it came about happily that in a library of the Minor Friars Observants of that castle there fell into his hands a book at the end of which there was a criticism or defense (he does not well remember) of an epigram by a gentleman of canon's rank named Massa. It included a discussion of the marvelous poetic meters especially observed in Virgil. This so captivated Vico that he was seized with a desire to study the Latin poets, starting with their prince. Then, beginning to be displeased with his own modern style of versifying, he turned to cultivation of the Tuscan tongue by study of its princes, Boccaccio in prose and Dante and Petrarch in verse. On successive days he would study Cicero side by side with Boccaccio, Virgil with Dante, and Horace with Petrarch, being curious to see and to judge for himself the differences between them. And he learned how far in all three cases the Latin tongue surpasses the Italian, by reading their most cultivated writers always three times each on the following plan: the first time to grasp each composition as a whole, the second to note the transitions and the sequence of things, the third in greater detail to collect the fine turns of thought and expression, which he marked in the books themselves instead of copying them into commonplace or phrase books. This practice, he thought, would lead him to make good use of them as his needs recalled them to mind in their contexts: which is the sole measure of effective thought and expression.

Then, reading in Horace's *Art [of Poetry]* that the richest source of poetical suggestion is to be found in the writings of the moral philosophers, he applied himself seriously to the ethics of the ancient Greeks, beginning with that of Aristotle, to which, as he had observed in his reading, the authorities on the various principles of the civil institutes frequently referred. And in this study he noticed that Roman jurisprudence was an art of equity conveyed by innumerable specific precepts of natural law which the jurists had extracted from the reasons of the laws and the intentions of the legislators. But the science of justice taught by moral philosophers proceeded from a few eternal truths dictated in metaphysics by an ideal justice, which in the work of cities plays the rôle of architect and commands the two particular justices, the commutative and the distributive, as it were two divine artisans, to measure utilities by two eternal measures, namely the two proportions demonstrated in mathematics, the arithmetical and the geometrical. Thus he began to realize how the legal discipline is less than half learned by the method of study which is commonly observed. Hence he was again brought round to the study of metaphysics, but since in this connection that of Aristotle, which he had learned from Suarez, was of no help to him, nor could he see the reason why, he proceeded to study that of Plato, guided only by his fame as the prince of divine philosophers. Only after he had made considerable progress did he understand why the metaphysics of Aristotle had been of no avail to him in the study of moral philosophy, as indeed it had not availed Averroes, whose *Commentary* left the Arabs no more humane or civilized than they had been before. For the metaphysics of Aristotle leads to a physical principle, which is matter, from which the particular forms are drawn; and indeed makes God a potter who works at things outside himself. But the metaphysics of Plato leads to a metaphysical principle, which is the eternal idea, drawing out and creating matter from itself, like a seminal spirit that forms its own egg. In conformity with this metaphysic he founds a moral philosophy on an ideal or architectonic virtue or justice. Consequently he devoted himself to meditating an ideal commonwealth, to which he gave, in his laws, an equally ideal justice. So that from the time that Vico felt himself dissatisfied with the metaphysic of Aristotle as an aid to the understanding of moral philosophy, and found himself instructed by that of Plato, there began to dawn on him, without his being aware of it, the thought of meditating an ideal eternal law that should be observed in a universal city after the idea or design of providence, upon which idea have since been founded all the commonwealths of all times and all nations. This was the ideal republic that Plato should have contemplated as a consequence of his metaphysic; but he was shut off from it by ignorance of the fall of the first man.[139]

At the same time the philosophical writings of Cicero, Aristotle and Plato, all worked out with a view to the good ordering of mankind in civil society, caused him to take little or no pleasure in the moral philosophies of the Stoics and Epicureans. For they are each a moral philosophy of solitaries: the Epicurean, of idlers inclosed in their own little gardens; the Stoic, of contemplatives who endeavor to feel no emotion. And the leap which he had made at the start from logic to metaphysics caused Vico thereafter to esteem lightly the physics of Aristotle and Epicurus and finally of René Descartes; whence he found himself disposed to look with favor on the physics of Timaeus adopted by Plato, which holds the world to be made of numbers. Nor could he bring himself to despise the physics of the Stoics, which holds the world to consist of points,[140] for between this and the Timaean there is no substantial difference; later indeed he tried to reestablish it in his book *On the Most Ancient Wisdom of the Italians*. And finally he could not accept either seriously or playfully the mechanical physics of Epicurus or Descartes, for both start from a false position.

When Vico saw how both Plato and Aristotle often employ mathematical proofs to demonstrate what they discuss in philosophy, he realized that he fell short of being able to understand them well, so he decided to apply himself to geometry and to penetrate as far as the fifth proposition of Euclid. And reflecting that its demonstration turned on a congruence of triangles, the sides and angles of one triangle being shown one by one to be equal to the corresponding sides and angles of the other, he found in himself that it was an easier matter to grasp all those minute truths together, as in a metaphysical genus, than to understand those particular geometrical quantities. And to his cost he learned that that study proper to minute wits is not easy for minds already made universal by metaphysics. So he gave up this study as one which chained and confined his mind, now accustomed through long study of metaphysics to move freely in the infinite of genera; and in the constant reading of orators, historians and poets his intellect took increasing delight in observing between the remotest matters ties that bound them together in some common relation. It is these ties that are the beautiful ornaments of eloquence which make subtleties delightful.

With reason the ancients considered the study of geometry suitable for children and judged it to be a logic appropriate to that tender age whose difficulty in comprehending the genera of things is proportional to its facility in apprehending the particulars and how to dispose them in sequence. Aristotle himself, though he had abstracted the syllogistic art from the method employed in geometry, agrees with this when he says that children should be taught anguages, histories and geometry as subjects suitable for exercising memory, imagination and perception.[141] Hence we can easily understand how much undoing, what sort of culture, youth derives from two pernicious practices in use today.

The first is in introducing philosophy to children barely out of grammar school with the so-called logic "of Arnauld," full of rigorous judgments concerning recondite matters of the higher sciences, remote from vulgar common sense. The result is a blasting of those youthful mental gifts which should be regulated and developed each by a separate art, as for example memory by the study of languages, imagination by the reading of poets, historians and orators, perception by plane geometry. This last indeed is in a certain sense a graphic art which at once invigorates memory by the great number of its elements, refines imagination with its delicate figures as with so many drawings described in the subtlest lines, and quickens perception which must survey all these figures and among them all collect those which are needed to demonstrate the magnitude which is required: all this to bear fruit, at the time of mature judgment, in an eloquent, lively and acute wisdom. But when by these logics lads are led prematurely into criticism (that is to say, are led to judge before properly apprehending, against the natural course of ideas—for they should first apprehend, then judge, and finally reason), they become arid and dry in expression and without ever doing anything set themselves up in judgment over all things. On the other hand, if in the age of perception, which is youth, they would devote themselves to Topics, the art of discovery that is the special privilege of the perceptive (as Vico, taking his cue from Cicero, did in his youth), they would then be furnished with matter in order later to form a sound opinion on it. For one can not form a sound judgment of a thing without having complete knowledge of it; and topics is the art of finding in anything all that is in it. Thus nature itself would aid the young to become philosophers and good speakers.

The other practice consists in teaching youth the elements of the science of magnitudes by the algebraic method. For this numbs all that is most exuberant in youthful natures: it obscures their imagination, enfeebles their memory, renders their perception sluggish, and slackens their understanding. And these four things are all most necessary for the culture of the best humanity: the first for painting, sculpture, architecture, music, poetry and eloquence; the second for learning languages and history; the third for inventions; and the fourth for prudence. But this algebra seems to be an Arabic device for reducing the natural signs of magnitudes to certain ciphers at will. Thus the signs for numbers, which among the Greeks and Latins had been the letters [of their alphabets], which in both (at least the capitals) are regular geometric lines,—were reduced by the Arabs to ten minute ciphers. So perception is stricken by algebra, for algebra sees only what is right under its eyes; memory is confounded, since when the second sign is found algebra pays no further attention to the first; imagination goes blind because algebra has no need of images; understanding is destroyed because algebra professes to divine. The result is that young men who have devoted much time to algebra find themselves later, to their great dismay and regret, less apt in the affairs of civil life. Wherefore, in order that it should afford some advantages and produce none of these evil effects, algebra should be studied for a short time at the end of the mathematics course, and it should be used as the Romans did with numbers. For in the case of immense sums they represented them by points. Similarly, where to find required magnitudes our human understanding would be obliged to undergo desperate labor by the synthetic method, we should take refuge in the oracle of the analytic. On the other hand, so far as the latter is essential to good reasoning, it is best to form the habit of it by metaphysical analysis. In every question one should look for truth in the infinity of being; then, descending by regular steps through the genera of substance, one should keep eliminating what the thing is not for all the species of each genus, until one arrives at the ultimate differentia which constitutes the essence of the thing one desires to know.

(This rather long digression is an annual lecture which Vico gave to the young men that they might know how to make choice and use of the sciences for eloquence.)

Returning now to the matter in hand: when he had discovered that the whole secret of the geometric method comes to this: first to define the terms one has to reason with; then to set up certain common maxims agreed to by one's companion in argument; finally, at need, to ask discretely for such concessions as the nature of things permits, in order to supply a basis for arguments, which without some such assumption could not reach their conclusions; and with these principles to proceed step by step in one's demonstrations from simpler to more complex truths, and never to affirm the complex truths without first examining singly their component parts,—he thought the only advantage of having learned how geometricians proceed in their reasoning was that if he ever had occasion to reason in that manner he would know how. And indeed later he followed it closely in the work *On the One Principle of Universal Law,* which in the opinion of Jean Le Clerc "is composed by a strict mathematical method," as will be narrated later in its proper place.

Now to follow in order the steps of Vico's progress in philosophy, we must here turn back a little. For at the time he left Naples the philosophy of Epicurus had begun to be cultivated in Pierre Gassendi's version; and two years later news that the young men had become its devotees made him wish to study it in Lucretius. By reading Lucretius he learned that Epicurus, because he denied any generic difference of substance between mind and body and so for want of a sound metaphysic remained of limited mind, had to take as the starting point for his philosophy matter already formed and divided into multiform ultimate parts composed of other parts which he imagined to be inseparable because there was no void between them. This is a philosophy to satisfy the circumscribed minds of children and the weak ones of silly women. And though Epicurus had no knowledge even of geometry, yet, by a well-ordered deduction, he built on his mechanical physics a metaphysics entirely sensualistic just like that of John Locke, and a hedonistic morality suitable for men who are to live in solitude, as indeed he enjoined upon all his disciples. And, to give him his due, Vico followed his explanation of the forms of corporeal nature with as much delight as he felt ridicule or pity on seeing him under the hard necessity of going off into a thousand inanities and absurdities to explain the operations of the human mind.[142] This reading therefore served only to confirm him still further in the doctrines of Plato, who from the very form of our human mind, without any hypothesis, establishes the eternal idea as the principle of all things on the basis of the knowledge and consciousness [*scienza e coscienza*] that we have of ourselves. For in our mind there are certain eternal truths that we cannot mistake or deny, and which are therefore not of our making. But for the rest we feel a liberty by thinking them to make all the things that are dependent on the body, and therefore we make them in time, that is when we choose to turn our attention to them, and we make them all by thinking them and contain them all within ourselves. For example, we make images by imagination, recollections by memory, passions by appetite; smells, tastes, colors, sounds and touches by the senses; and all these things we contain within us. But for the eternal truths which are not of our making and have no dependence on our bodies, we must conceive as principle of all things an eternal idea altogether separate from body, which, in its consciousness, when it wills, creates all things in time and contains them within itself, and by containing them sustains them. By this principle of philosophy Plato establishes, in metaphysics, abstract substances as having more reality than corporeal ones. From it he derives a morality well adapted throughout for civil life, so that the school of Socrates, both in itself and through its successors, furnished the greatest lights of Greece in the arts both of peace and of war. And he approves the Timaean physics, which is that of Pythagoras and holds the world to consist of numbers, which in a certain respect are more abstract than the metaphysical points that Zeno hit upon for explaining the things of nature, as Vico has shown in his *Metaphysics* in a way to be pointed out later.

A short time after this he learned of the growing prestige of experimental physics, for which the name of Robert Boyle was on everyone's lips; but, profitable as he thought it for medicine and spagyric, he desired to have nothing to do with this science. For it contributed nothing to the philosophy of man and had to be expounded in barbarous formulas, whereas his own principal concern was the study of Roman laws, the main foundations of which are the philosophy of human customs and the science of the Roman language and government, which can only be learned in the Latin writers.

Toward the end of his period of solitude, which lasted a good nine years, he heard that the physics of René Descartes had eclipsed all preceding systems, so that he became inflamed with a desire to have knowledge of it; whereas, by a pleasant deception, he was already acquainted with it. For among other books he had brought from his father's bookstore the *Natural Philosophy* of Henri Du Roy, under whose mask Descartes had first published it in Utrecht.[143] Turning from Lucretius to the study of Du Roy, a philosopher whose profession was medicine but who showed that he had no erudition save in mathematics, he thought him a man no less ignorant of metaphysics than Epicurus had been, who never wished to learn anything of mathematics at all. For he too sets up in nature a principle falsely postulated: namely, body already formed. The only differences are that Epicurus halts the divisibility of body at the atoms, while Du Roy makes its three dimensions infinitely divisible; Epicurus makes motion take place in a void, Du Roy in a plenum; Epicurus starts the formation of his infinite worlds with a casual swerve of atoms from the downward motion due to their own weight and gravity, Du Roy starts the formation of his limitless vortices with an impetus impressed on a piece of inert, and so as yet undivided, matter, which under the impressed motion is divided into particles and, though impeded by its weight, is compelled to attempt to move in a straight line. Since this is prevented by the plenum, it begins, divided as it is into particles, a rotation of each particle about its own center. As then by the casual swerve of his atoms Epicurus leaves the world to the discretion of chance, so from this necessity of René's first corpuscles to attempt rectilinear motion it seemed to Vico that this system would be acceptable to those who subject the world to fate.

He had cause to congratulate himself on this opinion when, after he had returned to Naples and learned that Du Roy's physics was that of René, the latter's *Metaphysical Meditations* were being cultivated. For René, over-ambitious for glory, as on the one hand he tried to make himself famous among professors of medicine with a physics contrived on a pattern like that of Epicurus and presented for the first time from the chair of a European university so famous as that of Utrecht, by a physician, so on the other he sketched a few first outlines of metaphysics in the manner of Plato. In the latter he labors to establish two kinds of substances, one extended the other thinking, so as to subject matter to an immaterial agent like Plato's God, in order one day to reign in the cloisters too, where the metaphysics of Aristotle was introduced as long ago as the eleventh century. For although, in virtue of what that philosopher had himself contributed, his metaphysics had previously served the purposes of the impious Averroists, yet since its ground plan was Plato's the Christian religion easily bent it to the pious intents of its Master. So that as it had ruled with the metaphysics of Plato from its beginning to the eleventh century, it has ruled ever since with that of Aristotle. And indeed, returning to Naples at the time when the Cartesian physics was most in vogue, Vico heard this assertion [that Descartes's metaphysics would drive Aristotle's from the cloisters] often made by Gregorio Caloprese,[144] a great Cartesian philosopher, who held Vico very dear.

But in respect of the unity of its parts the philosophy of Descartes is not at all a consistent system; for his physics calls for a metaphysics that should set up a single kind of substance, the corporeal, operating, as we have said, by necessity, just as that of Epicurus calls for a single kind of substance, corporeal, operating by chance. For Descartes and Epicurus agree in this, that all the infinitely various forms of bodies are modifications of corporeal substance, and have themselves no substantial being. Nor did his metaphysics yield any moral philosophy suited to the Christian religion. Certainly the few things he himself wrote on the subject do not constitute such a philosophy, and his treatise on the *Passions* is more useful to medicine than to ethics. Even Father Malebranche was unable to work out from them a system of Christian morality, and the *Thoughts* of Pascal are merely scattered lights. Nor does a distinctively Cartesian logic emerge from his metaphysics, for Arnauld erects his on the basis of Aristotle's. Nor is it useful even to medicine itself, for the anatomists do not find the Cartesian man in nature. So that, compared to that of Descartes, the philosophy of Epicurus makes a more consistent system, although the latter knew nothing of mathematics. For all these reasons, of which Vico took note, he was soon much elated that, as the reading of Lucretius had made him a partisan of the Platonic metaphysics, so that of Du Roy had confirmed him in it.

These systems of physics were for Vico as so many diversions from his serious meditations on the Platonic metaphysicians and they served to give his fancy scope in his exercises in verse-making. For he was given to the practice of working out canzoni, still following his early habit of composing in Italian, but with an eye to drawing into them luminous Latin ideas, under the guidance of the best Tuscan poets. For example, prompted by the panegyric of Pompey the Great which Cicero wove into his oration on the Manilian Law (than which there is no more solemn oration of its kind in the Latin language), and in imitation of the "three sisters" of Petrarch, he composed the panegyric, divided into three canzoni, *In Praise of the Elector Maximilian of Bavaria;* these canzoni may be found in Lippi's *Selection from the Italian Poets,* printed at Lucca in the year 1709. And in Acampora's *Selection from the Neapolitan Poets,* printed at Naples in the year 1701, there is another canzone written on the occasion of the marriage of Donna Ippolita Cantelmo [145] of the house of the dukes of Popoli to Don Vincenzo Carafa, Duke of Bruzzano and now Prince of Rocella. This was composed on the pattern of that most graceful song of Catullus: *Vesper adest.* Vico later read that this poem had been imitated before him by Torquato Tasso in a canzone with a similar subject, and he was glad not to have known of this before, partly because of the reverence he felt for such a great poet and partly because, had he known that he had been anticipated, he would hardly have dared to undertake the composition and would certainly have taken no pleasure in it. In addition to these canzoni Vico composed yet another, on Plato's idea of the "Great Year," on which Virgil had constructed his learned eclogue *Sicelides musae.* The occasion for this canzone was the marriage of the

Duke of Bavaria to Princess Theresa of Poland, and it is included in the first volume of Albano's *Selection from the Neapolitan Poets,* printed at Naples in the year 1723.

With this learning and erudition Vico returned to Naples a stranger in his own land, and found the physics of Descartes at the height of its renown among the established men of letters. That of Aristotle, on its own account but much more because of the excessive alterations made in it by the schoolmen, had now become a laughingstock. As for metaphysics, which in the sixteenth century had placed in the highest rank of literature such men as Marsilio Ficino, Pico della Mirandola, Agostino Nifo and Agostino Steuchio, Giacopo Mazzoni, Alessandro Piccolomini, Matteo Acquaviva, and Francesco Patrizi,[146] and contributed so much to poetry, history, and eloquence that all Greece in the time of its utmost learning and grace of speech seemed to have risen again in Italy,—it was now thought worthy only of being shut up in the cloisters; and as for Plato, an occasional passage was turned to poetic use, or quoted to parade an erudite memory, and that was all. Scholastic logic was condemned and Euclid's *Elements* approved to replace it. Medicine, because of the frequent revolutions in systems of physics, had declined into scepticism, and doctors had begun to take their stand on acatalepsy or the impossibility of comprehending the truth about the nature of diseases, and to "suspend judgment" or withhold assent when it came to diagnosis or application of effective remedies. Galenic medicine, which when studied in the light of Greek philosophy and in the Greek language had produced so many incomparable doctors, had now, because of the great ignorance of its followers, fallen beneath contempt. The medieval interpreters of the civil law had fallen from their high repute in the academies, and the modern humanists had taken their place, to the great detriment of the courts; for just as the latter are needed for the criticism of Roman laws the former are equally necessary for legal "topics" in cases of doubtful equity. The most learned Don Carlo Buragna had reintroduced the praiseworthy style of composing verses, but he had too tightly confined it by his imitation of Giovanni della Casa, deriving nothing delicate or robust from Greek and Latin springs, or from the limpid streams of Petrarch's *rime,* or from the great torrents of Dante's canzoni. The most erudite Lionardo di Capua had restored good Tuscan prose, and clothed it with grace and beauty; but in spite of these virtues there was never to be heard an oration either animated by Greek wisdom in the treatment of manners, or invigorated by Roman grandeur in stirring the emotions. And finally a man incomparable for his Latinity, Tommaso Cornelio, by the extreme purity of his *Progymnasmata* had dismayed the minds of the young rather than giving them courage to go on in later years with the study of the Latin language.[147]

So for all these reasons Vico blessed his good fortune in having no teacher whose words he had sworn by, and he felt most grateful for those woods in which, guided by his good genius, he had followed the main course of his studies untroubled by sectarian prejudice; for in the city taste in letters changed every two or three years like styles in dress. The common neglect of good Latin prose made him all the more determined to cultivate it. Learning that Cornelio had not been strong in Greek, had paid scant attention to Tuscan, and had found little or no pleasure in criticism—perhaps because he had observed that polyglots for all the languages they know never use any one of them correctly, and critics never attain to the virtues of a language because they are always pausing to note the defects in its writers—Vico likewise decided to abandon Greek, in which he had progressed somewhat from Gretser's *Rudiments* [148] studied in the second grade of the Jesuits, and Tuscan as well (and for the same reason he never cared to learn any French), and to concentrate on Latin. And because he had also observed that by the publication of lexicons and commentaries Latin had fallen into decay, he resolved never again to take into his hands any such book, excepting only Junius's *Nomenclator* [149] for the understanding of technical terms; but to read the Latin authors completely free of notes, entering into their spirit by means of philosophical criticism, just as the Latin authors of the sixteenth century had done. Among these he particularly admired Giovio for his fluency and Navagero for his delicacy as far as we can judge from the little that he left, and also for his exceedingly elegant taste which makes us lament the great loss of his *History*. [150]

For these reasons Vico lived in his native city not only a stranger but quite unknown. His solitary tastes and habits did not prevent his venerating from afar as sages the older men who were recognized for their knowledge of letters, and envying with a genuine vexation other young men who had the good fortune to enjoy their conversation. With this attitude which is necessary to young men who wish to make further progress and not on the say of malicious or ignorant teachers to remain all their lives satisfied with a knowledge suited to another's taste and capacity, he first came to the attention of two men of importance. One was Father Don Gaetano d' Andrea, a Theatine, who later died a most reverend bishop; he was a brother of Francesco and Gennaio [d' Andrea], both of immortal name. [151] In a conversation which he had with Vico in a bookstore on the history of collections of canons, he asked him if he were married. And when Vico answered that he was not, he inquired if he wanted to become a Theatine. On Vico's replying that he was not of noble birth, the father answered that that need be no obstacle, for he would obtain a dispensation from Rome. Then Vico, seeing himself obliged by the great honor the father paid him, came out with it that his parents were old and poor and he was their only hope. When the father pointed out that men of letters were rather a burden than a help to their families, Vico replied that perhaps it would not be so in his case. Then the father closed the conversation by saying: "That is not your vocation."

The other was Don Giuseppe Lucina, a man of great erudition in Greek, Latin and Tuscan and in all branches of divine and human knowledge. He had made some trial of the young man's ability, and in his kind way was regretting that it was not put to some good use in the city, when a good occasion offered itself to him for advancing the youth. For Don Nicola Caravita, leader of the bar in sharpness of intellect, severity of judgment and purity of Tuscan style, and a great patron of men of letters, had decided to make a collection of literary tributes to the Count of San Estevan, viceroy of Naples, on the occasion of his departure. This was the first collection of its kind that appeared in Naples within our memory, and it had to be printed in the narrow limits of a few days. Lucina, whose opinion was respected by all, suggested that Vico should write the oration to serve as preface to all the other compositions. And having secured this commission for the young man, he brought it to him, pointing out to him his opportunity to make himself favorably known to a patron of letters such as he had found to be his own greatest protector; and indeed the youth needed no prompting to be most eager for it. And so, because he had given up Tuscan studies, he worked out a Latin oration for that collection at the printing establishment itself of Giuseppe Roselli, in the year 1696. From then on he began to rise in fame as a man of letters; and among others Gregorio Caloprese, whom we have above mentioned with honor, was wont to call him (as Epicurus was called) the "autodidact" or "teacher of himself." Later, for the *Funeral Rites of Donna Caterina d' Aragona,* mother of the Duke of Medinaceli, viceroy of Naples, for which the most learned Carlo Rossi wrote the Greek, and the celebrated sacred orator Don Emmanuel Cicatelli the Italian, Vico wrote the Latin oration. Along with the other compositions it was published in a folio volume printed in the year 1697.

A short time later, by the death of the incumbent professor, the chair of rhetoric fell vacant. It yielded not more than a hundred ducats annually, with the addition of another smaller and varying sum derived from fees on the habilitation certificates which the professor gives his students for their admission to the law course. Caravita told him that he should forthwith enter the competition for this chair. At first he declined because he had failed in another candidacy a few months previously, in which he had sought the post of town clerk. But Don Nicola, gently reproaching him as a man of little spirit (as indeed he is as far as practical affairs are concerned), told him that he need only attend to preparing his lecture, for he (Don Nicola) would make the application for him. So Vico competed with an hour's lecture on the opening lines of Fabius Quintilian's long chapter *De statibus causarum,* limiting himself to the etymology of the term *status* and the distinction of its meanings. The lecture was full of Greek and Latin erudition and criticism, and won him the chair by an ample number of votes.

Meanwhile the viceroy, the Duke of Medinaceli, had restored literature in Naples to a glory not seen since the time of Alfonso of Aragon, by founding an academy [152] for its cultivation, composed of the very flower of men of letters. This had been suggested to him by Don Federico Pappacoda, a Neapolitan gentleman of good taste in letters and a great esteemer of scholars, and by Don Nicola Caravita. Since the most cultured literature had begun to rise into great favor among the noble classes, Vico, urged thereto the more by the honor of having been numbered among the academicians, now applied himself wholly to the profession of humane letters.

The reason that fortune is said to be friendly to young men is that they choose their lot in life from among those arts and professions that flourish in their youth; but as the world by its nature changes in taste from year to year, they later find themselves in their old age strong in such wisdom as no longer pleases and therefore no longer profits. Thus there came about a great and sudden revolution in literary affairs in Naples. Just when it was thought that the best literature of the sixteenth century was to be reestablished there for a long time to come, the departure of the duke-viceroy gave rise to a new order of things which cast it down in a very short time and contrary to every expectation. For those valiant men of letters who had declared a few years before that metaphysics should remain immured in the cloisters, now began to cultivate it intensively. But they studied it not, as Marsilio and others had done, in the works of men like Plato and Plotinus (which had made fruitful so many great men of letters in the sixteenth century), but in the *Meditations* of René Descartes and its companion piece his book *On Method,* wherein he disapproves the study of languages, orators, historians and poets, and by setting up only his metaphysics, physics and mathematics, reduces literature to the wisdom of the Arabs, who in all these three fields produced men of great learning—men like Averroes in metaphysics, and so many famous astronomers and physicians that they bequeathed to both sciences the very terms necessary to expound them. Now the savants of the day, however great and learned, since they had all first and for a long time occupied themselves with corpuscular physics, experiments and machines, must have found the *Meditations* so abstruse that it was difficult for them to withdraw their minds from the senses enough to meditate on them; so that the highest praise of a philosopher was: He understands the *Meditations* of Descartes.

At this time both Vico and Don Paolo Doria [153] were frequent visitors in the home of Caravita, which was a rendezvous for men of letters; and Doria, as fine a philosopher as he was a gentleman, was the first with whom Vico could begin to discuss metaphysics. What Doria admired as sublime, great and new in Descartes, Vico remarked to be old and common knowledge among the Platonists. But in Doria's discourse he perceived a mind that often gave forth lightning-like flashes of Platonic divinity, so that thenceforth they remained linked in a noble and faithful friendship.

Up to this time Vico had admired two only above all other learned men: Plato and Tacitus; for with an incomparable metaphysical mind Tacitus contemplates man as he is, Plato as he should be. And as Plato with his universal knowledge explores the parts of nobility which constitute the man of intellectual wisdom, so Tacitus descends into all the counsels of utility whereby, among the infinite irregular chances of malice and fortune, the man of practical wisdom brings things to good issue. Now Vico's admiration of these two

great authors from this point of view was a foreshadowing of that plan on which he later worked out an ideal
eternal history to be traversed by the universal history of
all times, carrying out on it, by certain eternal properties of civil affairs, the development, acme and decay of all
nations. From this it follows that the wise man should be
formed both of esoteric wisdom such as Plato's and of common wisdom such as that of Tacitus. And now at length
Vico's attention was drawn to Francis Bacon, Lord Verulam,
a man of incomparable wisdom both common and esoteric,
at one and the same time a universal man in theory and in
practice, a rare philosopher and a great English minister of
state. Leaving aside his other works, on whose subjects there
were perhaps writers as good or better, from his *De augmentis
scientiarum* Vico concluded that, as Plato is the prince of
Greek wisdom, and the Greeks have no Tacitus, so Romans
and Greeks alike have no Bacon. He marveled that one sole
man could see in the world of letters what studies remained
to be discovered and developed, and how many and what
kinds of defects must be corrected in those it already contained; and that without professional or sectarian bias, save
for a few things which offend the Catholic religion, he did
justice to all the sciences, and always with the design that each
should make its special contribution to that *summa* which the
universal republic of letters constitutes. Vico now proposed
to have these three unique authors ever before him in meditation and writing, and so he went on elaborating his works
of discovery, which culminated in *The One Principle of Universal Law.*

Accordingly he was wont, in his orations delivered in successive years at the annual opening of studies in the Royal
University, to propose universal arguments brought down

from metaphysics and given social application. From this point of view he treated of the ends of the various studies, as in the first six orations, or of the method of study, as in the latter part of the sixth and in the entire seventh. The first three treat principally of the ends suitable to human nature, the next two principally of the political ends, the sixth of the Christian end.[154]

The first, delivered the 18th of October 1699, proposes that we cultivate the force of our divine mind in all its faculties. Its thesis is: "That the knowledge of oneself is for each of us the greatest incentive to the compendious study of every branch of learning." It proves that the human mind is by analogy the god of man, just as God is the mind of the whole [of things]. It shows severally how the marvelous faculties of the mind, whether senses or imagination or memory or invention or reason, perform with divine powers of quickness, facility and efficiency the most numerous and varied tasks at one and the same time. How children, free of evil affections and vices, at the end of three or four years of idle play are found to have learned the entire vocabulary of their native tongues. How Socrates did not so much bring down moral philosophy from heaven as elevate our spirit to it, and how those who for their inventions were raised to heaven among the gods are but the intelligence which each of us possesses. How it is a matter for astonishment that there should be so many ignorant persons when ignorance or being misled or falling into error is as repugnant to the mind as smoke is to the eyes, or a foul stench to the nose; wherefore negligence is especially to be condemned. How it is only because we do not wish to be that we are not instructed in everything, seeing that by our efficacious will alone, when transported by inspiration, we do things which when accomplished we wonder at as if they had been done not by ourselves but by a god. And therefore it concludes that if in a few years a youth has not run through the whole round of the sciences it is only because he did not want to, or if he had the desire he has failed for lack of teachers or of a good order of study, or because the end of his studies was something other than cultivating a kind of divinity in our mind.

The second oration, delivered in 1700, urges that we inform the spirit with the virtues by following the truths of the mind. Its argument is: "That there is no enmity more dire and dangerous than that of the fool against himself." It represents this universe as a great city in which God by an eternal law condemns the foolish to wage against themselves a war thus conceived: "Its law has as many chapters, written out by an omnipotent hand, as there are natures of all things. Let us recite the chapter on man. 'Let man be of mortal body and eternal soul. Let him be born for two things, truth and goodness, that is to say for Me alone. Let his mind distinguish the true from the false. Let not his senses impose upon his mind. Let reason be the principle, guide and lord of his life. Let his desires submit to his reason. . . . Let him win praise for himself by the good arts of his spirit. By virtue and constancy let him attain to human felicity. If anyone foolishly breaks these laws, whether through malice or luxury or sloth or mere imprudence, he is guilty of treason: let him wage war against himself.' " And it proceeds to a tragic description of the war. From this passage it is quite clear that as far back as this time Vico was turning over in his mind the theme which he later developed in his *Universal Law*.

The third oration, delivered in the year 1701, is a kind of practical appendix to the two preceding ones. Its argument is: "That the society of letters must be rid of every deceit, if you would study to be adorned with true not feigned, solid not empty, erudition." It points out that in the republic of letters one must live justly; it condemns the wilful critics who wrongfully exact tribute from this public treasury of letters, the stubborn sectarians who keep it from growing, and the impostors who counterfeit their contributions to it.

The fourth oration, delivered in the year 1704, has this for its argument: "He who would reap from the study of letters the greatest advantages, combined always with honor, let him be educated for the glory and good of the community." It is directed against the false scholars who study for advantage alone and therefore take more pains to seem learned than to be so. When the advantage they seek has been attained, they grow lazy and stoop to the lowest arts to keep up their reputation as scholars. Vico had delivered half of this discourse when Don Feliz Lanzina Ulloa, president of the Sacred Council and the Cato of the Spanish ministers, joined the audience. In his honor Vico with great presence of mind gave a new and briefer turn to what had gone before and united it with what he had left to say. A similar quickness of wit had been exercised by Clement XI when he was an abbé speaking in Italian before the Academy of the Umoristi in honor of Cardinal d'Estrées, his protector. Thus he began his fortunate career under Innocent XII, which later carried him to the pontificate.[155]

In the fifth oration, delivered in the year 1705, it is proposed "That commonwealths have been most renowned for military glory and most powerful politically when letters have most flourished in them." And the argument is vigorously proved by good reasons and then confirmed by this continuous series of examples. In Assyria there arose the Chaldeans, the first learned men in the world, and there the first monarchy was established. When Greece shone with wisdom more than in all preceding times, the monarchy of Persia was overthrown by Alexander. Rome established her world empire on the ruins of Carthage, whom she destroyed under Scipio, whose knowledge of philosophy, eloquence and poetry appears in the inimitable comedies of Terence, which Scipio wrote in collaboration with his friend Laelius. (Considering them unworthy to appear under his own great name, he had them published under that of Terence, who doubtless put into them something of his own.) And of course the Roman monarchy was established under Augustus, in whose time all the wisdom of Greece shone forth at Rome in the splendor of the Roman language. The most luminous kingdom of Italy threw out its beams under Theodoric, who enjoyed the counsel of men like Cassiodorus. With Charlemagne the Roman Empire rose again in Germany, because letters, long since dead in the royal courts of the West, began to arise in his in the persons of Alcuin and others. Homer fashioned an Alexander who burned to follow the example of Achilles in valor, and Alexander's example in turn inspired Julius Caesar to great deeds; so that these two great commanders (and none dared say which was the greater) are pupils of a Homeric hero. Two cardinals, both great philosophers and theologians and one of them a great sacred orator as well—Jiménez and Richelieu—drew up the plans for the monarchies of Spain and France respectively. The Turk has founded a great empire on barbarism, but with the counsel of one Sergius, a learned and impious Christian monk who gave the stupid Mohammed the law on which to found it. And when the Greeks, first in Asia and then everywhere, had declined into barbarism, the Arabs cultivated metaphysics, mathematics, astronomy and medicine, and with this scholarly knowledge, although not with that of the most cultured humanity, they roused to a high glory of conquests the wild and barbarous Al Mansurs, and helped the Turk establish an empire in which all study of letters was abolished. But this vast empire, had it not been for the perfidious Christians, first Greek and later Latin, who supplied it from time to time with the arts and stratagems of warfare, would have fallen to ruin of its own accord.

In the sixth oration, delivered in the year 1707, he treats of this argument, which is partly on the ends of the various studies and partly on the order of studying them. "The knowledge of the corrupt nature of man invites us to study the complete cycle of the liberal arts and sciences, and propounds and expounds the true, easy and unvarying order in which they are to be acquired." In it he leads his hearers to meditate on themselves, how man under pain of sin is divided from man by tongue, mind and heart. By the tongue, which often fails and often betrays the ideas through which man would but cannot unite himself to man. By the mind, through the variety of opinions springing from diversity of sensuous tastes, in which men do not agree. And finally by the heart, whose corruption prevents even the conciliation of man with man by uniformity of vice. Whence Vico proves that the pain of our corruption must be healed by virtue, knowledge and eloquence; for through these three things only does one man feel the same as another. This brings Vico to the end of the various studies, and fixes the point of view from which he considers the order of study. He shows that as languages were the most powerful means for setting up human society, so the studies should begin with them, since they depend altogether on memory which in childhood is marvelously strong. The age of childhood, weak in reason, is regulated only by examples, which to be effective must be grasped with vividness of imagination, for which childhood is marvelous. Hence children should be occupied with the reading of history, both fabulous and true. The age of childhood is reasonable but it has no material on which to reason; let children then be prepared for the art of good reasoning through a study of the quantitative sciences, which call for memory and imagination and at the same time check the tendency to corpulence of the imaginative faculty, which when swollen is the mother of all our errors and woes. In early youth the senses prevail and draw the pure mind in their train; let youths then apply themselves to physics, which leads to the contemplation of the corporeal universe and has need of mathematics for the science of the cosmic system. Thus by the vast and corpulent physical ideas and by the delicate ideas of lines and numbers let them be prepared to grasp the abstract metaphysical infinite by the science of being and the one. And when they have come to know their mind in this science let them be prepared to contemplate their spirit and in consequence of eternal truths to perceive that it is corrupt, so that they may be disposed to amend it naturally by morality at an age when they have had some experience of the evil guidance of the passions, which are most violent in childhood. And when they have learned that by its nature pagan morality is insufficient to tame and subdue philauty or self-love, and when by experience in metaphysics they understand that the infinite is more certain than the finite, mind than body, God than man (who cannot tell how he himself moves, feels or knows), then with humbled intellect let them make ready to receive revealed theology, from which let them descend to Christian ethics, and thus purged let them finally pass to Christian jurisprudence.

From the time of the first oration of which we have spoken,

it is evident both in it and in all that followed but above all in this last, that Vico was agitating in his mind a theme both new and grand, to unite in one principle all knowledge human and divine. But all these arguments of which he had discoursed fell too far short of it. He was therefore glad that he had not published these orations, for he thought the republic of letters, stooped under so great a pile of books, should not be burdened with more, but should only be offered books of important discoveries and useful inventions. But in the year 1708 the Royal University resolved to have a solemn public inauguration of studies and to dedicate it to the king with an oration to be delivered in the presence of Cardinal Grimani, viceroy of Naples. The oration for this occasion was therefore to be published,[156] and it gave Vico a happy opportunity to devise an argument that should bring some new and profitable discovery to the world of letters,—a desire worthy to be numbered among those of Bacon in his *New Organ of the Sciences.* It turns on the advantages and disadvantages of our manner of studying as compared with that of the ancients in all branches of knowledge: which disadvantages of our way could be avoided, and by what means; and as for the unavoidable ones, by what advantages of the ancients they might be compensated (so that by adding only a Plato, for example, to what we possess beyond the ancients, we should have a complete university of today); to the end that all divine and human wisdom should everywhere reign with one spirit and cohere in all its parts, so that the sciences lend each other a helping hand and none is a hindrance to any other. The dissertation appeared the same year in duodecimo from the press of Felice Mosca. Its argument is in fact a first draft of what he later worked out in his *The One Principle of Universal Law,* with its appendix *The Consistency of the Jurisprudent.*

And because Vico always had the aim of winning distinction for himself and the university in the field of jurisprudence by other means than lecturing on it to youngsters, he discussed at length in this dissertation [156] the secrecy of the laws of the ancient Roman jurisprudents and essayed a system of jurisprudence for interpreting even the private laws from the point of view of the constitution of the Roman government. With reference to this part of the work Monsignor Vincenzo Vidania, prefect of the royal studies, a man most learned in Roman antiquities and especially in the matter of the laws, being at that time in Barcelona took exception in a most praiseworthy dissertation to this point which Vico had maintained: that the ancient Roman jurisconsults had all been patricians. Vico answered privately at the time and later publicly in the work on *Universal Law,* in a footnote to which may be found the illustrious Vidania's dissertation with Vico's replies. But Hendrik Brenkmann, a most learned Dutch jurist, was greatly pleased with Vico's views on jurisprudence; and while he was staying in Florence to consult the Florentine *Pandects* he spoke favorably of them in conversations with Antonio Rinaldi, who had gone there from Naples to plead the case of a Neapolitan nobleman. [157]

When this dissertation was published, [156] with the addition of what could not be said in the presence of the cardinal viceroy without misusing the time which is so precious to princes, it led Domenico d' Aulisio, [158] the head afternoon lecturer on law and a man of universal knowledge in languages and sciences, to call Vico to him at a public competition for professorships and invite him to sit beside him. D' Aulisio then told him he had read "that little book" (he had not attended the inauguration of studies because of a quarrel with the head lecturer on canon law as to who should precede) and considered Vico "no grubbing compiler but a man whose every page would furnish matter for others to spin out into large volumes." Now d' Aulisio had hitherto looked askance at Vico in the university, not indeed for any fault of the latter but because he was a friend of those men of letters who had been partisans of di Capua against d' Aulisio in a great literary contest which had raged in Naples a long time before and which there is no need to discuss here.[159] This generous act and kindly judgment, on the part of a man otherwise so stern and sparing of praise, showed therefore a singular magnanimity toward Vico; and from that day they contracted a very close friendship which lasted as long as that great man of letters lived.

Meanwhile Vico, by the reading of Bacon of Verulam's treatise *On the Wisdom of the Ancients,* more ingenious and learned than true, was incited to look for its principles farther back than in the fables of the poets. He was moved to do this by the example of Plato who in the *Cratylus* had sought to track them down within the origins of the Greek language. An added incentive was the feeling he had begun to entertain, that the etymologies of the grammarians were unsatisfactory. He applied himself therefore to search out these principles in the origins of Latin words; for certainly the wisdom of the Italic sect had in the school of Pythagoras a much earlier flowering and a greater depth than that which began later in Greece itself. From the word *coelum,* which means both "chisel" and the "great body of the air," he conjectured that perhaps the Egyptians,[160] by whom Pythagoras was instructed,[161] had been of the opinion that the instrument with which nature makes everything was the wedge, and that this was what they meant their pyramids to signify. Now the Latins called nature *ingenium,*[162] whose principal property is

sharpness; [163] thus intimating that nature forms and deforms
every form with the chisel of air. It would form matter by
shaving lightly, and deform it by gouging deeply, with the
chisel by which the air ravages everything. The hand that
moves this instrument would be the ether, whose mind by all
accounts was Jove. And the Latins used the word *anima* for
air as the principle which gives the universe motion and life,
and on which the ether acts as male on female. The ether insinuated into living beings the Latins called *animus;* hence
the common Latin distinction, "anima vivimus, animo senti-
mus": by the soul we have life, by the spirit sensation. Accordingly the soul, that is the air insinuated into the blood, would
be the principle of life in man, and the ether insinuated into
the nerves would be the principle of sensation. In proportion
as ether is more active than air, the animal spirits would be
more mobile and quick than the vital. And just as soul is acted
on by spirit, so spirit would be acted on by what the Latins
called *mens,* meaning thought; hence the Latin phrase "mens
animi," the mind of the spirit. And this thought or mind
would come to men from Jove, who is the mind of the ether.
Finally, if all this were so, the operating principle of all things
in nature would be corpuscles of pyramidal shape. And certainly ether united [separated off and condensed] is fire.

On the basis of these principles, in conversation with Doria
one day in the home of Don Lucio di Sangro, Vico remarked
that perhaps those effects which the physicists marvel at as
strange in the magnet, are, if they would but reflect, common
enough in fire. For the most marvelous magnetic phenomena
are three: the attraction of iron, the communication of magnetic power to the iron, and the pointing to the pole. Yet
nothing is more commonplace than that heat at distances proportional [to its intensity] begets fire; that fire in whirling

begets flame, which communicates light to us; and that flame points to the vertex of its heaven. Thus if the magnet were as rarefied as the flame and the flame as dense as the magnet, the latter would not point to the pole but to its zenith, and the flame would point to the pole and not to its vertex. Might it not be then that the magnet points to the pole because that is the highest part of the heaven to which it can raise itself? For it is readily observable in fairly long needles whose points have been magnetized, that while they turn to the pole they can be clearly seen trying to rise toward the zenith. Perhaps therefore, if travelers would observe the magnet in this respect and determine wherever it rose higher than elsewhere, it might give us those accurate measurements of latitude which are now so much sought in order to bring geography to its perfection.[164]

Doria was highly pleased by this reasoning, so Vico sought to extend it to the advantage of medicine. For those same Egyptians who represented nature by the pyramid had a distinctive mechanical medicine, that of "slack and tight" which the most learned Prospero Alpino set forth with great learning and erudition. And when Vico saw that no physician had made use of heat and cold as defined by Descartes [165] (cold being motion inward from without and heat the reverse motion outward from within), he was moved to build thereon a system of medicine. May not ardent fevers be caused by air in the veins [i.e., arteries] moving from the heart at the center to the periphery and distending, more than is compatible with good health, the diameters of blood vessels clogged at the opposite or outer end? On the other hand, may not malignant ["bad-air" or malarial] fevers be motion of air in the blood vessels [i.e., veins] inward from without, likewise distending more than is compatible with good health the diame-

ters of vessels clogged at the opposite or [in this case] inner
end? Thus the heart, center of the animate body, would lack
the air it needs for such motion as health requires; and as the
heart's motion became weaker the blood would clot, which
is the chief cause of acute fevers. Is not this the "divine something" that Hippocrates [166] said gave rise to such fevers? This
view is supported by reasonable conjectures from all nature.
For instance, cold and heat contribute alike to the generation
of things. Cold promotes the germination of grain seeds, the
generation of worms in dead bodies, and that of other animals in dark and damp places. Excessive cold as well as heat
causes gangrene, and in Sweden gangrene is treated with ice.
It is supported also by the symptoms of malignant fevers, cold
touch and colliquative sweats, which indicate great enlargement of the excretory vessels; and by those of ardent fevers,
hot and rough touch, the roughness indicating that the vessels
are too shriveled and shrunken toward the outer end. May it
not then be that the Latin practice of reducing all diseases to
the all-embracing genus *ruptum* derived from an ancient
medical tradition in Italy that all illness starts from deteriora-
tion of solid parts and leads in the end to what these same
Latins called *corruptum*? [167]

For the reasons set forth in the little book which he afterwards published,[168] Vico now undertook to ground his physics on a suitable metaphysics. By similar treatment of the
origins of Latin words, he purged Zeno's points [169] of Aristotle's garbled reports, and showed that these points are the
only hypothesis for descending from abstract to bodily things,
just as geometry is the only way to proceed scientifically from
bodily things to the abstract things by which the bodies are
constituted. The definition of the point as that which has no
parts amounts to the founding of an infinite principle of ab-

stract extension. As the point, which is not extended, by an excursion makes the extension of the line, so there must be an infinite substance that as it were by its excursion, that is by generation, gives form to finite things. And as Pythagoras will have the world constituted by numbers, which in a certain way are more abstract than lines, for the reason that one is not number yet generates number and in every odd number is indivisibly present (whence Aristotle said essences are indivisible like numbers, for to divide them is to destroy them), so the point, which stands equally under [is equally the substance of] lines of unequal extension (so that the diagonal and side of a square, for example, though otherwise incommensurable are cut in the same [infinite number of] points [by lines parallel to the adjacent side]), is a hypothesis of an unextended substance that stands equally under unequal bodies and equally supports them.

This metaphysics would have as sequels the logic of the Stoics in which they were taught to reason in sorites, which was their way of arguing as it were by a geometric method, and also their physics which posits as principle of all corporeal forms the wedge, in the same way that the first composite figure generated in geometry is the triangle, just as the first simple figure is the circle, symbol of God's perfection. Thus we might easily come out with the physics of the Egyptians, who conceived nature as a pyramid, which is a solid with four triangular faces. The Egyptian medicine of slack and tight would also fit in. Vico wrote on the latter a short book with the title *On the Equilibrium of Living Bodies* addressed to Domenico d' Aulisio, as learned a man as ever was in medical matters. He also had frequent discussions on this subject with Lucantonio Porzio, which won him the latter's high esteem and intimate friendship, maintained until the death of this last Italian philosopher of the school of Galileo. Porzio was wont to say among his friends that he was (to use his own expression) dismayed by Vico's meditations. But the *Metaphysics* alone was printed at Naples in duodecimo in the year 1710 by Felice Mosca and dedicated to Don Paolo Doria, as the first book of the treatise *On the Primitive Wisdom of the Italians to be recovered from the Origins of the Latin Language.* This book gave rise to a controversy between the Venetian critics and the author, and the latter's *Reply* and *Rejoinder* were published at Naples by Mosca in 1711 and 1712 respectively, both in duodecimo.[170] This debate was carried on honorably by both parties and concluded with good grace. But the dissatisfaction with grammatical etymologies which Vico had begun to feel was an indication of the source whence later, in his most recent works, he was to recover the origins of languages, deriving them from a principle of nature common to all on which he establishes the principles of a universal etymology to determine the origins of all languages living or dead. And his slight satisfaction with Bacon's book attempting to trace the wisdom of the ancients in the fables of the poets, was a sign of the source whence Vico, also in his latest works, was to recover principles of poetry different from those which the Greeks and Latins and the others since them have hitherto accepted. On these he establishes the only principles of mythology according to which the fables bore historical evidence as to the first Greek commonwealths, and by their aid he explains all the fabulous history of the heroic commonwealths.

A short time later he was honored by the request of Don Adriano Caraffa, Duke of Traetto, in whose education he had been employed for many years, to write the life of Marshal Antonio Caraffa his uncle. Vico, who cherished a truthful spirit, accepted the commission because the Duke was able to provide an enormous quantity of good and reliable documentary material that was in his keeping. Since his duties consumed all his time during the day, he had only the night to spend on this task, and it took him two years: one to prepare his commentaries from the confused and scattered source material, the other to weave his history out of these commentaries. During this whole period he was wracked by the cruelest hypochondriac cramps in the left arm. And as everyone could see of evenings while he was writing the book [in Latin], he had nothing before him on his desk save the commentaries, as if he were writing in his native language, in the midst of the turmoil and distraction of the household and often in conversation with his friends. Yet he carried out the work with proper honor to the subject, reverence for princes, and the justice we owe to the truth. The work was magnificently printed by the press of Felice Mosca in one volume quarto in the year 1716, and was the first book published by any press of Naples in the style of the Dutch printers. The Duke sent it to the supreme pontiff Clement XI, who in his letter of acknowledgment praised it as an "immortal history." Moreover it earned for Vico the esteem and friendship of a most illustrious Italian man of letters, Gianvincenzo Gravina, with whom thenceforth he carried on an intimate correspondence as long as Gravina lived.[171]

While preparing to write this life Vico found himself obliged to read Hugo Grotius *On the Law of War and Peace.* And here he found a fourth author to add to the three he had set before himself. For Plato adorns rather than confirms his esoteric wisdom with the common wisdom of Homer. Tacitus intersperses his metaphysics, ethics and politics with the facts, as they have come down to him from the times, scattered and confused and without system. Bacon sees that the sum of human and divine knowledge of his time needs supplementing and emending, but as far as laws are concerned he does not succeed with his canons in compassing the universe of cities and the course of all times, or the extent of all nations. Grotius, however, embraces in a system of universal law the whole of philosophy and philology, including both parts of the latter, the history on the one hand of facts and events, both fabulous and real, and on the other of the three languages, Hebrew, Greek and Latin; that is to say, the three learned languages of antiquity that have been handed down to us by the Christian religion. And Vico had occasion to penetrate much more deeply into this work of Grotius when he was asked to write some notes for a new edition of it. He set out to write them less in correction of Grotius than of Gronovius's notes on him, which had been added more to please free governments than to give justice its due. Vico had covered the first book and half of the second when he abandoned the task, reflecting that it was not fitting for a man of Catholic faith to adorn with notes the work of a heretical author.

Prepared by all these studies and the knowledge he had acquired, and by these four authors whom he admired above all others and desired to turn to the use of the Catholic religion, Vico finally came to perceive that there was not yet in the world of letters a system so devised as to bring the best philosophy, that of Plato made subordinate to the Christian faith, into harmony with a philology exhibiting scientific necessity in both its branches, that is in the two histories, that of languages and that of things; to give certainty to the history of languages by reference to the history of things; and to bring into accord the maxims of the academic sages and the practices of the political sages. By this insight Vico's mind arrived at a clear conception of what it had been vaguely seeking in the first inaugural orations and had sketched somewhat clumsily in the dissertation *On the Method of the Studies of Our Time,* and a little more distinctly in the *Metaphysics.*

At the solemn public opening of studies in 1719 he therefore proposed this argument: "All divine and human learning has three elements: knowledge, will and power, whose single principle is the mind, with reason for its eye, to which God brings the light of eternal truth." [172] And he divided the argument thus: "Now as to these three elements, which we know to exist and to belong to us as certainly as we know that we ourselves live, let us explain them by that one thing of which we cannot by any means doubt, that is of course by thought. That we may the more easily do this, I divide this entire discourse into three parts. In the first of these let us demonstrate that all the principles of the sciences are from God. In the second, that the divine light or eternal truth, by the three elements above set forth, permeates all the sciences, disposes them all in an order in which they are linked by the closest ties one with another, and relates them all to God as their source. In the third, that whatever has been written or said concerning the foundations of divine and human learning, if it agrees with these principles, is true, if it disagrees is false. Three further matters concerning the knowledge of divine and human things I shall also treat: its origin, circularity, and consistency; [173] and I shall show that the origins of all things proceed from God, that all return to God by a circle, that all have their consistency in God, and that apart from God they are all darkness and error." And he discoursed on this argument for an hour and more.

Some considered the argument, particularly in the third part, more magnificent than effectual, saying that Pico della

Mirandola had not assumed such a burden when he proposed to sustain "conclusions concerning all the knowable," for he left aside the great and major part of it, namely philology [= historiography], which, treating of countless matters of religions, languages, laws, customs, property rights, conveyances, sovereign powers, governments, classes and the like, is in its beginnings incomplete, obscure, unreasonable, incredible, and without hope of reduction to scientific principles.[174] Whereupon Vico, in order to give a preliminary idea of it that would show that such a science could indeed come into being, published a prospectus which circulated among the men of letters of Italy and beyond the Alps.[175] Some gave unfavorable opinions of it, but since they did not maintain these opinions when the work later appeared adorned with very complimentary opinions of learned scholars, whose praises weighed in its favor, they are hardly worth mentioning here. Anton Salvini, a great glory of Italy, deigned to make some objections to the work on the score of philology. These were conveyed to Vico by means of a letter addressed to Francesco Valletta, a most learned man and worthy heir of the celebrated Valletta library left by his grandfather Giuseppe. Vico made courteous reply in his *On the Consistency of Philology*. Other objections on the score of philosophy were made by Ulrich Hüber and Christian Thomasius, men famous for their learning in Germany, and were conveyed to Vico by Baron Ludwig von Gemmingen;[176] but he found he had answered them in the work itself, as can be seen at the end of the book *On the Consistency of the Jurisprudent*.

When the first book appeared with the title *On the One Principle and the One End of Universal Law* in the same year 1720, printed in quarto by the same Felice Mosca, in which Vico proves the first and second parts of the dissertation, there reached the author's ears objections voiced by critics unknown to him, and others were made to him in person by certain people. None of these objections undermined the system itself; they had to do with small details, and for the most part they derived from old opinions against which the system had been designed. So that he might not seem to be feigning enemies merely to strike them down, Vico answered these critics without naming them in the book he next published, *On the Consistency of the Jurisprudent,* in order that these unknown adversaries, if ever the book fell into their hands, should understand in solitude and privacy that they had been answered. This second volume, with the title *On the Consistency of the Jurisprudent,* came out the following year, 1721, likewise published in quarto by Mosca. Here are given more detailed proofs of the third part of the dissertation, divided in this book into two parts, one *On the Consistency of Philosophy,* the other *On the Consistency of Philology.* In the latter part some were displeased by the chapter entitled "A New Science is Essayed," wherein he begins to reduce philology to scientific principles. But it was found that the promise made by Vico in the third part of the dissertation was by no means vain, either on the side of philosophy or, what was more, on that of philology. Moreover by this system many important discoveries were made, all new and far removed from the opinion of the scholars of all times. So the work suffered no other reproof than that of being unintelligible. But scholars of the city attested to the world that it was eminently intelligible, by approving it publicly and giving it their grave and effectual praise. Their eulogies may be read in the work itself.

About this time a letter was written to Vico by Jean Le Clerc of the following tenor:

A few days ago, distinguished sir, the ephor of the illustrious Count Wildenstein delivered to me your work on the origin of law and on philology. Though I was then at Utrecht, I was scarcely able to skim through it. For I was compelled by certain business affairs to return to Amsterdam before I had time to immerse myself in its limpid fountain. At a glance, however, I saw many excellent things, both philosophical and philological, which will give me occasion to show our northern scholars that acumen and erudition are to be found among the Italians no less than among themselves; indeed, that more learned and acute things are being said by Italians than can be hoped for from dwellers in colder climes. Tomorrow I return to Utrecht, to stay there a few weeks and to enjoy your work to the full in that retreat, where I am less interrupted than at Amsterdam. When I have adequately grasped your thought, in the second part of volume eighteen of the *Bibliothèque Ancienne et Moderne* I shall show how highly it is to be prized. Farewell, distinguished sir, and number me among those who justly esteem your remarkable erudition. Written in haste at Amsterdam, September 8, 1722.[177]

This letter delighted the able men who had judged favorably the work of Vico, and by the same token displeased those who were of the contrary opinion. The latter persuaded themselves that Le Clerc was simply paying a private compliment, and would give the book such justice as they thought it deserved when he came to his public criticism of it in the *Bibliothèque*. They said it was impossible that as a result of this work of Vico's Le Clerc should be willing to retract what he had been saying for nearly fifty years, namely that Italy produced no works that could stand comparison for wit or learning with those published in the rest of Europe. Vico, meanwhile, to prove to the world that while cherishing the esteem of distinguished men he did not make it the end and goal of his work, read both the poems of Homer in the light of his principles of philology; and by certain canons of mythology which he had conceived, he gives these poems an aspect different from that which they have hitherto borne, and shows how divinely the poet weaves into the treatment of his two subjects two groups of Greek stories, the one belonging to the obscure period and the other to the heroic, according to Varro's division. These interpretations of Homer, along with the canons of mythology, he had printed in quarto by Mosca in the following year, 1722, with this title: *Notes by Giambattista Vico on two books, one On the Principle of Universal Law, the other On the Consistency of the Jurisprudent.*[178]

A short time later the chair of the head morning lecturer on law fell vacant.[179] This was inferior to that of the afternoon lecturer, and carried a stipend of six hundred ducats a year. Vico's hopes of winning it were quickened by the above related accomplishments, particularly in the field of jurisprudence, through which he had prepared himself for such advancement in his university. He is moreover its oldest member in point of professorial tenure, for he alone holds his chair by appointment of Charles II, and all the others hold theirs by later appointments. He relied too on the life he had led in his native city, where by the work of his intellect he had honored all, been of service to many, and harmed none. On the day preceding the competition, as the custom was, the *Digestum vetus,* from which on this occasion the laws were to be drawn by lot, was opened, and these three fell to Vico: one from the title *Laying claim to a thing,* one from *The peculium,* and lastly the first law under [*Actions using*] *prescribed words.* Since all three were texts full of matter, Vico, wishing to show Monsignor Vidania, prefect of studies, his readiness for the trial (although he had never taught jurisprudence), asked him to be so kind as to assign one of the three passages as the text for his lecture twenty-four hours hence. When the prefect declined to make the selection, Vico chose for himself the last of the three,[180] because, he said, it was taken from Papinian who of all jurisconsults had the loftiest faculties, and had to do with the definitions of legal terms, which in jurisprudence is the hardest task to carry out well. He foresaw that only a rash and ignorant man would calumniate him for choosing that law, for it would amount to reproaching him for choosing so difficult a subject. Cujas indeed when he defines legal terms waxes proud (and rightly so), and bids all come and learn from him, as in his *Paratitles to the Digest,* the title *On codicils.* He considers Papinian the prince of Roman jurisconsults precisely because none defines better than he and none has furnished jurisprudence with more or better definitions.

The other competitors had placed their hopes in four things as rocks to shipwreck Vico. All were led by their inward respect for his services to the University to feel sure that he would begin with a long and grandiloquent account of them. A few, who knew that he could readily do so, prophesied that he would base his interpretation of the text on his own *Principles of Universal Law,* and by thus breaking the rules for competitions in jurisprudence would arouse the audience to protest. The majority, who think the only masters of a subject are those who teach it to the young, fondly expected him to base his argument on Hotman, since his text was one that Hotman had discussed with much erudition; or else, since Favre had attacked all the early interpretations of this law and had not been answered by any later interpreters, to fill his lecture with Favre or at least not to attack him. But Vico's lecture turned out quite different from anything they had expected. He began with a brief, grave and moving introduction; then he recited the *principium* or beginning of the law, restricting his lecture to it and excluding the other paragraphs. After giving a summary and outline, he proceeded immediately to interpret the words of the law one by one, in a style as unusual in such competitions as it was common among the Roman jurisconsults. For they are always repeating "The law says," "The senate decree says," "The praetor says"; and he used the similar formula, "The jurisconsult says." This he did to escape the charge, so often made in these competitions, of wandering (however slightly) from the text. Only an ignorant and malicious person would depreciate his lecture on the ground that he was allowed to base it on the *principium* of the title, for the laws of the *Pandects* are not at all organized according to any scholastic method employed by the institute writers. And though Papinian happened to be cited in that *principium,* it might have been some other jurisconsult defining in other words and in another sense the action under discussion. From the interpretation of the words he elicited the sense of Papinian's definition, illustrated it by reference to Cujas, and showed how it agreed with the definition of the Greek interpreters. Then he dealt with Favre and showed how slight, carping and empty were his reasons for reprehending Accursius, Paolo di Castro, the old ultramontane interpreters, and finally Andrea Alciati. Though he had named Hotman before Cujas in the list of those attacked by Favre, in the sequel he forgot Hotman and after Alciati took up the defense of Cujas. When he realized what he had done, he interpolated these words: "I see that by a lapse of memory I have placed Cujas before Hotman; but now that Cujas is absolved, we shall proceed to vindicate Hotman from Favre's charges." So firmly had he relied on carrying the day with

Hotman! Finally, just as he was coming to the defense of Hotman, the lecture hour ended.

He had prepared his lecture the evening before, working until five in the morning in the midst of the conversation of his friends and the cries of his children, as his custom was, whether reading, writing, or thinking. He had reduced the lecture to main heads which could be set down on a single page, and he delivered it with as much facility as if he had taught nothing else all his life, and with such a copiousness of expression as might have served another for a two hours' harangue. He used the very finest legal expressions of the most erudite jurisprudence, including the Greek technical terms; indeed, when he required a scholastic expression, he chose the Greek term in preference to the barbarian. Once only, because of the difficulty of the word *progegrammenōn,* he hesitated for a moment, but then continued: "It is no wonder that I was brought to a halt, for the very *antitupia* [harshness] of the word put me off." Many thought he had allowed himself to seem confused only in order to recompose himself with so apt and elegant a Hellenism. The next day he wrote out his lecture just as he had delivered it, and distributed copies. He gave one to Don Domenico Caravita, leading advocate of these tribunals and very worthy son of Don Nicola, for he had been unable to be present.

For taking this step Vico supposed his qualifications and trial lecture were sufficient warrant. The general applause of the lecture had made him feel almost certain of obtaining the chair. But now he was forewarned of the unhappy outcome (so it proved even for the students who were presently graduated in that faculty), and the said Domenico Caravita, a sagacious man who was very well disposed toward him, agreed that it behooved him to retire from the field. By his authoritative advice, therefore, he magnanimously went and announced that he was withdrawing his candidacy. This he did in order not to lay himself open to the charge of false delicacy and pride in abstaining from going about soliciting and doing all the other things that are expected of the candidates.

For this misfortune of Vico's, which made him despair of ever holding a worthier position in his native city, there was some consolation in Jean Le Clerc's review. In Article VIII of the second part of Volume XVIII of the *Bibliothèque ancienne et moderne,* as if he had heard the charges some had brought against Vico's work, he expressed himself as follows (his words are here translated literally from the original French). As if addressing those who said the work was unintelligible, he gives it as his general opinion that it is "full of recondite matter considered from quite various points of view, and written in a very compact style"; that countless passages [are incapable of further condensation and] could only be represented by long quotations; that it is constructed by "mathematical method," which "from few principles draws infinite consequences"; that one must read it with care and without interruption from beginning to end, accustoming oneself to the author's ideas and style; that as its readers thus meditate upon it, "they will find besides, as they get farther into it, many discoveries and interesting observations beyond their expectations." As touching the matters which had caused such a stir when first presented in the third part of Vico's dissertation, Le Clerc says with reference to the philosophy: "Of all that has ever been said about the principles of divine and human erudition, so much is necessarily true as is found to agree with what has been written in the preceding book" [on universal law]. And with reference to the philology: "In brief compass he gives us the principal eras from the deluge to Hannibal's invasion of Italy, for here and there throughout the book he discusses various things which took place in that space of time, and makes many philological observations on a great number of matters, correcting a quantity of common errors which the ablest critics have passed over." And finally, addressing the public generally, he concludes: "There is a continuous mingling of philosophical, juridical and philological matters, for Signor Vico has devoted himself particularly to these three sciences and pondered them well, as all who read his works will agree. There is such a close relationship between these three sciences that one cannot boast of having penetrated and understood any one of them in all its ramifications without having also a very good knowledge of the others. We are not surprised therefore to read at the end of the volume the tributes that Italian scholars have bestowed on the work. From these we gather that the author is regarded as an expert in metaphysics, law and philology, and his work as original and full of important discoveries."

[PART B, 1725, 1728]

THAT Vico was born for the glory of his native city and therefore of Italy (since, being born there and not in Morocco, he became a scholar) is evidenced by nothing so much as by this: that after this blow of adverse fortune, which would have made another henceforth renounce all learning if not repent of having ever cultivated it, he did not even suspend his labors on other works. Indeed he had already written one divided into two parts, which would have made two sizeable volumes in quarto.[181] In the first part he set out to find the principles

of the natural law of the peoples within those of the humanity
of the nations, by way of [a critique of] the improbabilities,
absurdities and impossibilities which his predecessors had
rather imagined than thought out. As a sequel to this in the
second part he set forth the generation of human customs
by means of a certain rational chronology of the obscure and
fabulous periods of the [history of the] Greeks, to whom we
owe all we know of gentile antiquity. The work had indeed
already been read through by Don Giulio Torno,[182] a learned
theologian of the Neapolitan church, when Vico decided that
this negative form of exposition, though intriguing to the
imagination, is repugnant to the understanding, since by it
the human mind is not enlarged. On the other hand, by a
stroke of bad luck [183] he found himself in such straits that he
could not afford to print the work and yet felt only too obliged to do so as a matter of honor, since he had promised its
publication. So he bent all his faculties toward finding, by
intense meditation, a positive method [of exposition] which
would be more concise and thus more efficacious.

At the close of the year 1725 he published in Naples, from
the press of Felice Mosca, a book in duodecimo consisting of
only twelve sheets [288 pages] set up in brevier type and
entitled: *Principles of a New Science of the Nature of Nations, from which are derived New Principles of the Natural
Law of Peoples;* [184] and in an inscription he addresses the
book to the universities of Europe. In this work he finally discovers in its full extent that principle which in his previous
works he had as yet understood only in a confused and indis-
tinct way. For he now recognizes an indispensable and even
human necessity to seek the first origins of this science in the
beginnings of sacred history. And because philosophers and
philologians alike acknowledge their despair of tracing the

steps of its progress in the first founders of gentile nations, he made ample, nay vast, use of one of the remarks Jean Le Clerc had made about his previous work. Vico, he said, "has given us a summary of the principal eras from the flood to the Second Punic War, discussing various things that took place in that space of time, making many philological observations about a great number of matters, and correcting a quantity of common errors which the ablest critics have passed over." For he discovers this new science by means of a new critical method for sifting the truth as to the founders of the [gentile] nations from the popular traditions of the nations they founded. Whereas the writers to whose works criticism is usually applied came thousands of years after these founders. By the light of this new critical method the origins of almost all the disciplines, whether sciences or arts, which are necessary if we are to discuss with clarity of ideas and propriety of language the natural law of nations, are discovered to be quite different from those that have previously been imagined.

Hence he divides these principles into two parts: one of ideas, the other of languages. In the part devoted to ideas he discovers new historical principles of geography and chronology, the two eyes of history, and thence the principles of universal history hitherto lacking. He discovers new historical principles of philosophy, and first of all a metaphysics of the human race. That is to say, a natural theology of all nations by which each people naturally created by itself its own gods through a certain natural instinct that man has for divinity. Fear of these gods led the first founders of nations to unite themselves with certain women in a lifelong companionship. This was the first human form of marriage. Thus he discovers the identity of the grand principle of gentile theology with that of the poetry of the theological poets, who were the world's first poets as well as the first poets of all gentile humanity. From this metaphysics he derives a morality and thence a politics common to all the nations, and on this he bases a jurisprudence of the human race, varying with certain sects of the times,[185] as the nations unfold the ideas of their nature, with consequent developmental changes in their governments. The final form of the latter he shows to be monarchy, in which the nations by nature come at last to rest. In this way he fills up the great void left in the principles of universal history, which begins with Ninus and the monarchy of the Assyrians.

In the part devoted to languages he discovers new principles of poetry, both of song and of verse, and shows that both it and they sprang up by the same natural necessity in all the first nations. By following up these principles, he discovers new origins of heroic insignia, which were the dumb language of all the first nations at a time when they were incapable of articulate speech. Thence he discovers new principles of the science of heraldry, which he shows to be the same as those of numismatics. Here he observes the heroic origins of the two houses of France and Austria with their four thousand years of continuous sovereignty. Among other results of the discovery of the origins of languages, he finds certain principles common to all, and by a specimen essay reveals the true causes of the Latin language. By this example he opens the way for scholars to do the same for all other tongues. He gives an idea of an etymologicon common to all original languages, and then an idea of another etymologicon for words of foreign origin, in order finally to develop an idea of a universal etymologicon for the science of language which is necessary if we are to be able to discuss with propriety the natural law of the peoples.

By means of these principles of ideas and tongues, that is by means of this philosophy and philology of the human race, he develops an ideal eternal history based on the idea of the providence by which, as he shows throughout the work, the natural law of the peoples was ordained. This eternal history is traversed in time by all the particular histories of the nations, each with its rise, development, acme, decline and fall. Thus from the Egyptians, who twitted the Greeks for being always children and knowing nothing of antiquity, he takes and puts to use two great fragments of antiquity. One of these is their division of all preceding times into three ages: the age of gods, the age of heroes, and the age of men. The other is their reduction of the languages spoken before their time to three types, coeval respectively with the three ages. First, the divine, a dumb language of hieroglyphics or sacred characters. Second, the symbolic, consisting of metaphors as the heroic language did. Third, the epistolographic [demotic], consisting of expressions agreed upon for the everyday uses of life.

He shows that the first age and the first language coincide with the time of the families, which certainly preceded the cities among all nations, and out of which it is agreed the cities arose. These families were ruled by the fathers as sovereign princes under the government of the gods, ordering all human affairs according to the divine auspices. Vico sets forth their history with the greatest naturalness and simplicity by reference to the divine fables of the Greeks. He observes in this connection that the Oriental gods, raised to the stars by the Chaldeans, brought into Greece by the

Phoenicians (which he shows happened after the Homeric period), found the names of the Greek gods ready to receive them, just as when they were later brought to Latium they found ready the names of the Latin gods. Thus he shows that the same pattern was repeated among Latins, Greeks and Asians, though [not simultaneously but] one after another.

Then he shows that the second age and the second or symbolic language coincide with the period of the first civil governments. These he shows were those of certain heroic kingdoms or ruling orders of nobles, whom the ancient Greeks called "herculean races" and held to be of divine origin. The first plebeians, their subjects, on the other hand, were held to be of bestial origin. The history of these kingdoms he easily exhibits as delineated for us by the Greeks in the character of their Theban Hercules. He certainly was the greatest of the Greek heroes and the progenitor of the Heraclids, by whom, under its two kings, the Spartan kingdom, beyond question an aristocratic one, was governed. And since the Egyptians and the Greeks alike observed that every nation had a Hercules (and as for the Latins, Varro enumerated as many as forty), Vico concludes that after the gods the heroes reigned everywhere among the gentile nations. Now according to a great fragment of Greek antiquity the Curetes emigrated from Greece into Crete, Saturnia (i.e., Italy), and Asia. He shows that these were the Latin Quirites, one group of which were the Roman Quirites, who were bands of men armed with spears. Hence the Law of the Quirites was the law of all the heroic peoples. He shows the vanity of the tale that the Law of the Twelve Tables came from Athens, and in three indigenous laws of the heroic races of Latium, introduced and observed in Rome and later fixed in the Tables, he discovers the basic causes of Roman government, virtue and justice, enforced in peace by law and in war by conquest. For otherwise ancient Roman history, interpreted by ideas now current, is even more incredible than the fabulous history of the Greeks. In the light of all this he sets forth the true principles of Roman jurisprudence.

Finally he shows that the third age, that of common men and vernacular languages, coincides with the times of the ideas of a human nature completely developed and hence recognized as identical in all men. This developed human nature brought with it forms of human government, which he shows to be the popular and the monarchical. To this period belonged the Roman jurisconsults under the emperors. Thus he shows that monarchies are the final governments in which nations come to rest. On the fanciful hypothesis that the first kings were monarchs such as those of the present are, the commonwealths could not have begun. Nor could the nations have begun by fraud and force, as has been imagined hitherto.

Equipped with these and other less important discoveries, of which he makes a great number, he proceeds to discuss the natural law of the peoples, and shows at what certain times and in what determinate ways the customs were born that constitute the entire economy of this law. These are religions, languages, property rights, conveyances, classes, sovereign powers, laws, arms, trials, penalties, wars, peaces and alliances. And from the times and ways in which they were born he unfolds the eternal properties which show that the nature of each, that is the time and way of its origin, is such and not otherwise.

He always takes account of the essential differences between the Hebrews and the gentiles. The former from the beginning arose and stood steadfast on the practices of an eternal justice. The pagan nations, however, by the sole guidance of divine providence, underwent with constant uniformity the successive variations of three kinds of laws corresponding to the three ages and languages of the Egyptians. The first law was divine, under the government of the true God among the Hebrews and of various false gods among the gentiles. The second was heroic, or peculiar to the heroes who stood midway between gods and men. The third was human, or peculiar to human nature as fully developed and recognized as alike in all men. Not until this last law already holds sway is it possible for philosophers to arise among the nations and perfect it by reasoning from the maxims of an eternal justice.

On this last point Grotius, Selden and Pufendorf have erred together. For lack of a critical method applicable to the founders of the nations, they believed them to be wise in esoteric wisdom and did not see that for the gentiles providence was the divine teacher of a common wisdom, out of which among them after the lapse of centuries the esoteric wisdom [of the philosophers] emerged. Thus our three authorities have failed to distinguish the natural law of the nations, which was coeval with their customs, from the natural law of the philosophers, which the latter grasped by force of reasoning, without ascribing any privilege to a people chosen by God for [the preservation of] his true cult [when it was] lost by all the other nations. The lack of this critical method had likewise earlier misled the learned interpreters of the Roman law into accepting the fable of the introduction of the Twelve Tables from Athens and reading into Roman jurisprudence, against its very genius, the sects of the philosophers, especially those of the Stoics and Epicureans, whereas there is nothing more contrary to the principles not merely of

Roman jurisprudence but of civilization itself than those of these two schools. This precluded their treating it in the light of its own sects, which were those of the times,[185] as the Roman jurisconsults themselves expressly claim to have done.

By this work, to the glory of the Catholic religion, the principles of all gentile wisdom human and divine have been discovered in this our age and in the bosom of the true Church, and Vico has thereby procured for our Italy the advantage of not envying Protestant Holland, England or Germany their three princes of this science. For these reasons the book has had the good fortune to be graciously received by His Eminence Cardinal Lorenzo Corsini, to whom it is dedicated; and he has praised it in these (not the meanest) terms: "A work, certainly, that for antiquity of language and for soundness of doctrine will suffice to show that there still lives in Italian spirits today a native and peculiar gift for Tuscan eloquence as well as a robust and happy boldness for undertaking new productions in the most difficult disciplines. Therefore I congratulate upon it the fatherland that it so adorns."

CONTINUATION BY THE AUTHOR

[1731]

WHEN the *New Science* was published, the author was careful to send it to Jean Le Clerc among others, and chose the Leghorn route as being the safest. Along with a letter addressed to Le Clerc, he inclosed it in a package to Giuseppe Attias, with whom he had formed a friendship here in Naples. Among the Hebrews of this age, Attias is reputed to be the most learned in the study of the sacred tongue, as is shown by his edition of the *Old Testament* published in Amsterdam, a work which has won acclaim in the republic of letters.[186] In the following reply he graciously accepted the commission.

I am unable to express the pleasure I felt in receiving your affectionate letter of November 3, which has renewed the memory of my happy sojourn in your most charming city. It will suffice to say that I was continually overwhelmed by the kindness and favors shown me by its celebrated men of letters, and especially by you, who have honored me with your excellent and sublime works. I have mentioned this with pride to the friends of my own circle and to the men of letters that I have met in my travels in France and Italy. I shall send the package and letter for M. Le Clerc to a friend of mine in Amsterdam who will give them to him personally. Thus I shall have fulfilled my duty and carried out your excellency's esteemed commands. I am infinitely obliged for your courtesy in giving me a copy of your book. It has been read by my friends and has been much admired for the sublimity of its subject and the abundance of new thoughts which (as M. Le Clerc puts it) [187] it suggests on many matters, great and wonderful for their rarity and sublimity, over and above the pleasure and profit yielded by all your works when attentively read. In closing, I beg you to remember me respectfully to Father Sostegni.

But Vico had no response from Le Clerc, perhaps because he was dead or because old age had compelled him to give up his scholarly pursuits and literary correspondence.[188]

In the midst of these severe studies Vico had no lack of lighter tasks as well. When King Philip V came to Naples, the Duke of Escalona, who was then governing the Kingdom of Naples, through Serafino Biscardi, who had been a pre-eminent advocate and was then Grand Chancellor, commissioned Vico, as Royal Professor of Eloquence, to write an oration on the King's coming. He had barely eight days before the King's departure, so that he had to compose it in

great haste. It was printed in duodecimo with the title
Panegyric addressed to Philip V, King of the Spaniards.

Later when this kingdom came under Austrian rule, Count
Wierich von Daun, commander of the imperial armies in this
kingdom, commanded him as follows in this flattering letter:

Most illustrious signor Giovan Battista di Vico, Professor in the
Royal University of Naples.—His Catholic Majesty (whom God
preserve) having ordered me to see that the funerals of Don
Giuseppe Capece and Don Carlo di Sangro are solemnized with
the dignity becoming his royal magnificence and the great valor
of the deceased gentlemen, the composition of the funeral oration
has been entrusted to Father Don Benedetto Laudati, Bene-
dictine prior. Since other compositions must be made for the
funeral inscriptions, I, admiring your lofty style, have thought
this matter might well be entrusted to your recognized skill. I
assure you that in addition to the honor you will achieve in such
a worthy work, I shall keep a lively memory of your noble
labors. Hoping that I may be of use to you on some occasion,
I pray that Heaven may favor you. I am, illustrious sir, your
excellency's devoted servant,   COUNT VON DAUN.

From this palace in Naples, October 11, 1707 (by my own
hand).

So Vico composed for this occasion the inscriptions, em-
blems and mottoes and the account of the funeral ceremonies,
and Father Laudati, the prior, a man of excellent life and
very learned in theology and canon law, pronounced the oration. The contributions of both were published in an illustrated volume, magnificently printed in folio at the expense
of the royal treasury, entitled *Funeral Rites of Carlo di Sangro
and Giuseppe Capece.*[189]

Not long after, by the gracious command of Count Carlo
Borromeo the viceroy, Vico composed the inscriptions for the
funeral rites that were celebrated in the royal chapel on the
death of the Emperor Joseph.

Adverse fortune later dealt a blow to his scholarly repute,[190] but since the matter was beyond his control this very adversity gained him an honor which a subject is not even permitted to desire under a monarchy. For the funeral rites of the Empress Eleanor he was commanded by Cardinal Wolfgang von Schrottenbach, the viceroy, to compose the inscriptions which follow. He planned them in such a way that, read separately, each is sufficient to itself, and, taken together, they compose a funeral oration. The one that was to be inscribed over the door of the royal chapel, on the outside, contains the proemium, as follows:

TO HER IMPERIAL HIGHNESS ELEANOR/OF THE HOUSE OF THE DUKES OF NEUBURG/BELOVED WIFE OF KAISER LEOPOLD/AND NOBLE MOTHER OF CHARLES VI OF AUSTRIA/EMPEROR OF THE ROMANS, KING OF THE SPANIARDS AND NEAPOLITANS/HE HAS RENDERED DUE FUNERAL HONORS/YOUR PRINCE, DELIGHT OF THE STATE/ IS IN MOURNING/HITHER DO YOU, O CITIZENS/BRING YOUR TRIBUTE/OF PUBLIC MOURNING

Of the four inscriptions meant to be set up inside over the four arches of the chapel, the first contains the eulogy:

YOU WHO BEHOLD THIS EMPTY TOMB/CONSIDER IT EMPTY INDEED/FOR AMID THE DELIGHTS OF ROYAL FORTUNE/SHE TURNED AWAY FROM TRANSITORY PLEASURES/AND AT THE HEIGHT OF WOMANLY DIGNITY/SHE HUMBLED HERSELF TO THOSE OF THE LOWLIEST STATION/AMONG MORTALS OF THE HUMAN RACE THE MARK OF CULTURE/IS CARE OF THOSE ETERNAL THINGS/WHICH/WHEREVER ON EARTH THEY BE NEGLECTED/HERE/HER IMPERIAL HIGHNESS ELEANOR HAVING DIED/ARE HEAPED WITH THE HIGHEST HONORS

The second sets forth the magnitude of the loss:

IF THERE ARE WORTHY KINGS ON EARTH/WHO BY EXAMPLES RATHER THAN BY LAWS/AMEND THE CORRUPTED CUSTOMS OF PEOPLES AND RACES/AND PRESERVE THE CIVIL FELICITY OF STATES/

ELEANOR/AS MUCH BY HER OWN VIRTUE AS BY THE FORTUNE OF
A ROYAL HUSBAND/WAS A WOMAN TRULY ABOVE ALL OTHERS IN
THE WORLD/WHO AS WIFE AND MOTHER OF KINGS/BY THE
SANCTITY OF HER LIFE/ACCORDING TO HER WOMANLY ABILITY
CONTRIBUTED SO MUCH/TO THE HAPPINESS OF A CHRISTIAN
EMPIRE/ALAS! HOW DEEPLY MUST EVERY GOOD PERSON MOURN
HER LOSS!

The third evokes grief:

YOU CITIZENS/WHOSE GREATEST JOY/IS IN CHARLES YOUR NOBLE
PRINCE AND EMPEROR/LET YOUR SORROW BE AS GREAT/IN THE
DEATH OF HER IMPERIAL HIGHNESS HIS MOTHER ELEANOR/WHO
BY HER BLESSED FRUITFULNESS/GAVE YOU YOUR GREAT DESIRE/A
PRINCE OF THE HOUSE OF AUSTRIA/AND BY THE RARE AND SPLEN-
DID EXAMPLES OF HER QUEENLY VIRTUES/GAVE YOU YOUR
GREATEST DESIRE/A PRINCE OF NOBLE CHARACTER

The fourth and last promises solace:

WITH TEARS/O CITIZENS/LET YOUR MOST EARNEST VOWS BE
OFFERED/THAT THE SPIRIT/OF ELEANOR/RECEIVED IN HEAVEN/
MAY OBTAIN BY DIVINE FAVOR/AN OFFSPRING/FOR THE EMPEROR
CHARLES FROM HER IMPERIAL HIGHNESS ELIZABETH/SUCH AS SHE
HERSELF GAVE TO LEOPOLD/SO THAT SHE MAY NOT LEAVE/THE
CHRISTIAN WORLD/IN GRIEF FOR HER/FOREVER UNASSUAGED

These inscriptions were not put up; but scarcely had the
first day of the funeral ceremonies passed when Don Nicola
d'Afflitto, a noble Neapolitan gentleman, formerly an eloquent advocate and at this time judicial assessor to the courts-
martial, besought Vico to remain at home that evening so that
he might call upon him. (This gentleman was in the cardinal's service, and this responsibility, with the great labors
attendant upon it, later brought on his death, mourned by
all worthy men.) On the occasion of his visit to Vico he had
the following to say to him: "I have broken off the discussion
of a most important matter with my lord the viceroy in order

to come here, and I must shortly return to the palace to resume it." In the course of the brief conversation that followed he said to Vico: "My lord the cardinal has told me that he is much distressed by this mischance which you have suffered through no fault of your own." To this Vico replied that he was infinitely grateful to the cardinal for such nobility of soul, befitting a grandee in relation to a subject, whose greatest glory is ever the homage he gives his prince.

Among these many occasions of mourning there came to him a festive one: the nuptial rites of Don Giambattista Filomarino,[191] a pious and liberal gentleman of praiseworthy habits and cultivated mind, and Donna Maria Vittoria Caracciolo of the family of the marquises of Sant' Eramo. For the collection of compositions made on this occasion and printed in quarto, Vico wrote an epithalamium of an original nature. It is a dramatic monody entitled *Juno in Dance,* in which the goddess of marriage is the sole speaker. She invites the other major gods to dance, and improves the occasion to expound the principles of that historical mythology which is fully worked out in the *New Science.*

On these same principles he composed a Pindaric ode in free verse. Its subject was *The History of Poetry* from its origin to our day, and it was dedicated to the excellent and wise Donna Marina della Torre, of a noble Genoese family, duchess of Carignano.

And now his youthful study of good writers in the vulgar tongue, though since neglected for so many years, enabled him in his old age not only to compose these poems but also to put together two orations, as well as to make splendid use of that tongue in writing the *New Science.* The first of these orations was written on the occasion of the death of Anna d'Aspermont, Countess d'Althann, mother of Cardinal d'Althann, at that time viceroy. This he wrote to show his gratitude for a favor done him by Don Francesco Santoro, then secretary of the kingdom. Santoro was also one of the judges of the civil Vicaria [or viceroyal court] and a suit against a son-in-law of Vico had been assigned to him. It was tried at joint sessions [of the two divisions of the civil Vicaria] on two successive Wednesdays. On Wednesdays the criminal Vicaria sits with the Royal Collateral Council to hear cases, but Don Antonio Caracciolo, Marquis dell' Amorosa, who was then regent of the Vicaria [and as such would ordinarily have sat with its criminal branch] attended both sessions [of the civil branch] expressly to be of service to Vico. (Caracciolo's government of the city found favor with four viceroys because of his integrity and prudence.) Santoro stated the case so fully, clearly and precisely before him that Caracciolo was spared the sifting of the facts, which, had it been necessary, would have enabled the adversary to prolong and entangle the case. Vico pleaded it in masterly form with such thoroughness that against an instrument of a notary still living he found thirty-seven presumptions of falsehood. Indeed he had to group them under several heads to keep them in order and thus remember them. He made his plea with such passion that all the judges in their great kindness not only maintained silence during the course of the pleading but did not even so much as glance at each other. Finally the regent was so deeply moved that, tempering his feelings with the gravity befitting such a great magistrate, he made a gesture combining, in proper degree, compassion for the defendant and scorn for the plaintiff. Thereupon the Vicaria, which is somewhat strict in rendering judgment, acquitted the defendant without adjudging that the criminal falsity of the accusation had been proved.[192]

Remembering this occasion with gratitude, Vico wrote the oration mentioned above. It is found in the collection of pieces that Santoro himself had made and printed in quarto. In this oration, speaking of the two sons of this saintly princess who were taking part in the war of the Spanish succession, he makes a digression in a style half way between that of poetry and that of prose. (Such indeed should be the historical style, in the opinion of Cicero, as indicated in the brief but pregnant remark he makes concerning the writing of history. For history should use, he says, "words for the most part taken from the poets"; perhaps because the historians were still clinging to their ancient possession, for, as is clearly demonstrated in the *New Science,* the first historians of the nations were the poets.) In this digression Vico takes in the entire war of the Spanish succession: its causes, strategy, occasions, episodes, and consequences. He compares it in all these respects to the Second Punic War, the greatest ever fought in the memory of the centuries, and shows how the Spanish war is greater. Speaking of this digression, Prince Giuseppe Caracciolo of the house of the marquises of Sant' Eramo, a gentleman of grave manners, wisdom and fine literary taste, was graciously pleased to say that he would like to see it bound in a great volume on white paper with the binder's title: *History of the War of the Spanish Succession.*

The other oration was written on the death of Donna Angiola Cimmino, marchioness della Petrella. This noble and wise lady, in the conversations in her house,[193] lofty in thought and shared for the most part by men of learning, both by her actions and by her discourse unobtrusively expressed and inspired in others the most laudable moral and civil virtues; whence all who knew her were naturally and almost unconsciously led to regard her with loving reverence and reverent love. Vico was desirous of presenting with truth and dignity the intimate thesis "that she had, by her own life, taught the sweet austerity of virtue." And he wished here to try how well the delicate sensibility of the Greeks could be united with the grandeur of Latin expression, and how much of both the Italian tongue could combine. This oration is included in an ingeniously and magnificently printed quarto volume, in which the first letter of each author's contribution is engraved on copper, with an emblem supplied by Vico appropriate to its subject. The introduction was written by Father Don Roberto Sostegni, Florentine canon of the Lateran, a man whose fine scholarship and charming manners endeared him to his native city. Though suffering from an excess of the choleric humour (which often made him mortally ill and finally, abscessing in his right side, caused his death, to the universal grief of those who knew him), he nevertheless controlled his temperament so well by his wisdom that he seemed by nature the mildest of men. As a student of the illustrious Abbé Anton Maria Salvini, he had acquired a knowledge of oriental languages and Greek, and great skill in Latin, especially in verse composition. He wrote Tuscan in a very robust style like that of Casa. Of other languages, aside from French which has now become fairly common, he was familiar with English and German and knew something of Turkish. His prose was persuasive and eloquent. He came to Naples especially because (as he was kind enough to say publicly) he had read the *Universal Law* which Vico had sent to Salvini, and so had learned that in Naples a profound and severe study of letters was cultivated. Vico was the first whose acquaintance he was anxious to make; he established an intimate correspondence with him; and on this account Vico now honors him with this eulogy.

It was about this time that Vico heard from Count Gian Artico di Porcía, brother of Cardinal Leandro di Porcía and distinguished for learning and nobility. He had conceived the idea of guiding young men with greater security in their course of study by setting before them the intellectual autobiographies of men celebrated for erudition and scholarship. Among the Neapolitans whom he considered worthy for this purpose, he deigned to include Vico. (There were eight in all, but we omit their names in order not to give offense to other very illustrious scholars whom he passed over perhaps because he did not know them.) He wrote a very gracious letter from Venice (forwarded through Rome by the Abbé Giuseppe Luigi Esperti) to Lorenzo Ciccarelli, asking him to obtain the autobiography of Vico. The latter, partly from modesty and partly because of his ill fortune, refused several times to write it, but the repeated and courteous pleading of Ciccarelli finally won his consent. And, as may be seen, he wrote it as a philosopher, meditating the causes, natural and moral, and the occasions of fortune; why even from childhood he had felt an inclination for certain studies and an aversion from others; what opportunities and obstacles had advanced or retarded his progress; and lastly the effect of his own exertions in right directions, which were destined later to bear fruit in those reflections on which he built his final work, the *New Science,* which was to demonstrate that his intellectual life was bound to have been such as it was and not otherwise.

Meanwhile the *New Science* had already become famous in Italy and especially in Venice. The Venetian Resident in Naples had acquired all the copies left in the shop of Felice Mosca the printer, and had enjoined him, on account of the many requests there had been for it in that city, to deliver to

him as many more as could be found. Thus in three years the
work had become so rare that, though a little book of 288
pages in duodecimo, it frequently brought a price of two
ducats and even more.

About that time Vico learned there were letters waiting
for him at the post office, which he was not in the habit of
visiting. One of these was from Father Carlo Lodoli of the
Minor Observants, a theologian of the sovereign state of Venice. It bore the date of January 15, 1728, and seven couriers had
left Naples since it had arrived at the post office. In this letter
Father Lodoli invited Vico to have his work reprinted in
Venice, using these words:

Here in Venice your profound book on the *Principles of a New
Science concerning the Nature of Nations* is circulating among
men of distinction and winning unmeasured applause. The
further they read into it the greater becomes their admiration
and esteem for your intellect which composed it. As the praises
of the book and the discussions about it spread its fame abroad,
it becomes increasingly sought after, and when there are no
copies to be had in the city some are ordered from Naples. But
since this is inconvenient because of the distance, some have considered having it reprinted in Venice. Since in this project I too
concur, I have thought it fitting to take counsel in advance with
your excellency, the author, first to see if this is agreeable to you,
and then to learn if you have any additions or corrections to
make, and, in that event, if you would have the kindness to
communicate them to me.

The Father had reinforced his request by including a letter from the Abbé Antonio Conti, a Venetian nobleman, a
great metaphysician and mathematician, rich in esoteric wisdom. In the course of travels in search of knowledge, he had
won the high esteem of Leibniz and Newton and other leading scholars of our time; and his tragedy *Caesar* had made

him famous in Italy, France and England. With a courtesy
equal to such nobility and learning, he had written Vico under date of January 3, 1728, as follows:

You could not find, illustrious sir, a correspondent more at home
in all kinds of studies nor one more influential with booksellers
than the Reverend Father Lodoli, who is offering to have your
Principles of a New Science reprinted. I myself was one of the
first to read it and enjoy it and to have my friends enjoy it. They
are unanimously agreed that we do not have in the Italian
language a book containing more erudite and philosophical
matters, all original in their kind. I have sent a short abstract of
it to France to show the French that there is room for many
additions and many corrections in the ideas of chronology and
mythology, as well as of ethics and jurisprudence, to which they
have given so much study. The English, when they see the book,
will be obliged to confess the same; but it is necessary to give it
wider circulation by reprinting it in better type. Your excellency
has the opportunity to add whatever you think proper, either to
extend the range of its erudition and scholarship, or to develop
certain ideas touched upon only lightly. I should advise you to
put at the beginning of the book a preface which would set forth
the several principles of the various matters of which the book
treats, and the harmonious system which results from them and
which extends even to the future, which depends throughout on
the laws of that eternal history of which the idea you have given
is so sublime and so fruitful.

The other letter, which had also been lying in the post
office, was from Count Giovan Artico di Porcía, whom we
have praised above; he had written Vico on December 14,
1727, as follows:

I am assured by Father Lodoli (who with the Abbé Conti sends
his respects to your excellency, both reaffirming the high esteem
in which they hold your virtues) that he will find someone who
will reprint your admirable work on the *Principles of the New
Science*. If you would like to add something you are perfectly

free to do so. You have now an opportunity to expand your thought in this work in which men of science declare they apprehend much more than is actually expressed, and which they all consider a masterpiece. I offer you my sincerest congratulations and I assure you that I take an infinite pleasure in seeing that productions of the spirit with the pith and depth that yours possesses, sooner or later come into recognition, and that they do not lack fortune so long as they do not lack intelligent and discerning readers.

In view of the courteous insistence and responsible encouragement of so many and such gifted men, Vico felt himself obliged to consent to this reprinting and to write the notes and additions suggested by them. By the time his answers to these first letters arrived in Venice (for, on account of the reason mentioned above, they were very late in being sent), the Abbé Conti, moved by a special affection for Vico and his works, had honored him with this second letter under date of March 10, 1728:

Two months ago I wrote your excellency a letter, which must have reached you, inclosed with one from the Reverend Father Lodoli. Having had no answer, I take the liberty of troubling you again, moved solely by the desire that you should know how much I admire you and how anxious I am to profit by the illumination so abundantly shed in your *Principle of a New Science*. Immediately after returning from France I read it with the greatest pleasure, and your discoveries along critical, historical and moral lines seemed to me no less new than instructive. There are some who would like to undertake the reprinting of this book, in better type and handsomer format. Father Lodoli had this design, and told me he had already written you about it, in order to beg you to add to it further dissertations on the same subject, or further illustrative material to the present chapters, if by chance you had prepared such material. Count Porcía sent Father Lodoli your *Autobiography,* containing numerous erudite comments on the development of the historical and critical system established in your other books.

This edition is much in demand, and many Frenchmen, to whom I have given a rough outline of the book, are eagerly requesting it.

This gave Vico an even greater stimulus to write notes and comments on his work. And during the time he was working on them (a period of about two years) it came about that Count Porcía, on an occasion which need not here be recalled, wrote that he wanted to print a certain *Proposal to the Scholars of Italy,* addressed to those most distinguished either by their published works or by their reputation as savants. The proposal was the one we have mentioned above, that they should write their intellectual autobiographies in such fashion as to promote a new method in the studies of the young, which would make their progress more certain and efficacious. He wanted to append as a model, he said, the autobiography which Vico had already sent him, for of the many he had received this one seemed to him the perfect realization of his idea. Whereupon Vico, who had thought his was to be printed along with the others and had indeed told Porcía in sending it that he felt greatly honored to be even the last in so glorious a company, begged and adjured him not to carry out his plan, for he would not accomplish his purpose, and Vico, through no fault of his own, would have to suffer from the envy of others. The Count remained firm in his intention, however, so that Vico repeated his protests through the Abbé Giuseppe Luigi Esperti at Rome and through Father Lodoli at Venice. Lodoli had learned from the Count that he was arranging to print this *Proposal* along with Vico's autobiography. And indeed Father Calogerà, who printed it in the first volume of his *Collection of Scientific and Philological Monographs,* has published to the world these protestations of Vico in a letter, by way of preface, to Signor Vallisnieri. The kindness of Father Calogerà to Vico in this connection was matched by the unkindness of the printer, who bungled the typesetting and made numerous errors, even in important passages. Furthermore, at the end of the catalog [194] of Vico's works, appended to the autobiography, this announcement was published: *"Principles of a New Science concerning the Nature of Nations,* in course of reprinting with the author's *Annotations* at Venice."

Still further, at about the same time it happened that a gross misrepresentation of Vico and his *New Science* appeared in the book notices of the Leipzig *Acta* [*Eruditorum*] for August, 1727. The notice there given of it does not give the name of the book, which is the first duty of a reviewer, but calls it merely *New Science,* omitting [that part of the title which explains] the subject with which it deals. It misdescribes the book as being in octavo whereas it is really in duodecimo. It lies about the author and says on the authority of "an Italian friend" that he is a certain "abbé" of the Vico family, whereas Vico is of course no abbé but a father and even a grandfather. It says that the author treats of a system or rather "fables" of natural law. It fails to distinguish between the natural law of the peoples, which the book discusses, and that of the philosophers, which our moral theologians have discussed; it implies that the latter is the subject of the *New Science,* whereas it is merely a corollary. It asserts that the work is based on principles quite different from those which philosophers have hitherto employed; and indeed in this it confesses the truth without meaning to, for a science deriving from old principles would not be a "new science." It observes that the work is suited to the taste of the Roman Catholic Church, as if the conception of a Divine Providence were not basic to the Christian religion in all its forms, or indeed to all religions. Thus the reviewer confesses himself an Epicurean or Spinozist, and instead of the reproach he intended, he pays the author the highest compliment, that of being pious. Though he notes that the book labors to impugn the doctrines of Grotius and Pufendorf, he says nothing of Selden, who was the third prince of these doctrines, perhaps because Selden was an expert in the Hebrew language. He judges that the author has indulged his wit at the expense of truth. On this last point Vico digresses in his reply to treat the profounder origins of wit and laughter, of acute and argute sayings. He says that wit always has truth for its object and is the father of acute sayings, whereas feeble fancy is the mother of argute sayings; and he proves that derision is more bestial than human. The reviewer further states that the author staggers under the weight of his conjectures, thereby confessing that his conjectures are not lacking in weight. He states that the author exercises his new critical art on the founders of the nations; but surely, since writers sprang up in these nations only after a thousand years at least, the new art could hardly take them at face value. He concludes by saying that the work was received even by the Italians with more tedium than applause, whereas the book had become very rare in Italy within three years of its printing, and if a copy was found it brought a high price, as we have seen above. Yet an Italian with impious mendacity informed the learned Protestants of Leipzig that his entire nation was displeased by a work containing Catholic doctrine!

Vico was obliged to reply, and did so in a small volume in duodecimo entitled *Notes on the Leipzig Reviewers*.[195] At the time he heard of the review he was undergoing treatment for a gangrenous ulcer of the throat. He was persuaded by Domenico Vitolo, a most learned and experienced physician, to submit to the dangerous remedy of cinnabar, though he

was then an old man of sixty and the remedy is likely to
cause apoplexy even in the young if by mischance it affects
the nerves. In his reply Vico finds many excellent reasons for
applying the term "unknown vagabond" to the author of this
tissue of falsehoods. He penetrates to the bottom of the ugly
calumny and proves that it was fabricated for five reasons.
Firstly, to do something displeasing to the author; secondly,
to make the readers of Leipzig indifferent about obtaining a
book described as false, vain, Catholic, and of unknown au-
thorship; thirdly, if by chance any might still wish to acquire
it, to make it difficult to find by either omitting or falsifying
the title, the format, and the identity of the author; fourthly,
if they should get hold of the book, to make them consider it
the work of another author when they found it so different
from what it was described to be; fifthly, in order to get himself regarded as a good friend by these excellent Germans.
Vico treats the Leipzig critics with the courtesy that is due
the scholars of a famous nation. He warns them in future to
be on their guard against such a friend, who confounds those
whose friend he professes to be, and has laid them open to
two serious charges: one of putting into their *Acta* reviews
and opinions of books they have not read, the other of passing
contradictory judgments on one and the same book. Addressing the "unknown vagabond" himself, he exhorts him seriously, as the kind of man who treats his friends worse than
his enemies, gives false information about his own nation and
basely misleads foreigners, to take his departure from the
world of men and to go and live with the wild beasts in the
African desert. He had intended to send to Leipzig a copy of
this reply, along with the following letter addressed to Burkhard Mencken, president of the academy there and prime
minister of the present king of Poland:

Giambattista Vico to the distinguished Leipzig Academy of Sciences and to its honorable President, Burkhard Mencken, greeting. It is a matter of great regret to me that my own misfortune should have involved you also, distinguished sirs, in the adverse fortune of being deceived by your pretended Italian friend into all the vain, false and unjust things you say of me and my book entitled *Principles of a New Science concerning the Humanity of the Nations* in reviewing it in your *Acta*. But my sorrow has been softened by this consolation, that the whole affair has of itself arisen in such a way that your innocence, magnanimity and good faith put me in a position to castigate his malice, envy and bad faith. Thus it has been possible in the slender book which I send you herewith to embrace at the same time his offences and their correction, your own civil virtues and their praise. Since therefore I have published these *Notes* largely in your behalf to vindicate the honor of your scholarship, I hope they may give occasion for no offense but rather for my obtaining great favor with you, and above all with your excellency, Burkhard Mencken, who by virtue of your outstanding erudition have won the chief place in your Academy of distinguished scholars. I wish you all prosperity. Given at Naples, October 19, 1729.

This letter, as the reader can see, was written in terms of the utmost courtesy. However, considering that even so it would openly convict these learned men of a grave breach of duty, since, making it their business as they do to examine whatever comes off the presses of Europe, they should take special pains with those books that come within their province, Vico decided that it would be still more courteous not to send it.

To return now to the matter in hand. Feeling himself obliged to reply to the honorable critics of Leipzig, Vico thought that it would be necessary to mention the new printing of his book which was under way in Venice. He wrote Father Lodoli for his permission, which was given. Accordingly, in his reply it was again made public in print that the

Principles of the New Science, with the annotations of the author, was being reprinted in Venice.

At this juncture certain Venetian printers, pretending to be scholars, and working through Gessari the bookseller and Mosca the printer in Naples, tried to obtain copies of all Vico's works, published and unpublished, as described in the aforesaid catalog. They said they wished to adorn their libraries with these works, but in fact they wanted to reprint them in a collected edition, in the hope that the inclusion of the *New Science* would insure a ready sale for such an edition. To show them that he knew them for what they were, Vico gave them to understand that of all the poor works of his exhausted genius he wished only the *New Science* to remain to the world; and that work, they must know, was already being reprinted in Venice. Moreover, in order to protect the printer of the new edition even after his own death, Vico generously offered Father Lodoli a manuscript of nearly a thousand pages, in which he had set about proving his *Principles* by a negative method. By using this material the *New Science* might have been expanded into a much larger book. Indeed, Don Giulio Torno, a canon and a most learned theologian of our Neapolitan church, with a magnanimous concern for Vico's interests, wanted, with some of his associates, to print such an edition here in Naples. But Vico dissuaded him by pointing out that the principles had already been established by the positive method.

Finally, in the month of October, 1729, Father Lodoli in Venice received all the material requested: the corrections of the first edition, the annotations, and the comments; altogether, a manuscript of nearly six hundred pages.

Now, since the public had twice been informed in print that the *New Science* was being reprinted with additions in

Venice, and since the entire manuscript was already in hand, the person in charge of the printing began to treat Vico as if he were obliged to have it printed there. Vico, feeling affronted, thereupon recalled all the material he had sent; and the restitution was finally made, but only after six months, when the printing [in Naples] was more than half finished. In the meantime, since for the reasons set forth above he could not find either here in Naples or elsewhere a publisher who would reprint the work at his own expense, Vico hit upon a new plan which was perhaps the best of all, though save for this necessity he would not have thought of it. By comparing it with that of the first edition, one may see how completely different it is. For everything that he had split up and dispersed in the Annotations to preserve the plan of the first edition, and a great deal of new material besides, is now composed and ordered by a single spirit. By virtue of this consecutive order, which even more than propriety of style is a principal cause of brevity, the second edition exceeds by only six pages the first plus the manuscript [that was sent to Venice]. An example of this may be seen in the passage on the properties of the natural law of the peoples. On the first plan (Book II, Chapter VII) his discussion of this took up almost twelve pages, and on the second only a few lines.

But the first edition was left standing for the sake of three passages with which Vico found himself fully satisfied.[196] It is principally for these three passages that the first edition of the *New Science* is [still] necessary. It is to this edition that he refers when he cites the *"New Science"* or "the work with the Annotations"; whereas when he cites his "other work," the reference is to the three books of the *Universal Law*. Accordingly, when the *Second New Science* is reprinted, the *First* should be printed along with it, or at least, in order that they may not be missed, these three passages should be printed. On the other hand, in order that the *Universal Law* should not be missed, since Vico was much less satisfied with it than with the *First New Science,* of which it was but a sketch, and since he considered it necessary for two passages only—one on the fable that the Law of the Twelve Tables came from Athens, the other on Tribonian's fable of the "Royal Law"—he reworked these into two *Discourses,*[197] composed with more unity and greater vigor. These two fables are among those errors of which Jean Le Clerc, reviewing the *Universal Law* in his *Bibliothèque ancienne et moderne,* says that "in a great number of matters a quantity of popular errors are corrected, which the most expert have never noticed."

It must not be laid to pride that Vico, not content with the favorable judgments passed by certain men on his works, afterwards disapproved and rejected them; for this is evidence of the great reverence and respect he has for these men, rather than otherwise. Crude and arrogant writers defend their works even against just criticisms and reasonable corrections; others, faint of heart perchance, fill themselves with the favorable judgments given to their works, and, by reason of these, take no steps to perfect them. But the praises of great men made Vico's desire the greater to correct, supplement, and even to recast in better form this work of his. Thus he condemns the Annotations, which followed the negative method in seeking these Principles, because that method finds its proofs in inconsistencies, absurdities, impossibilities, which, with their ugly aspects, offend rather than feed the understanding, to which the positive method on the other hand commends itself by bringing forward the consistent, the harmonious, the uniform, which beautify the truth in which alone the human mind delights and finds nourishment. Vico is dissatisfied further with the *Universal Law* because he tried therein to descend from the mind of Plato and other enlightened philosophers into the dull and simple minds of the founders of the gentile peoples, whereas he should have taken the opposite course; whence he fell into error in certain matters. In the *First New Science* he erred, if not in the matter, then certainly in the arrangement, because he treated the origins of ideas apart from the origins of languages, whereas they were by nature united. Furthermore he discussed separately the methods of deriving the matters of this Science from these two sources, whereas he ought rather to have derived them from the two together; whence many errors of arrangement came about.

All this was corrected in the *Second New Science*. But he was constrained to meditate and write this work in a very short time, almost in the course of the printing itself. An almost fatal fury drove him to meditate and write it so rapidly, indeed, that he began it Christmas morning [1729] and finished it at nine o'clock Easter Sunday evening [April 9, 1730]. And then, after more than half of it had been printed [in Naples], a final communication from Venice [198] constrained him to suppress eighty-six pages of what had been printed. These pages contained an advertisement in which all the letters of Father Lodoli and his own in connection with this affair were printed in full and in order, with the reflections suggested by them. For this advertisement he now substituted an engraved frontispiece and an explanation of it long enough to fill the void. Besides all this there was the long and serious illness which Vico contracted from the epidemic of catarrh [i.e., grippe] which was then abroad in Italy, and finally the very solitude in which he lives. All these causes prevented his exercising diligence, [that virtue] which must lose itself in laboring over arguments of any considerable size, because it is a minute and therefore a tardy virtue. For all these reasons he was unable to attend to certain expressions which were confused and ought to have been set in order, or were left in the rough and ought to have been polished, or were too short and ought to have been expanded; nor to a multitude of passages in verse rhythms, which ought to be avoided in prose; nor finally to several slips of memory, which however were verbal only and did no harm to the sense. Therefore at the end of the book in the First Annotations, along with the corrections of typographical errors (of which, for the aforesaid reasons, there were very many), he included certain Meliorations and Additions, designated by the letters M and A. He followed the same plan in his Second Annotations, which, a few days after the appearance of the book, he wrote when Don Francesco Spinelli,[199] Prince of Scalea (a sublime philosopher adorned with cultivated erudition, especially in Greek), called his attention to three errors which he had observed in the course of going through the entire work in three days. Vico cordially thanked him for his kindness in the following letter (printed with these Second Annotations), by which he tacitly invited other learned men to do the same, because their corrections would be gratefully received.

I owe your excellency infinite thanks for having read through the latest edition of my *New Science* in scarcely three days after I had sent you a copy by my son, taking the precious time which you are wont to spend in sublime philosophic meditation or in the reading of the most profound writers, particularly the Greeks. Because of the marvelous acuteness of your intellect and the depth and breadth of your understanding, you have been able to read it straight through and yet to penetrate, as it were, to its marrow, and to grasp it in all its extent. Passing over in modest silence the flattering opinions that you were led to express by the loftiness of mind which befits your exalted rank, I profess myself highly indebted to your kindness in pointing out to me the following passages in which you have observed some errors. Your excellency was kind enough to say that these were merely slips of memory which did no harm to the sense of the matters under discussion.

The first is on page 313, line 19. Here in my version Briseis belongs to Agamemnon and Chryseis to Achilles; Agamemnon has commanded that Chryseis be restored to Chryses her father, priest of Apollo, who on her account has been wreaking havoc among the Greeks with his pestilence, and Achilles has not consented to obey him in this. Now this episode is told by Homer in quite a different fashion. But this error into which I fell was in fact an unconscious emendation of Homer in the most important matter of morality; for indeed Achilles would not have been willing to obey, and Agamemnon would have commanded him for the safety of the army. But in this matter Homer himself really preserved decorum, for, though he had made his chieftain wise, he imagined him no less strong; having yielded Chryseis as if under compulsion by Achilles, and so feeling his honor offended, to regain his prestige he took Briseis unjustly from Achilles, and by this deed many of the Greeks were brought to their downfall; so that in the *Iliad* Homer is giving us a very stupid chieftain. Thus our error was really a great disadvantage to us in that it prevented us from seeing this further great disproof of the esoteric wisdom hitherto ascribed to Homer, which offered confirmation of our discovery of the true Homer. And Achilles also, though celebrated by Homer with the recurrent epithet "blameless" and presented as a model of heroic virtue, does not meet the conception of hero as the term is defined by scholars. For, however justifiable the grief of Achilles may have been, none the less on leaving the camp with his men and taking his ships from the common fleet he expresses the most impious wish that Hector may destroy the Greeks that were spared by the plague, and he takes pleasure in seeing this wish on the way to fulfilment (as in the passage you suggested to me in the course of our discussion, Achilles tells Patroclus of his desire that all the

Greeks and Trojans should die and only the two of them survive the war), which is the revenge of a traitor.

The second error is on page 314, line 38, and page 315, line 1. Here you have called my attention to the fact that the Manlius who defended the fortress of the Capitoline against the Gauls was called Capitolinus, and after him came the other Manlius with the cognomen Torquatus who had his son beheaded. It was the former and not the latter who, by his efforts to introduce a new reckoning in favor of the debt-ridden plebs, made the nobles suspect that he was trying to make himself tyrant of Rome by popular favor, and so was condemned and hurled from the Tarpeian rock. This lapse of memory was harmful to us in that it deprived us of this powerful proof of the uniformity of the aristocratic state of ancient Rome and Sparta: in the latter too the valorous and great-souled King Agis, a Spartan Capitolinus, because of a similar debt-canceling law (rather than for any agrarian law) and because of another testamentary law, was executed by the ephors.

The third error is at the end of Book V, page 445, line 37, where one should read "Numantines" (for it is they who are there referred to).

Because of your kind observations I proceeded to reread the work and have written a second set of corrections, meliorations and additions.

These first and second annotations, along with some other (few but important) notes [200] written from time to time as the author discussed the book with his friends, can be incorporated in the places indicated when a third edition is printed.

While Vico was engaged in writing and seeing through the press the *Second New Science,* Cardinal Corsini, to whom the first edition had been dedicated, was elevated to the papacy. It was accordingly to His Holiness [Clement XII] that this second edition was dedicated. When it was presented to him, it was his wish, since it came inscribed to him, that his nephew Cardinal Neri Corsini, when he thanked the author for the copy which he had himself received without any covering letter, should make the following reply in his name:

MOST ILLUSTRIOUS SIR:

Your excellency's work on the *Principles of a New Science* had already in its first edition called forth all the praise of our lord, at that time Cardinal; and now, in its new edition, further illumined and enriched in erudition by your genius, it has met with the greatest approval in the most clement mind of His Holiness. I have desired to give you the comfort of this assurance on the same occasion on which I am moved to express my thanks for the copy you have had presented to me, which I hold in the esteem it merits. Expressing my eagerness to be of service to you at any opportunity, I pray God that He may prosper your affairs.

Always your excellency's affectionate

Rome, January 6, 1731 N. CARD. CORSINI

Overwhelmed by this great honor, Vico had nothing further to hope for in this world; wherefor, on account of his advanced age, worn out as he was by so many labors, afflicted by so many domestic cares and suffering from spasmodic pains in the thighs and legs and from a strange disease devouring all the tissues between the palate and the lower bone of the head, he definitely abandoned his studies. To Father Domenico Lodovico,[201] an incomparable Latin elegiac poet of the purest character, he gave the manuscript of the annotations he had written on the *First New Science,* with the following inscription:

TO THE CHRISTIAN TIBULLUS/FATHER DOMENICO LODOVICO/THESE MISERABLE REMAINS/OF THE UNHAPPY NEW SCIENCE/TOSSED TO AND FRO BY LAND AND SEA/GIAMBATTISTA VICO/AGITATED AND AFFLICTED/BY THE CEASELESS STORMS OF FORTUNE/AS TO SAFE PORT AT LAST/TORN AND TIRED/DELIVERS.

In the teaching of his subject Vico was always most interested in the progress of the young men, and to open their eyes and prevent them from being deceived by false doctors he was willing to incur the hostility of pedants. He never discussed matters pertaining to eloquence apart from wisdom, but would say that eloquence is nothing but wisdom speaking; that his chair was the one that should give direction to minds and make them universal; that others were concerned with the various parts of knowledge, but his should teach it as an integral whole in which each part accords with every other and gets its meaning from the whole. No matter what the subject, he showed in his lectures how by eloquence it was animated as it were by a single spirit drawing life from all the sciences that had any bearing upon it. This was the meaning of what he had written in his book *On the Method of the Studies:* that a Plato (to take a conspicuous example) among the ancients was the equivalent of an entire university of studies of our day, all harmonized in one system. Thus Vico lectured every day with as much elegance and profundity in various branches of scholarship as if famous men of letters had come from abroad to attend his classes and to hear him.[202]

Vico was choleric to a fault. Though he guarded himself from it as best he could in his writing, he publicly confessed this failing. He would inveigh too violently against the errors of thought or scholarship or against the misconduct of those men of letters who were his rivals, which as a charitable Christian or a true philosopher he should rather have overlooked or pitied. But if he was bitter toward those who belittled him and his works, he was correspondingly grateful to those who formed a just opinion of both; and the latter were always the best and the most learned men of the city. Among the caitiff semi-learned or pseudo-learned, the more shameless called him a fool, or in somewhat more courteous terms they said that he was obscure or eccentric and had odd ideas. The more malicious damned him with such compliments as these: some said he was a good teacher for young men when they had completed their course of study, that is when their studies had made them quite satisfied with their own knowledge (as if Quintilian had not wished that the children of the great might like Alexander be entrusted from boyhood to men like Aristotle); others went so far as to pay him the compliment, as dangerous as it was flattering, that he would make an excellent instructor of teachers themselves. He however blessed all these adversities as so many occasions for withdrawing to his desk, as to his high impregnable citadel, to meditate and to write further works which he was wont to call "so many noble acts of vengeance against his detractors." These finally led him to the discovery of his *New Science*. And when he had written this work, enjoying life, liberty and honor, he held himself more fortunate than Socrates, on whom Phaedrus has these fine lines:

> I would not shun his death to win his fame;
> I'd yield to odium, if absolved when dust.[203]

VICO'S LAST YEARS

(Continuation by the Marquis of Villarosa, 1818)

Now that Vico had become, as he himself tells us, the father of a large family, and his children had grown up, he began to suffer those vexations and distresses that a fortunate father is not infrequently compelled to undergo. He beheld the indigence of his family daily increasing for the reason that, as he himself confesses, from his earliest days Providence had been unwilling to establish him in comfortable circumstances and had cut off all honorable means to which he had resorted

to improve his condition. Indeed he writes as follows on the
back of a reply he had received from Cardinal Lorenzo Corsini,[204] his Maecenas, whose patronage he had vainly solicited
for the printing of the first edition of the *New Science:*

Letter from his eminence Corsini, who has not the means to assume the expense of printing the work that preceded the *New
Science*. Thus I was compelled by my poverty to think of this last
[the *New Science*], for it reduced my spirit to printing only this
small book, parting for the purpose with a ring I had which was
set with a five-grain diamond of the purest water. With the price
it brought I was able to pay for the printing and binding of the
copies of the book, which, because I found myself committed to its
publication, I dedicated to this same Cardinal.

He was entirely dependent for livelihood on the small
stipend of his professorship, and since this by no means suf-
ficed he found himself obliged to give private lessons at his
home in Latin rhetoric and literature. The finest gentlemen
of our capital city were glad to send their sons to him, being
sure that from Vico better than from any other professor of
these subjects they would get sound instruction along with the
best moral training. To those who came to Vico's house for
lessons we must add the many sons of the principal gentlemen
of this kingdom whom Vico visited in their own homes to
give them lessons. Among these I will mention for brevity's
sake only the Carafas of Traetto, the Spinellis of the house of
the princes of Scalea, and the Gaetanis of the house of the
dukes of Laurenzano. For the magnates of our city at that
time overlooked no means to have their sons and heirs grow
wise and learned, rightly believing that nothing so ill becomes
a man of noble blood and ample means as to be undistin-
guishable from the numberless troop of the foolish and ignorant.

But such aids were insufficient for the urgent needs by which he was continually oppressed and discouraged. He had taken to wife by the greatest ill-fortune a woman endowed indeed with a pure and innocent character but wanting in those talents which are required even in a mediocre wife and mother. Unable even to write, she took very little care of household matters, so that the learned professor was obliged to plan and provide not only for the clothes but for whatever else his children might need.[205]

He was very indulgent toward them, and showed a special predilection for the two girls. Perceiving that the elder, Luisa, was endowed with talents beyond those necessary in a woman, and that she displayed an inclination to the liberal arts and especially to poetry, he undertook to instruct her himself with the greatest care and attention. He had the satisfaction of seeing that his efforts were not in vain, for on reaching womanhood she distinguished herself in poetry, as is evidenced by some charming compositions of hers which appear in various printed anthologies. It was a happy sight to see our philosopher playing lightheartedly with his daughters in the few hours that he had free from constant and trying daily tasks. Father Don Benedetto Laudati, a monk of the order of Mount Cassino greatly esteemed for his venerable character and his knowledge, was eye-witness of such a scene. He was a frequent visitor, and finding Vico one day at play with his little girls he could not refrain from quoting to him these verses from Tasso:

> Here can be seen, midst the Maeonian maidens,
> Alcides with a distaff, gossiping.

At this quip the fond father laughed merrily.

The comfort which his daughters brought him was however alloyed with bitterness by the bad character which one of his sons (whose name I shall not here reveal) [206] showed from childhood. When he had grown up, far from applying himself to studies and sober habits, he became addicted to a soft and lazy life, and as time went on to all sorts of vices, so that he became the dishonor of the entire family. No measure was overlooked by the good father to bring his son back from his erring ways and set him again on the right path. Repeated and affectionate admonishments, authoritative warnings from men of wisdom and reputation, all proved useless efforts to reform the errant youth. Things came to such a pass indeed that the sorrowing father found himself against his will in the hard necessity of calling in the police to have his son imprisoned. But at the last minute, when he heard the police coming up the stairs of his house and bethought himself of their errand, he was carried away by paternal love, ran to his unhappy son and said to him, trembling: "Save yourself, my son." But this act of fatherly tenderness did not prevent justice from taking its inevitable course; for the boy was taken to prison and spent a long time there before he gave clear signs of having really mended his ways.

This domestic calamity—no light matter in itself—was accompanied by another no less grave: the failing health of his other daughter,[207] who began to suffer grievously from painful infirmities. While his daughter's illness caused the greatest affliction to the unhappy father, it also drove him to continual expenditures for doctors and medicine; expenditures made in sorrow but without stint, and perhaps vainly thrown away. Such grave preoccupations as these never diverted Vico from regular attendance at his classes, to which honor and duty called him. He endured everything with heroic patience, and only occasionally to some intimate friend allowed himself to say sadly that "misfortune would pursue him even after his death." A presage of doom that unhappily came true, as we shall see later.

With the auspicious arrival in this kingdom of the immortal Charles of Bourbon, a ray of hope for the improvement of his condition began to gleam for him. This magnanimous and beneficent sovereign, to whose grand and swiftly enacted enterprises (brought to final fulfilment by his worthy son and successor now on the throne) this kingdom owes so much, made it not the least of his concerns to be, like his predecessor Alfonso, the highest patron of scholars and learned men. When therefore he was informed of the rare qualifications of our Vico, he issued this flattering diploma appointing him Royal Historiographer with an annual stipend of a hundred ducats.[208]

In consideration of the learning your excellency possesses and of the labors you have performed in instructing over a long period of years the youth of this Royal University, His Majesty has deigned to appoint you his historiographer, with the title and duties appertaining thereto, confident because of your well known ability that you will perform them with the credit that has marked the learned works you have already published, and assigning you also for the present a hundred ducats above your University stipend. I am pleased to announce to you his royal order, so that you may know the favor you have acquired in His Majesty's eyes.

May God preserve your excellency for many years, as I fervently hope.   JOSEPH JOACHIM DE MONTEALEGRE.
     Naples, July 21, 1735.
Señor Don Juan Baptista Vico.

Our Vico would certainly have experienced further evidences of his sovereign's beneficence, had not his increasing years been marked by an increase of those infirmities which had threatened him even in his prime. His nervous system began to be noticeably weakened, to the extent that he could walk only with difficulty; and a greater affliction to him was the realization that his memory was growing feebler day by day. On this account he was compelled to give up his private lessons and also his lectures in the University. He thereupon petitioned the king that he might be pleased to appoint his son Gennaro at least interim successor to his chair. Gennaro, he said, had given sufficient evidence of his competence by several times expounding the institutes of oratory in his father's presence to the satisfaction of the public.[209] The petition was deferred for a time to consult Monsignor Don Nicola de Rosa, Bishop of Pozzuoli and Grand Chaplain, since the latter office then carried with it that of University Prefect. The wise prelate, to whom the competence and probity of the young Gennaro Vico were well known, was not slow to advise his sovereign that, having regard to the long years of Giambattista Vico's service in the Royal University and to the good qualities which were united in his son, he might properly deign to confer on the latter the chair of rhetoric. Since his most clement majesty concurred in this opinion, the chair of rhetoric was conferred on Gennaro Vico, to the inexpressible satisfaction of his aged and infirm father.

Meanwhile the exhausted body of the old scholar grew weaker from day to day. His memory was so far gone that he forgot the nearest objects and confused the names of the most familiar things. No longer did he take pleasure, as he had in the early days of his illness, in the Latin authors read to him by his devoted Gennaro. He would spend the entire day sitting in a corner of his house, not merely calm but silent as well; and his nourishment, taken with difficulty, was light and infrequent. He scarcely greeted the friends who came often to see him, and he no longer engaged them, as had been his wont, in open and jovial conversation. It was impossible to cure or even to check this pertinacious disease by any recourse to medicine. To no avail were the efficacious remedies suggested by his able medical colleagues in the University. On the contrary, his desperate infirmity kept getting worse, until the unhappy Vico was reduced to such a state that he did not recognize his own dearly beloved children. In this wretched state he continued for a year and two months.[210] By that time his aversion from any sort of food had so far sapped his strength that he had to keep to his bed, drinking death in slow and painful draughts. Some days before breathing his last he recovered his senses, and as if awakened from a long sleep recognized his children and those who were about him. What joy this gave them need hardly be asked. But his only benefit from the improvement was the realization that his end was approaching. Perceiving for himself that all human remedies were now vain and fruitless, overcome as he was by a congestion of the lungs to which in his greatly weakened condition he could offer no resistance, he sent for Father Antonio Maria da Palazzuolo,[211] a learned Capuchin and intimate friend, to administer the last friendly offices and assist him in the dread passage. With the most perfect submission to the divine will and a prayer for the pardon of his sins, comforted by the powerful aid that Holy Church affords her beloved children and which he himself had eagerly requested, continually reciting the psalms of David, he died peacefully on the 20th of January, 1744,[212] having passed the seventy-sixth year of his age.

After his death it fell out as he had foretold many years before, as if by prophetic inspiration; that is, that misfortune would follow him even after death. The prediction was fulfilled by a mishap till then unheard of, but which to our shame we have seen repeated in our own day, in spite of the enlightenment on which we pride ourselves.

It was the custom for the professors of the Royal University to accompany to the sepulcher the remains of their departed colleagues; a praiseworthy custom which has survived the lapse of so many others. When the hour for Vico's funeral rites had been set, almost all the professors were eager to pay this last tribute to their deceased colleague and came to his house to accompany the remains. The Confraternity of Santa Sophia, of which Vico had been a member, were to carry the coffin as they regularly did for their deceased members. When the Confraternity arrived at his house, they began to murmur that they would not allow the professors of the University to bear the pall. The professors on the other hand contended they had the right to that honor, and adduced many precedents. Meanwhile the corpse was carried down into the courtyard of the house and laid on the bier, which bore the arms of the Royal University. Hereupon there began a great uproar between the members of the Confraternity and the professors of the University, neither side being willing to yield to the other, and both showing in the presence of the dead how far human weakness and pride can go. As no amicable understanding could be reached, the Confraternity, with small regard for human decency, decided to take their leave, abandoning the corpse where it lay. The professors alone were unable to carry out the funeral rites, and the corpse had to be carried back into its old dwelling. How this incident must have shocked the grief-stricken son, who, after losing so dear a father, was obliged to see him brought back into the house in this fashion, may be easily imagined. On the following day, after giving vent to his grief, he decided to ask the cathedral chapter to conduct his father's remains to the sepulcher, incurring the additional expense which is imperatively required in such mournful circumstances. The professors were not reluctant to accompany their deceased colleague to the tomb, and he was buried in the church of the Oratorians called Gerolamini, as being the church most frequented by the illustrious man in his lifetime, and the one he had chosen to receive his ashes.

His remains lay neglected and unknown, as is the usual fate of men of learning in our city, down to the year 1789. In that year Gennaro, the surviving son of his great father, had a brief inscription carved for him in a remote corner of the church. This might well have provided an occasion for recalling the ancient complaint of the poet on beholding a pretentious monument raised in honor of a petty man:

> In a marble tomb Licinus lies; in a poor one, Cato;
> Pompey in none at all. . . .

The inscription he placed there reads as follows:

TO GIAMBATTISTA VICO
ROYAL PROFESSOR OF RHETORIC
AND ROYAL HISTORIOGRAPHER

*

WHAT MANNER OF MAN HE WAS IN LIFE
BY GENIUS LEARNING AND CHARACTER
IS MANIFEST IN THE WRITINGS
ON WHICH HIS FAME RESTS

*

WHERE HE LIES IN DEATH
BY THE SIDE OF CATERINA DESTITO
HIS BELOVED WIFE
THIS TABLET SHOWS

*

HE DIED JANUARY 19, 1744
AGED SEVENTY-FOUR YEARS

*

PLACED BY HIS GRIEVING SON
GENNARO

The Arcadia of Rome, of which Vico was a member under the name Laufilo Terio, erected the following memorial inscription in the Bosco Parrasio:

BY ORDER OF THE GENERAL ASSEMBLY OF ARCADIA
TO LAUFILO TERIO SHEPHERD OF ARCADIA
PHILOLOGIAN
RENOWNED FOR LEARNING IN UNIVERSAL LAW

*

ERECTED IN HIS HONOR
UNDER THE CARE OF DORALBO TRIARIO SHEPHERD OF ARCADIA
IN THE FOURTH YEAR
OF THE SIX HUNDRED THIRTY-SECOND OLYMPIAD
BEING THE THIRD YEAR OF THE SIXTEENTH OLYMPIAD
FROM THE FOUNDING OF THE ARCADIA

NOTES

TO THE INTRODUCTION

1. *Philosophische Schriften,* ed. Gerhardt, III, 567 f.

2. On Conti see J. G. Robertson: *Studies in the Genesis of Romantic Theory in the Eighteenth Century,* Cambridge, 1923, ch. IV.

3. *"Vita . . . da lui stesso descritta."* In our translation of the Autobiography we use the convenient modern term for similar circumlocutions.

4. Below, pp. 113, 182.

5. *The Philosophy of Giambattista Vico,* London, 1913, p. 266.

6. *English Works,* ed. Molesworth, I, viii, ix.

7. The recent histories of historical writing by Harry Elmer Barnes and James Westfall Thompson, and the earlier works of European scholars, are useful only as bibliographical guides. Friedrich Meinecke's *Entstehung des Historismus,* München and Berlin, 1936, and Croce's various writings on historiography, are penetrating and provocative. The chapter on history in Leo Strauss: *Political Philosophy of Hobbes,* Oxford, 1936, is an example of the kind of work that must still be done.

8. *Advancement of Learning* (ed. W. A. Wright), I. iv. 5; iv. 2.

9. *Decline and Fall,* ed. Bury, VI, 444 n. 87.

10. *Philosophische Schriften,* ed. Gerhardt, III, 270; V, 452; VI, 198.

11. Quoted by Strauss, p. 82, n. 4.

12. *Lives,* tr. North, Temple Classics ed., I, 9 f.

13. *Advancement of Learning,* II. xx. 3; xxii. 3, 4, 5.

14. II. xxii. 4, 6; xxiii. 8; i. 2.

15. II. vii. 6.

16. Paris, 1566, p. 8.

17. *Latin Works,* I, xxiv.

18. *English Works,* VIII, viii.

19. By W. Nichols; see John Laird: *Hobbes,* London, 1934, p. 6.

20. *English Works,* VIII, vi, vii, viii, xxii.

21. *English Works,* IV, 30; III, 203; I, 10 f.; *Latin Works,* III, 66.

22. *Oeuvres,* ed. Adam & Tannery, VI, 6 f., 12 f.; X, 502 f.

23. *Autobiographies,* ed. John Murray, London, 1896, pp. 143, 235.

24. *Civil History of the Kingdom of Naples,* tr. Ogilvie, London, 1731, II, 842, in a chapter on "The State of our Jurisprudence, and of the other Arts and Sciences which flourished among us in the End of the seventeenth Century, and continue so at this time" (1723). See also Gilbert Burnet: *Some Letters, containing an account of what seemed most remarkable in travelling through Switzerland, Italy, some parts of Germany, &c., in the years 1685*

and *1686, written* . . . *to the Honourable R*[obert] *B*[oyle], 3d ed., Rotterdam, 1687, esp. pp. 195 ff. Fausto Nicolini: *La giovinezza di G. B. Vico,* 2d ed., Bari, 1932; *Aspetti della vita Italo-Spagnuola nel cinque e seicento,* Napoli, 1934, ch. IV; and article cited in n. 25 below.

25. Nicolini: "Sulla vita civile, letteraria e religiosa napoletana alla fine del Seicento," *Atti della R. Accademia di scienze morali e politiche di Napoli* 52 (1928), 175–255, esp. 203–230, 249–255.

26. *Vita di Pietro Giannone scritta da lui medesimo,* ed. Nicolini, Napoli, 1905, p. 31.

27. H. C. Lea: *The Inquisition in the Spanish Dependencies,* New York, 1908, ch. II, esp. pp. 98–108.

28. See the translation by H. P. Adams: *The Life and Writings of Giambattista Vico,* London, 1935, pp. 223 ff.

29. In the preface he contributed to Belli's Italian translation of Fracastorius: *Syphilis,* quoted by Croce in: *Rivista di Filosofia* n.s. 1 (1940), 144.

30. On Vico and Descartes see Nicolini: *Giovinezza,* pp. 116–120.

31. *Opere,* I, 35 f. (Laterza edition).

32. I, 274.

33. II–2, 318.

34. I, 85.

35. I, 136.

36. I, 150.

37. I, 136 f. On Vico's theory of knowledge see Robert Flint: *Vico,* 1884, pp. 86–111.

38. *Kritik der reinen Vernunft,* Vorrede zur zweiten Auflage, pp. xiii f.

39. *English Works,* VII, 183 f. Nicolini (*Fonti e riferimenti storici della seconda Scienza Nuova,* Bari, 1931, pp. 30, 46) thinks Vico had not read Hobbes but depended on the account in G. Pasch: *De novis inventis,* Leipzig, 1700, pp. 190–203. Some of Vico's direct references to Hobbes are not in Pasch, however, and it would seem that he must have known Hobbes's Latin works.

40. On Vico and Lucretius see Nicolini: *Giovinezza,* pp. 120–124.

41. Biblioteca Nazionale di Napoli, cod. seg. I. AA. 32, fol. 1; a deposition by a witness for the Inquisition.

42. On Vico and Bacon see Nicolini in *Atti della R. Accademia di scienze morali e politiche* 52 (1928), 136–145.

43. *Opere,* V, 155.

44. II–1, 33. Vico elsewhere speaks of Augustine as his "particular protector": V, 377.

45. *Advancement of Learning,* II. ii. 7.

46. *Opere,* IV–1, 117 f., §331.

47. Among previous interpretations of the New Science, the nearest approach to that offered here will be found in C. E. Vaughan: *Studies in the History of Political Philosophy,* Manchester, 1925, I, 207–253; see also his lecture, "Giambattista Vico: An Eighteenth Century Pioneer," *Bulletin of*

the John Rylands Library 6 (1921–22), 266–288. In lieu of documentation, which would require a reference for nearly every sentence, the reader is referred to the sixty-page analytic index in Nicolini's three-volume critical edition of the *Scienza nuova*, Bari, 1911–1916. See also Thomas Whittaker, "Vico's New Science of Humanity," *Mind* 35 (1926), reprinted in his: *Reason and Other Essays*, Cambridge, 1934, pp. 133–189; an essay based on Nicolini's edition.

48. *Opere*, IV–1, 113, §314.

49. III, 5.

50. IV–2, 164, §1108.

51. IV–1, 125, §342.

52. IV–1, 128, §349.

53. IV–2, 163, §1107.

54. IV–1, 28, §34.

55. IV–1, 123 f., §338.

56. IV–2, 125 f., §1040–§1043.

57. IV–1, 78, §146.

58. IV–2, 119, title.

59. IV–2, 171, §1119.

60. For continental Europe, the indispensable guide to such research is Croce's great Vico bibliography and its supplements, of which seven have so far appeared. *Bibliografia Vichiana raccolta di tre memorie presentate all' Accademia Pontaniana di Napoli nel 1903, 1907 e 1910, con appendice di Fausto Nicolini*, Bari, 1911. "Nuove ricerche sulla vita e le opere del Vico e sul Vichianismo," *La Critica* 15 (1917), 290–299; 16 (1918), 148–158, 214–216; 17 (1919), 109–111, 307–311; 18 (1920), 164–166, 229–235, 353–361; 19 (1921), 47–49, 107–108. "Quarto Supplemento alla Bibliografia Vichiana," *Atti della R. Accademia di scienze morali e politiche di Napoli* 51 (1927) 3–28. "Quinto Supplemento," ibid. 55 (1932), 5–39. G. F. Finetti: *Difesa dell' Autorità della Sacra Scrittura contro Giambattista Vico, dissertazione del 1768 con introduzione di Benedetto Croce, unitovi il sesto supplemento alla Bibliografia Vichiana* (pp. 95–108), Bari, 1936. "Settimo Supplemento," *Rivista di Filosofia* n.s. 1 (1940), 117–137. See also Croce's masterly sketches in: *The Philosophy of Giambattista Vico*, tr. Collingwood, London, 1913, ch. XX and app. II. The present survey breaks fresh ground in sections D, E, and F, and here and there in the earlier sections.

61. Croce in *Atti della Accademia Pontaniana* 33 (1903), 26–28. Hugh Quigley: *Italy and the Rise of a New School of Criticism in the 18th Century*, Perth, 1921, pp. 36 ff., 42 and passim. For Vico's influence on Pagano in particular see Croce in *La Critica* 17 (1919), 109–111.

62. *Lezioni di economia politica* (1757), in: *Scrittori Classici Italiani di Economia Politica* 8 (Milano, 1803), 273 n.

63. G. Natali: *Storia letteraria d'Italia: Il settecento* 1 (1928), 319.

64. Max Ascoli: "La filosofia giuridica di Emanuele Duni," *Annali dell' Università di Camerino* 2 (*Sezione giuridica*, Roma, 1929), 137–159.

Notes to the Introduction 213

65. Croce's introduction to a reprint of Finetti's *Difesa dell' Autorità della Sacra Scrittura contro Giambattista Vico*, Bari, 1936.

66. *Origine e progressi del cittadino*, Roma, 1763, II, 405–409.

67. *Saggio di giurisprudenza universale*, Roma, 1760, p. 5.

68. Elio Gianturco: *Joseph de Maistre and Giambattista Vico*, Columbia University thesis, 1937.

69. *Storia della Storiografia Italiana nel secolo decimonono*, 2a ed., Bari, 1930, I, 11 f.

70. Quoted by Croce in *La Critica* 18 (1920), 230.

71. Marcel Grilli: "The Nationality of Philosophy and Bertrando Spaventa," *Journal of the History of Ideas* 2 (1941), 339–371, esp. 361, 368.

72. M. H. Fisch: "Croce and Vico," in the forthcoming Croce volume in *The Library of Living Philosophers*, edited by Paul Arthur Schilpp.

73. Mario Palmieri: *The Philosophy of Fascism*, Chicago, 1936, ch. XIII, esp. p. 192. Cf. Aline Lion: *The Pedigree of Fascism*, London, 1927. But good work untouched by Fascism went on, e.g. Donati's cited in n. 86.

74. J. G. Hamann: *Schriften*, ed. Roth, V, 267 f.

75. J. F. Herder: *Werke*, ed. Suphan, XVIII, 245 ff.

76. R. Haym: *Herder*, 1885, II, 409.

77. *Italienische Reise*, under date of March 5, 1787.

78. F. H. Jacobi: *Von den göttlichen Dingen und ihrer Offenbarung*, Leipzig, 1811, pp. 121–123; cf. Vico: *Opere*, I, 150.

79. *Schweizerisches Museum* 1 (1816), 184 ff.

80. *Vermischte Schriften*, IV, 217 f.

81. *Kantstudien, Ergänzungsheft* 38 (1916), 17 ff.

82. Walter Witzenmann: *Politischer Aktivismus und sozialer Mythos: Giambattista Vico und die Lehre des Faschismus*, Berlin, 1935.

83. Paul Hazard: "La pensée de Vico, III. Les influences sur la pensée française," *Revue des cours et conférences* 33 (1931), 127–143.

84. Nicolini: "La teoria del linguaggio in Giambattista Vico e Giangiacomo Rousseau," *Revue de littérature comparée* 10 (1930), 292–298.

85. *Revue de littérature comparée* 12 (1932), 829–837.

86. G. Monod: *La vie et la pensée de Jules Michelet*, Paris, 1923, chs. VI–VIII. Benvenuto Donati: *Nuovi studi sulla filosofia civile di G. B. Vico*, Firenze, 1936, pp. 469–527. W. P. Dismukes: *Michelet and Vico*, University of Illinois thesis, 1936.

87. *Vico*, Edinburgh, 1884, p. 230.

88. Werner Kaegi: *Michelet und Deutschland*, Basel, 1936.

89. *Opere* IV-1, 214, §499; V, 265; I, 269; IV-2, 187 f., §1178; IV-1, 128, §347.

90. Nicolini: *Aspetti della vita Italo-Spagnuola*, Napoli, 1934, pp. 320 f.

91. *The Life, Unpublished Letters, and Philosophical Regimen of Anthony Earl of Shaftesbury*, ed. B. Rand, 1900, p. 479; cf. p. 497. See Croce: "Shaftesbury in Italia," *La Critica* 23 (1925), 1–34.

92. Fraser: *Life and Letters of George Berkeley*, 1871, pp. 78–85, 571–574.

93. Francesco Lomonaco: *Vite degli eccellenti Italiani,* Lugano, 1836, II, 296.

94. *Opere,* V, 55, n. 3.

95. René Wellek: *The Rise of English Literary History,* Chapel Hill, 1941, pp. 74, 86, and passim.

96. 3d ed., London, 1768, pp. 182, 204, 280, 286.

97. Details and documentation in M. H. Fisch: "The Coleridges, Dr. Prati, and Vico," *Modern Philology* 41 (1943–44), 111–122.

98. Lionel Trilling: *Matthew Arnold,* 1939, pp. 50 f.

99. C. C. J. Bunsen: *God in History,* London, 1870, III, 273, 275.

100. In 1848 Robert Blakey, in the third volume of his *History of the Philosophy of Mind,* devoted some seven pages to a summary of Vico's doctrines, not without mistakes, and probably at second hand. A shorter summary, partly repeated from this one, was offered in his *Historical Sketch of Logic* in 1851. And D. C. Heron in his *Introduction to the History of Jurisprudence* in 1860 included a deadly fifty-page digest of Vico. Neither Blakey nor Heron made any attempt to place Vico in the general movement of modern thought.

101. *Life of Frederick Denison Maurice,* 1884, I, 185.

102. *Lettres inédites de J. S. Mill à A. Comte,* ed. Lévy-Bruhl, 1899, pp. 383 ff.

103. *System of Positive Polity,* tr. Congreve, 1877, IV, calendar facing p. 348, and pp. 483–489; cf. III, 1876, 503 f.

104. J. H. Bridges: *Illustrations of Positivism,* ed. Jones, Chicago, 1915, pp. 352–358 at 353; cf. Vico: *Opere,* IV–1, 86, §180; 148, §377; 164 f., §405.

105. P. 473, n. 1; cf. Vol. II, p. 215, n. 1.

106. Ed. J. M. Robertson, London, 1904, p. 466 n. 131, p. 500, and p. 91 n. 8.

107. *A Memoir of the Right Hon. William Edward Hartpole Lecky,* by his Wife, New York, 1909, pp. 68 f.

108. J. M. Robertson: *A History of Freethought in the Nineteenth Century,* 1930, II, 355, 359 n. 1.

109. *Mind* 20 (1911), 442.

110. Flint: *Vico,* 1884, p. 230.

111. Since these two volumes on the philosophy of history have not been superseded, and since neither has an index, a list of references to Vico in them may be useful. 1874: 26, 77, 96 n. 1, 206, 286–287, 289, 290, 320–321, 324, 351 n. 1. 1894: 77, 124, 126, 158, 211, 227, 255–256, 264, 265–266, 321, 35?, 382, 383, 389–390, 480, 526, 530–532, 536, 568, 677, 684.

112. *Form in Modern Poetry,* New York, 1933, pp. 36–38; *In Defence of Shelley & Other Essays,* London, 1936, pp. 150–156.

113. Samuel Beckett: "Dante. . . Bruno. Vico. . Joyce," in: *An Exagmination of James Joyce,* 1939, pp. 3–22; Herbert Gorman: *James Joyce,* 1939, pp. 332–335; Harry Levin: *James Joyce,* 1941, index s.n. Vico. William Butler Yeats: *Wheels and Butterflies,* 1935, pp. 16 ff.; *A Vision,* 1938, pp.

261 f.; *On the Boiler,* 1938, p. 22; Louis MacNeice: *The Poetry of W. B. Yeats,* 1941, pp. 125 f.; Joseph Hone: *W. B. Yeats,* 1943, pp. 393 f., 444.

114. Croce in *La Critica* 18 (1920), 166.

115. E.g., Everett, A. H., "Progress and Limits of Social Improvement," *North American Review* 38 (1834), 502–538 at 513; unsigned, "State of Historical Science in France," *Eclectic Magazine* 1 (1844), 161–181, esp. 163 f. (reprinted from the *British and Foreign Review*); O., "Inductive Theory of Civilization," *American Review* 6 (1847), 381–398 at 390; Farrar, C. C. S., "The Science of History," *De Bow's Review* 5 (1848), 58–64, 127–134, 211–220, 346–357, 445–454, esp. 58 f., 133 f., 211–214; Wright, O. W., "Primary Law of Political Development in Civil History," *North American Review* 88 (1859), 387–429; Giles, Henry, "The Leading Theories on the Philosophy of History," *ibid.* 95 (1862), 163–188, esp. 167–170.

116. Hawkins, R. L.: *Auguste Comte and the United States,* 1936, pp. 119, 126. Parker, Theodore, in *The Christian Examiner,* March, 1858; reprinted in his *Works,* vol. XII, and in his *The American Scholar,* ed. G. W. Cooke, 1907, 364 ff. Clark, J. S.: *Life and Letters of John Fiske,* 1917, I, 285. Fiske: *Works,* XIV, 182, n. 1; XX, 138.

117. Sanborn, Frank B.: "Social Science in Theory and in Practice," *Journal of Social Science* 9 (1878), 1–13, esp. 2–3, and "Social Science in the Nineteenth Century," *ibid.* 30 (1892), 1–11 at 1.

117a. Gianturco, Elio: "Suarez and Vico," *Harvard Theological Review* 27 (1934), 207–210; another article on Suarez and Vico abstracted in *Italica* 13 (1936), 116: a review *ibid.* 132; and a review in *Journal of Modern History* 9 (1937), 514–516.

118. Lassalle: *Nachgelassene Briefe und Schriften,* ed. G. Mayer, III, 387 f.

119. *Marx/Engels Gesamtausgabe,* 3 Abt., III, 63.

120. Volksausgabe, Berlin and Moscow, 1922, I, 389 n. 89.

121. 2 (1896), 785–817, 906–941, 1013–1046. See also his essay, "Was man von Vico lernt," *Sozialistischen Monatsheften,* 1898, e. g. p. 270: "Of all the philosophers who wrote on history before Marx, there is none whose work is so much worth study as Vico's."

122. *Le système historique de Renan,* Paris, 1906.

123. *Réflexions sur la violence,* Paris, 1908.

124. *The Philosophy of Giambattista Vico,* p. 243.

125. *The Eighteenth Brumaire of Louis Bonaparte* (1852), 2d par. of ch. I.

126. Croce in *La Critica* 36 (1938), 38, 39.

127. *Le déterminisme économique: la méthode historique de Karl Marx,* Paris, 1907, ch. III; *Die Neue Zeit* IX-1 (1890), 15.

128. *Quinto supplemento alla Bibliografia Vichiana,* p. 38.

TO THE AUTOBIOGRAPHY

129. Actually 1668. (Vico's errors in dating are corrected in our Chronological Table, and some of his omissions are there supplied.) He was born in a

room over his father's small bookshop at 31 Via San Biagio dei Librai. His father was Antonio di Vico of Maddaloni (c. 1636–1708), a farmer's son who had come to Naples about 1656. His mother was Candida Masullo of Naples (1633–c. 1695), daughter of Giambattista Masullo, a carriage maker. She was Antonio's second wife, and Giambattista Vico was the sixth of the eight children she bore him.

130. Probably when reaching for a book on the top shelf of his father's shop.

131. Which he was attending before his fall.

132. I.e., in the *De institutione grammatica* of the Portuguese Jesuit Manuel Alvarez (1526–83). In the Jesuit schools the "lower studies" comprised three grades of grammar (chiefly Latin, with some Greek) and two of "humanity" and rhetoric; the "higher studies" included two or three years of philosophy (beginning with logic) and four of theology.

133. The Academy of the Infuriati, founded in the second decade of the seventeenth century and maintained until 1672, was revived in 1690 only to be transformed in 1692 into the Academy of the Uniti, of which Vico was shortly made a member on Valletta's motion. Vico here antedates its revival by about seven years. It was the Academy of the Investiganti that was revived in 1683, and Vico may have been invited to some of its meetings at that time. If that was the source of his early inspiration, the memory was suppressed after his alienation from the movement it represented, and by a Freudian substitution the Uniti took the place of the Investiganti.

134. *In institutiones iuris civilis a Iustiniano compositas commentarius.*

135. Father of Vico's close friend the Jesuit poet Nicola Partenio Giannettasio (1648–1715).

136. *Summa iuris canonici in quatuor institutionum libros contracta,* Ingolstadt, 1625.

137. On the Rocca family, its estate at Vatolla, and Vico's sojourn there, see Nicolini in *Archivio storico italiano,* serie VII, vol. 6 (1926), 61–111; Adams: *Life and Writings of Giambattista Vico,* ch. III.

138. I.e., the French Jesuit Étienne Deschamps (1613–1701), who under the pseudonym of Antonius Richardus wrote a *Disputatio de libero arbitrio* (1645) and the *De haeresi ianseniana ab apostolica sede proscripta* (1654). Vico's somewhat forced interpretation was probably not worked out until the decade 1710–20.

139. Vico's transition to Platonism (or rather Neoplatonism) did not long precede his *Ancient Wisdom of the Italians* (1710); his theory of justice was a still later development. Both are here antedated.

140. See n. 169 below.

141. *Ingegno* (Latin *ingenium*) is difficult to render. Perception, invention, the faculty of discerning the relations between things, which issues on the one hand in analogy, simile, metaphor, and on the other in scientific hypotheses.

142. As Adams (pp. 55 f.) remarks, "the plain meaning of this passage is,

not that Vico came afterwards to see that the atomists were wrong, but that he never thought they were right. But he certainly understates the extent of his intercourse" with the young Epicureans of Naples. It is scarcely too much to say that he was himself one of them. See our introduction, pp. 34–36 above.

143. Henricus Regius (Henri Du Roy): *Fundamenta physices* (1646), though largely plagiarized from Descartes, was repudiated by him in the preface to the French version of his *Principia.*

144. See Raffaele Cotugno: *Gregorio Caloprese,* Trani, 1910.

145. A poetess, later godmother of one of Vico's daughters, and through his influence elected a shepherdess of Arcadia. Adams, p. 101.

146. For what Vico saw in these writers see Adams, pp. 34–39.

147. On Di Capua and Cornelio, and on the intellectual atmosphere of Naples in the latter half of the seventeenth century, see M. H. Fisch: "The Quarrel of Ancients and Moderns at Naples," to appear shortly in the *Bulletin of the Medical Library Association.*

148. *Institutiones linguae graecae,* 1596 and many later editions.

149. Hadrianus Junius (de Jonch) (1511–1575): *Nomenclator omnium rerum,* Antwerp, 1567 and many later editions.

150. Paolo Giovio (1483–1552): *Historiarum sui temporis libri XLV,* of which the first ten books were never written. That the first six were lost in the sack of Rome (1527) seems to have been a story put in circulation by Giovio himself in order that his work might seem like Livy's even in fragmentariness. By a characteristic slip, Vico assigns the *History* to Bernardo Navagero (1507–65).

151. On Francesco d'Andrea see Adams, pp. 46 f.; on Gaetano, ibid., 61 f. Gennaro was counselor of the Sacro Real Consiglio and later regent of the Collaterale.

152. The Accademia Palatina or Academy of the Royal Palace, more commonly called the Accademia Medinaceli. Adams, pp. 64 f. Inaugurated March 20, 1698, suspended in September, 1701, because of the conspiracy of Macchia, and disbanded in February, 1702.

153. On Doria see Flint: *Vico,* pp. 78–80; Adams, pp. 65 f.

154. The inaugural orations summarized in the following paragraphs were first published in 1868, and may be found in *Opere,* I, 5–67. Good accounts of them in Flint, ch. V, and Adams, ch. VI. Some of Vico's dates have been corrected in our chronological table.

155. It must have been the third rather than the fourth oration which was attended by Lanzina Ulloa of Salamanca, who died March 30, 1703. The episode which led to the advancement of the future Clement XI took place not at the Academy of the Umoristi, but at the Roman residence of Christina of Sweden.

156. *De nostri temporis studiorum ratione,* Napoli, Felice Mosca, 1709. *Opere,* I, 69–121; Flint, pp. 58–63; Adams, ch. VII.

157. Diego Vincenzo Vidania of Huesca (1631–1732), lecturer in the

Universidad Sertoriana, then grand inquisitor at Barcelona and in Sicily, and finally chaplain major of the Kingdom of Naples and ex officio prefect of the University, wrote a treatise on the Justinian Code of which in 1713 he published anonymously a part which was highly praised by Brenckmann. The latter was in Naples in 1712 and probably made Vico's acquaintance there, for Vico had sent him at Florence in 1710 an inscribed copy of the *De antiquissima*. Rinaldi had gone to Florence at the instance of Vico's friend Basilio Giannelli to look after the interests of the Duchess of San Giovanni, whom Vico misremembers as "un napoletano magnate."

158. Domenico Aulisio, Hebrew, Greek and Latin scholar, jurist, philosopher, mathematician, physician, professor of law in the University of Naples, teacher of Pietro Giannone, one of the most learned men of his time.

159. This contest, provoked by Di Capua's claim that under certain conditions the complete circle of the rainbow could be seen, and by Aulisio's answering epigram, was an offshoot of the larger contest between the Capuists (or anti-Galenists) and Anti-Capuists, on which see the article by M. H. Fisch cited in n. 147 above.

160. As in the published first book of the *De antiquissima* (n. 168 below) Vico attributes to the ancient inhabitants of Italy his own epistemology and metaphysics, so in this sketch of the second book he attributes to the ancient Egyptians his own pantheistic physics.

161. At the time of which he speaks Vico still believed in the historicity of Pythagoras and his voyages in search of wisdom.

162. I.e., *natura* and *ingenium* were synonyms. Elsewhere (*Opere*, I, 212) Vico had said that as nature or the divine *ingenium* generates physical things, so the human *ingenium* generates mechanical objects or artifacts. For this parallel the *New Science* had later substituted that between the world of nature created by God and the world of nations created by men.

163. From the "acuteness" (*acutezza* in the metaphorical sense) of the human *ingenium* (cf. n. 141 above) Vico leaps to the "acuteness" (*acutezza* in the physical sense) of the cuneiform or wedge-shaped burin, the form assumed by feminine air when fecundated by masculine ether. (This whole passage derives ultimately from the Orphic theogony as interpreted by Stoicism and Neoplatonism and familiar to Vico in the *Philosophia perennis* of Agostino Steuco, bk. VII, ch. 10.)

164. In the *Giornale italiano* for October 6, 1804, Vincenzo Cuoco, reviewing rival British and French claims to the discovery that a magnetic sphere floating in mercury revolves on its axis in such a way as to indicate latitude and longitude, cited this paragraph as an anticipation of the principle involved. See his *Scritti vari*, ed. Cortese & Nicolini, Bari, 1924, pp. 243 f.

165. *L'homme* and *Description du corps humain*, passim; and (Vico's immediate source) Henri Du Roy: *Philosophia naturalis*, Amsterdam, 1661, bk. V, passim.

166. *Regimen in acute diseases*, Loeb Classical Library ed., vol. II.

167. If in ancient Latin *ruptum* was the generic term for diseases, must

there not have been (stemming from Pythagoras and influenced by Egyptian medicine) an ancient Italian medical school which held that diseases were caused by a rupture of some blood vessel (*vizio di solidi*) and derived the word *corruptum* (= *cum ruptum*) from the simultaneous (*cum*) rupture of all the blood vessels? Cf. *Opere*, IV–1, 336, §698.

168. The *Liber metaphysicus* or first book of the *De antiquissima*. Vico projected the *De antiquissima* as a complete system of philosophy in three books: (1) metaphysics (with an appendix on logic); (2) physics or philosophy of nature; (3) ethics. The first book (without the appendix on logic) was published in 1710. From his notes for the second book Vico put together in 1713 a manuscript *De aequilibrio corporis animantis,* referred to in the next paragraph below as having been dedicated to Aulisio. The third book was never drafted. The *De Aequilibrio* was laid aside for more than twenty years, but toward the end of 1735 Vico composed a fresh dedication for it, this time addressed to Charles of Bourbon. Not until the end of the eighteenth century, however, was it postumously published in the Neapolitan periodical *Scelta Miscellanea,* and read by Cuoco, who noted its parallels with John Brown's popular *Elementa medicinae* (1780), and urged in 1808 the publication of a "second edition." This did not materialize; the manuscript has since been lost; and no copies of the issues of the *Scelta* in which it was printed are known to be extant.

169. "Zeno, the founder of Stoicism, was currently represented in the time of Vico as having taught that the *materia prima* was composed of indivisible parts; Zeno, the Eleatic, had employed the notion of infinite divisibility in the construction of those famous puzzles on which Aristotle and so many subsequent philosophers have exercised their ingenuity; and Vico, in some inexplicable manner, fancied that these two were one, and so created for himself a Zeno who explained the origination of the many from the One by the hypothesis of indivisible metaphysical points."—Flint: *Vico*, p. 115; see pp. 115–129, and Croce: *The Philosophy of Giambattista Vico*, ch. XII, on this doctrine of metaphysical points.

170. *Opere*, I, 195–279.

171. On the Life of Caraffa, Adams, ch. IX; an essay by Croce in *Uomini e cose della vecchia Italia*, serie I, Bari, 1928, pp. 248–264; and one by Nicolini in: *Scritti vari dedicati a Mario Armanni*, Milano, 1938. On Gravina, J. G. Robertson: *Studies in the Genesis of Romantic Theory in the Eighteenth Century*, ch. II.

172. Coleridge used this sentence as a motto in his *Aids to Reflection*.

173. *Constantia* means both constancy or perpetuity and consistency or rigorously scientific character; similarly in the titles of Vico's *De constantia iurisprudentis* and of its two parts, *De constantia philosophiae* and *De constantia philologiae*, cited below.

174. So that if Vico succeeded in this he would be founding a new science.

175. This prospectus, printed without title, is known as the *Sinopsi del Diritto universale*. *Opere*, II–1, 1–16.

176. Hüber had been dead since 1694. Thomasius was still living, but Gemmingen was merely citing their works, not conveying their criticisms of the synopsis. See his letter, with Vico's marginalia, in *Opere*, V, 151 f.

177. For the parts of this letter which Vico here omits, see *Opere*, V, 42 f.

178. A copy was sent to Le Clerc, with a letter which may be found in *Opere*, V, 102 ff. There was no reply; cf. n. 188. The three volumes (*De uno, De constantia, Notae*) of which this was the third are printed in *Opere*, II-1, II-2, II-3, under the general title: *Il Diritto Universale*. Cf. Adams, chs. X–XI.

179. Actually the chair had been vacated in 1717, and Vico wrote the *Universal Law* to qualify himself for it, or for one of the seven other vacancies in the law faculty.

180. Digest 19.5.1. The other two titles were 6.1 and 15.1. (The *Digestum vetus* included books 1 through 24.2.)

181. The "new science in negative form," on which see Adams, pp. 143 f.

182. Giulio Nicola Torno (1672–1756), canon of the Naples cathedral, was ecclesiastical censor of all Vico's works from the *Universal Law* on. In 1723 he wrote a lengthy treatise against the *Civil History* of Giannone, which, though unpublished, may have given rise to Giannone's estrangement from Vico.

183. Corsini's failure to keep his promise.

184. The "first *New Science*." Adams, ch. XIII.

185. *sette de' tempi*. Cf. Whittaker: *Reason and Other Essays*, p. 169, n. 2: "What is meant is that the characteristic modes of feeling and acting in each age are as if derived from the doctrinal rule of a philosophical or religious sect concerning what is right or wrong, good or evil." Perhaps the most nearly equivalent English phrase is "climate of opinion."

186. It was not Giuseppe Attias of Leghorn, but Giuseppe ben Abraham Attias of Cordova, who published the famous edition of the Hebrew text of the Old Testament.

187. Vico notes that Attias must have reference to Le Clerc's review of the *Universal Law*.

188. The latter guess was the right one. Cf. n. 178.

189. Capece and Sangro were the outstanding leaders of the conspiracy of Macchia, whose history Vico had written. Cf. Adams, pp. 80 f.; Croce: *The Philosophy of Giambattista Vico*, pp. 250 f. Laudati was later Vico's ecclesiastical censor for the *De antiquissima* and for the two *Risposte al Giornale de' letterati*.

190. This blow of adverse fortune was the erection of another's inscriptions after Vico had been given the commission.

191. Filomarino, later Neapolitan ambassador to Spain, had been a pupil of Vico, who expounded the principles of the New Science at a gathering in his home in 1722. Croce has resided since 1911 in the Filomarino palace.

192. For an account of this case see Nicolini: *Vicende e traversie giudiziarie di Giambattista Vico*, Napoli, 1934 (estratto da *Il Tribunale*), 10–16.

193. On the Cimmino (or Cimini) salon see Adams, pp. 180 f., and the note in *Opere*, V, 122 f.

194. *Opere*, V, 89–91.

195. *Opere*, III, 291–322, with text of *Acta* notice on p. 295.

196. Bk. III, chs. 30, 38, 43; *Opere*, III, 185 ff., 204 ff., 216 f.

197. *Opere*, IV–2, pp. 275–306.

198. Probably a conciliatory letter from Lodoli.

199. Spinelli (1686–1752) had been a private pupil of Vico, and so were his sons after him. See his autobiography in: *Raccolta d'opuscoli scientifici e filologici* 49 (1753), 465–526.

200. These notes, expanded and multiplied, became the "Third Corrections, Meliorations and Additions," completed in August, 1731. A fourth set, incorporating parts of the third, was written in 1733 or 1734, and made the basis of a revision of the entire work in 1735 or 1736, the "third *New Science*," which Vico was seeing through the press at the time of his death in 1744.

201. A Jesuit father who wrote the couplet printed below Vico's portrait in the third edition of the *New Science*, and who on receiving a copy of the second edition had sent Vico a little wine from the cellar and a little bread from the oven of the Jesuit house of the Nunziatella, together with a graceful letter (*Opere*, V, 229) begging the author to accept "these trifles, simple as they are, since the infant Jesus himself did not refuse the rude offerings of rustic shepherds," and suggesting that at the side of the alphabet in the symbolic frontispiece a little dwarf should be added, dumb with astonishment like Dante's mountaineer, and that beneath him should be written, "with a significant diaeresis," the name Lodo-Vico ("I praise Vico").

202. On Vico as teacher, and on his personal appearance at this time, see the passages from Solla's life of him translated by Adams, pp. 181 f., and the notes in *Opere*, V, 127–129.

203. Phaedrus 3.9.

204. Corsini's letter is in *Opere*, V, 183 f.

205. On Vico's wife and children see Nicolini: "G. B. Vico nella vita domestica," *Archivio storico per le province napoletane* 50 (1925), 227–298.

206. Ignazio, who was a customs official at the time of his death in 1736.

207. Angela Teresa.

208. Vico's letter of application for this post is in *Opere*, V, 240 ff.; cf. Adams, pp. 197 f.

209. Vico's letter of petition is in *Opere*, V, 273 f. On Gennaro Vico see Giovanni Gentile: "Il figlio di G. B. Vico e gl'inizi dell' insegnamento di letteratura italiana nella Università di Napoli," *La Critica* 3 (1905), reprinted in: *Studi Vichiani*, Messina, 1915, 2d ed., Firenze, 1927. Gennaro's appointment was due not to Nicola de Rosa but to Celestino Galiani, who had been responsible also for Vico's appointment as royal historiographer; details in *Opere*, V, 131, 304–307; cf. Adams, pp. 199 f.

210. Villarosa's account of Vico's infirmities must be discounted in the

light of the facts that within the last fourteen months of his life Vico composed two sonnets, continued to revise the manuscript of the "third *New Science*" and began to correct the printer's proofs (making slight additions here and there), wrote out instructions for the frontispiece portrait, corresponded with Cardinal Troiano d'Acquaviva for permission to dedicate the work to him, and, only twelve or thirteen days before his death, wrote or dictated the dedication.

211. Palazzuolo had died in 1735. Vico entrusted the funeral arrangements to his father confessor, Don Nicola Merola. A document of March 2, 1744, clearing Merola of blame for the unseemly strife that delayed the funeral, is printed as an appendix in Raffaele Cotugno's *La sorte di Giovan Battista Vico*, Bari, 1914, pp. 235–241, and summarized in *Opere*, V, 132 f.

212. Vico died in the night between January 22 and 23, 1744. Besides debts and household goods, he left a collection of about a hundred paintings of the sixteenth, seventeenth, and eighteenth centuries, including a portrait of himself by Francesco Solimena. This was destroyed by fire in 1819, but Villarosa had had a copy made for the Academy of Arcadia. This copy still survives, and a photographic reproduction of it serves as frontispiece to *Opere*, V, from which our frontispiece in turn was taken.

SUPPLEMENTARY NOTES (1962)

A. In the eighteen years since our first edition appeared, Vichian studies have flourished. A revision extensive enough to take full account of the scholarship of those years was not practicable; and piety toward this first fruit of our collaboration would in any case have deterred us from changes that would make it no longer recognizable as a work of 1944. For the convenience of students, however, we mention here the major works of scholarship and of interpretation. Of scholarship: Fausto Nicolini's reworking and expansion of Croce's great bibliography of Vico (hereafter N:BV; see note T below), and his *Commento storico alla seconda Scienza nuova* (2 vols., Rome, 1949). Of interpretation: Franco Amerio, *Introduzione allo studio di G. B. Vico* (Turin, 1947; Catholic realist); Enzo Paci, *Ingens Sylva* (Milan, 1949; existentialist); Nicola Badaloni, *Introduzione a G. B. Vico* (Milan, 1961; Marxist); A. Robert Caponigri, *Time and Idea: The Theory of History in Giambattista Vico* (Chicago, 1953; reviewed by M. H. Fisch, *Journal of Philosophy* 54 [1957], 648–652). A few other works are mentioned in the following notes (nos. in parentheses after initial letters refer to pages, lines and notes of the present volume: 170.3fb means p. 170 l. 3 from bottom; 220.179 means p. 220 n. 179).

B ([v].22–26). The 1929 text and notes that we used are now superseded by those in Nicolini's one-volume *Opere* of Vico in the series *La letteratura italiana*, vol. 43 (Milan and Naples, 1953; hereafter N'53).

C (vi.11–12). Our translation of the *New Science* was published by

Cornell University Press in 1948 and, abridged and revised and with a new introduction, by Anchor Books in 1961. See notes G and S below.

D (8–10, 220.179). We relied here on the notes in the 1929 edition, but from a letter of Vico's discovered after that date (N'53, 114 f.) and from other evidence not known to us in 1944, it appears that the first morning chair of civil law was held by Domenico Campanile from 1689 until his death late in 1722, and that it was not from that chair but from one of canon law that Capasso was promoted in 1717 to the first afternoon chair of civil law, which Aulisio had held since 1694. The "first" chairs of law carried not only higher salaries but permanent tenure; the others, like Vico's chair of rhetoric, were subject to quadrennial reappointment. Aulisio's death and Capasso's promotion in 1717 gave Vico his first hope for a chair of law with tenure, and by the time of Campanile's death in 1722 Vico had reason to think himself qualified for the fulfillment of that hope. Nicolini has reconstructed his concourse speech in *Opere*, VIII, 288–297.

E (9–11). On the value of the *Universal Law* in its own right, see M. H. Fisch, "Vico on Roman Law," in *Essays in Political Theory Presented to George H. Sabine* (Cornell University Press, 1948), 62–88.

F (38–46). See Arthur Child, "Making and Knowing in Hobbes, Vico, and Dewey," *Univ. of Calif. Pubs. in Philosophy*, 16 (1953), 271–310.

G (48). A somewhat different, and we believe a more accurate, account of Vico's *diritto naturale delle genti* is given in the Anchor Book edition of the *New Science*, pp. xxx–xxxv. For reasons there given, we now render the phrase "natural law of the gentes"; and we recommend that the reader substitute "gentes" for "peoples" in this phrase above on pages 48 (twice), 53, 166 (twice), 169 (twice), 171, 187, 192, and for "nations" on 119 (but let "nations" stand on 167 and 172 where it translates *nazioni*); and substitute "gentes" for "peoples" at 170.5fb and for "races" at 170.3fb.

H (67 f.). Robert T. Clark, Jr., "Herder, Cesarotti and Vico," *Studies in Philology*, 44 (1947), 645–671, shows that some of Vico's ideas reached Herder as early as 1770 through Denis's German translation of Ossian with notes translated by Denis from Cesarotti.

I (69, 83, 214.97). The Scottish historian John Gillies refers to Vico in his *History of Ancient Greece* (1786), I, 42 n.; *A View of the Reign of Frederick II of Prussia* (1789), 30; *The History of the World* (1807), I, 652 n. See Duncan Forbes in *The Cambridge Journal* 7 (1954), 658 f.

J (72). Paul Hazard, *La pensée européenne au xviiième siècle* (Paris, 1946), 333, says, "Montesquieu in his personal notes was struck by a theory of Vico's, that of the *corsi* and *ricorsi*," but withholds his evidence.

K (85–87). For some further details and a correction, see Duncan Forbes, *The Liberal Anglican Idea of History* (Cambridge University Press, 1952), 17, 156 f. But Arnold's letter to Ellis (155) may refer to the second volume of Ellis's *Outlines of General History* (1830), pages 33, 37, 44, 45.

L (104–107). N:BV 704–705, 713–715, points out minor inexactnesses and finds the spiritual gulf between Vico and Marx greater, and the historical connections more tenuous, than is here acknowledged.

M (117.23–27). It is now agreed that this sentence does not belong in the text. Read: ". . . coherent in all its parts. For, though already . . ."

N (121.10fb). Following N'53, read "physical" for "metaphysical."

O (139, 154, 155). See Guido Fasso: *I "quattro auttori" del Vico* (Milan, 1949). The "new edition" of Grotius (155.14) has been identified by Dario Faucci in *Giornale storico della letteratura italiana* 136 (1959), 97–104.

P (144.12). Read: "invites and incites us" etc.

Q (157.11). Read: "published in 1720 a prospectus" etc.

R (180.4). N'53 reads *tanta*, great, in place of *santa*, saintly.

S (211.46; 212.48, 50–59). See the correspondingly numbered paragraphs of our translation of the *New Science*, preferably in the Anchor Book edition, in which we more frequently render *cose* "institutions," as we would now do above at 58.2 (in place of "things"); 139.5 (in place of "affairs"); 155.8 (read: "on the one hand the history, whether fabulous or certain, of institutions, and on the other hand the history of the three languages" etc.); 155.4fb and 3fb (in place of "things"); 156.8fb (read: "divine and human institutions I shall also treat: their origin" etc.); 157.4 (in place of "matters"); 165.4 and 167.5 (read: "various institutions that arose" etc.); 169.5fb (in place of "affairs"). We would now translate *stati* "maturity" instead of "acme" above at 55.3fb, 139.5, 169.9.

T (212.60). The bibliography and its supplements have been incorporated, rewritten, and expanded in Benedetto Croce, *Bibliografia Vichiana accresciuta e rielaborata da Fausto Nicolini* (2 vols., Naples, 1947–1948).

U (213.72). The plan for this volume was abandoned and the essay here referred to remains unpublished.

V (214.93). N:BV 238 f. thinks Lomonaco's story is incompatible with Vico's own statement at the bottom of p. 182 above, and guesses that in the oral tradition of the episode London was at some point substituted for Venice. (To 214.94 add: VIII, 264, 301.)

W (215.115). Add: *Encyclopaedia Americana* (1832), article on Vico; James M. Walker, review of Michelet's translations, *Southern Quarterly Review* 2 (1842), 404–416; George F. Holmes, "Schlegel's Philosophy of History," *ibid.* 3 (1843), 263–317, at 274–279; Orestes A. Brownson, "The Philosophy of History," *Democratic Review,* 1843, reprinted in his *Works,* IV, 361–423, at 393–401; Charles Sumner, *The Law of Human Progress* (Boston, 1849), 14–15.

X (215.128). See the essay on Vico by M. Lifshitz in *Philosophy and Phenomenological Research* 8 (1948), 391–414.

Y (217.147; 218.159). The promised essay appeared as "The Academy of the Investigators" in *Science, Medicine and History* (Oxford University Press, 1953), I, 521–563. See also Biagio de Giovanni, *Filosofia e diritto in Francesco D'Andrea* (Milan, 1958), and Badaloni (note A above).

Z (220.191). Croce died in 1952, but the Istituto Italiano per gli Studi Storici, using his library, lives on in the palace.

CHRONOLOGICAL TABLE

CHRONOLOGICAL TABLE

A.D.	VICO	NAPLES (Ruled by Spanish viceroys 1509-1707)	NORTHERN ITALY AND EUROPE
1668	Born at Naples June 23.	Academy of Investiganti (founded 1650) discontinued by order of viceroy.	Giornale de Letterati, first Italian periodical, founded at Rome.
1669			Hobbes: Leviathan (Latin ed.). Marchetti at Pisa revises his Italian translation of Lucretius.
1670		Death of Carlo Buragna.	Marchetti forbidden to publish; ms. copies begin to circulate and multiply. Spinoza: Tractatus theologico-politicus. Pascal: Pensées.
1671		Spread of Cartesianism alarms Inquisition. Nicola Capasso born.	More: Enchiridion metaphysicum.
1672		Academy of Infuriati lapses until 1690.	Addison and Muratori born. Pufendorf: De iure naturae et gentium. Cumberland: De legibus naturae.
1673 1674 1675 1676 1677	Falls and fractures his skull.	Giannone born.	Malebranche: Recherche de la vérité. Death of Spinoza. Antonio Conti born. Spinoza: Opera posthuma (Ethica, etc.).
1678 1679	Returns to grammar school. Skipped to second grade.		Cudworth: True Intellectual System. Death of Hobbes. Christian Wolff born. Bossuet: Histoire universelle.
1680	Transferred to Jesuit grammar school, second grade.		Borelli: De motu animalium.

1681	Completes grammar and "humanity" course by study of Alvarez at home; begins philosophy course under Balzo. Abandons studies for year and a half.	Lionardo di Capua: Parere. Di Capua-d'Aulisio controversy. Gravina at University.	Mabillon: De re diplomatica.
1682			Acta Eruditorum founded at Leipzig. Petty: Political Arithmetic.
1683	Returns to Jesuit school and is taught by Ricci.	Marquis of Carpio viceroy 1683–87. Academy of Investiganti revived.	
1684	Studies Suarez at home. Hears Aquadia at University. Attends private law course of Verde.	Di Capua: Lezioni . . . delle Mofete. Death of Tommaso Cornelio; public funeral secured by Francesco d'Andrea.	
1685	Studies Vulteius on civil and Canisius on canon law.	Scarlatti's first opera produced.	Berkeley born.
1686	Coached by Del Vecchio; defends father in court in June. Spends nine years as tutor to Roccas at Vatolla, with occasional visits to Naples (1686–1695).	Visits of Mabillon and Burnet. Inquisition prosecutes "atheists" (1686–93).	
1687			Newton: Principia. Bouhours: La manière de bien penser. Perrault: Parallèle des anciens et des modernes.
1688		Valletta's library opened to students. Cornelio: Progymnasmata physica (2d ed.).	Fontenelle: Digression sur les anciens et les modernes.
1689	Matriculated at University school of law.	Di Capua: Parere (2d ed.). Visit of Leibniz in November. Academy of Infuriati revived.	
1690	Conversation with Lubrano. Studies Deschamps.		Academy of Arcadia founded at Rome. Temple: Ancient and modern learning. Locke: Essay; Civil Government. Arnauld hears from Naples that "young fools are turned atheist and Epicurean by reading Gassendi."
1691		Papal delegate expelled. Caloprese: Concione di Marfisa.	
1692	Affetti di un disperato. Elected to Academy of Uniti.	Academy of Infuriati reorganized as Academy of Uniti. Vico's friends Cristofaro, Galizia and Giannelli stigmatized by Inquisition.	

CHRONOLOGICAL TABLE (*continued*)

A.D.	VICO	NAPLES (Ruled by Spanish viceroys 1509–1707)	NORTHERN ITALY AND EUROPE
1693	In morte di Antonio Caraffa.	Ravaged by plague and earthquake. Inquisition condemns Vico's friends.	Locke: Thoughts concerning education. Di Capua's Parere placed on Index. Death of Pufendorf.
1694	LL.D., University of Naples (Salerno). Panegyric of Elector Maximilian. Epithalamium Maximilian-Theresa.	Giovanni della Casa's poems published with notes by Caloprese and others.	Wotton: Reflections upon ancient and modern learning.
1695	Resumes residence at Naples. Epithalamium Mazzacane-Rocca.	Death of Di Capua; memorial meeting of Academy of Investiganti. Di Capua: Parere (3d ed.)	Leibniz: Système nouveau de la nature.
1696	Contributes to San Estevan volume. Epithalamium Carafa-Cantelmo.		Gravina: Discorso delle antiche favole.
1697	Funeral oration, Caterina d'Aragona. Defeated for city clerkship.		Bayle: Dictionnaire historique et critique.
1698	Competes for chair of rhetoric.	Academy Medinaceli founded. Death of Francesco d'Andrea. Visit of Montfaucon Oct. 28–Nov. 10.	Metastasio born.
1699	Professor of Rhetoric (1699–1741). Marries Teresa Caterina Destito. Elected to Academy Medinaceli. Reads "Delle cene suntuose de' Romani." Inaugural Oration I.		
1700	Inaugural Oration II. Daughter Luisa born.	Doria: Vita civile.	War of Spanish Succession 1700–13. Berlin Academy of Sciences founded with Leibniz as president.
1701		Visit of Addison. Conspiracy of Macchia, Sept. 23. Capece and Sangro executed. Gravina: De ortu et progressu iuris civilis.	

1702	Panegyric of Philip V. De parthenopea coniuratione.	Visit of Philip V, April 17–June 2. Academy Medinaceli disbanded.	
1703	Inaugural Oration III. Inaugural Oration IV. Professorship confirmed.	Reform of University.	Orsi: Considerazioni sulla maniera del ben pensare. Death of Locke and Bossuet.
1704			Addison: Remarks on Italy. Thomasius: Fundamenta iuris naturalis et gentium.
1705	Inaugural Oration V.		Muratori: Della perfetta poesia italiana.
1706	Inaugural Oration VI. Son Ignazio born. Begins to study Bacon.		
1707		Austrian occupation; Naples ruled by Austrian viceroys 1707–1734.	Death of Mabillon.
1708	Capece-Sangro memorial volume.		Gravina: Della ragion poetica. Montfaucon: Paléographie grecque. Berkeley: New theory of vision. Journal des savants reviews Vico's book.
1709	De nostri temporis studiorum ratione. Begins reading Grotius.		
1710	Elected to Academy of Arcadia. De antiquissima Italorum sapientia.	Nicola Amenta: Vita di Lionardo di Capua.	Berkeley: Principles of human knowledge. Leibniz: Théodicée. Giornale de' Letterati (Maffei & Zeno), 1710–36.
1711	Polemic with Giornale de' Letterati. De aequilibrio corporis animantium (ms. Liber physicus).	Shaftesbury in residence 1711–13.	Gravina secession from Arcadia. Shaftesbury: Characteristicks. Hume born.
1712	Institutiones oratoriae (ms.). Civil censor for Gravina: Tragedie cinque.	Visit of Brenckmann.	Addison & Steele: The Spectator.
1713	Dedicates De aequilibrio to Aulisio.	Death of Shaftesbury. Gravina: De origine iuris, 2d ed. Death of Valletta and Caloprese.	Conti and Martelli in France.
1714			Leibniz: Monadologie; letter to Bourguet.

CHRONOLOGICAL TABLE (*continued*)

A.D.	VICO	NAPLES (Ruled by Austrian viceroys *1707-1734*)	NORTHERN ITALY AND EUROPE
1715	Son Gennaro born.	Gravina: Della tragedia.	Conti in England. Death of Louis XIV. Death of Leibniz.
1716 1717	De rebus gestis Antonii Caraphaei. Annotates Grotius. Daughter Luisa married.	Sojourn of Berkeley 1717-19. Death of Caravita and Aulisio. Promotion of Capasso.	Marchetti's Lucretius printed in London.
1718	Made a grandfather by birth of Luisa's first child.	Metastasio enters law office of Vico's friend Castagnola.	Marchetti's Lucretius placed on Index. Death of Gravina. Conti returns to Paris, Martelli to Bologna.
1719 1720	Inaugural Oration on universal law. Edits Raccolta Carafa-Borghese. Sinopsi del Diritto Universale. De uno universi iuris principio et fine uno.	Schrottembach viceroy 1719-21.	Montfaucon: L'antiquité expliquée. Death of Addison.
1721	De constantia iurisprudentis. Giunone in danza.	Metastasio collaborates with Vico in Raccolta Filomarino-Caracciolo.	Montesquieu: Lettres Persanes.
1722	Notae (to De uno & De constantia). Receives letter from Jean Le Clerc.	Doria: Opere matematiche. Descartes: Principia, tr. by Giuseppa Barbapiccola. Althann viceroy 1722-28.	Pouilly: Dissertation sur l'incertitude de l'histoire des quatres premiers siècles de Rome.
1723	Defeated for chair of civil law. Origine, progresso e caduta della poesia italiana.	Giannone: Istoria civile del Regno di Napoli. Death of Lucantonio Porzio.	Muratori: Rerum Italicarum Scriptores (1723-51).
1724	"Scienza nuova in forma negativa." Funeral oration, Anna d'Aspermont.	Ciccarelli publishes Boccaccio's commentary on Dante.	Lafitau: Moeurs des sauvages amériquains comparées aux moeurs des premiers temps. Kant born.

1725	Autobiography, Part A sent to Porcia in June; Part B drafted in December. Scienza nuova, 1st ed, October. Appraises Valletta's library.		Hutcheson: Our ideas of beauty and virtue.
1726			Conti returns to Italy. Butler: Sermons. Voltaire in England 1726-29. Death of Newton.
1727	Funeral Oration, Angela Cimini.		
1728	Autobiography, Part B revised and sent to Porcia with corrections of Part A in March.	Doria: Filosofia di Paolo Mattia Doria, con la quale si schiarisce quella di Platone.	Porcia's "Proposal" and Vico's Autobiography published in Calogerà's Raccolta at Venice. Montesquieu in Venice. Wolff: Philosophia rationalis.
1729	Notae in Acta Eruditorum Lipsiensia. Demands return of ms. from Venice in December.	Visit of Montesquieu. Ignacio de Luzán studies at Naples 1729-33.	European epidemic of grippe, winter 1729-30. Metastasio becomes court poet at Vienna.
1730	Elected to Academy of Assorditi. Scienza nuova, 2d ed, December. Correzioni, miglioramenti e aggiunte (CMA) I. Notes on Horace: Ars poetica (ms.)		Hamann born. Cardinal Lorenzo Corsini elected Pope Clement XII. Wolff: Philosophia prima sive ontologia.
1731	Continues Autobiography to 1731. Contributes dedicatory epistle and preface to Belli's Italian translation of Fracastoro's Syphilis. CMA II, January; CMA III (ms.), August.		Cudworth: Eternal and Immutable Morality.
1732	Inaugural Oration "De mente heroica."	Doria: Difesa della metafisica degli antichi filosofi contro Giovanni Locke ed alcuni altri moderni autori. Academy of Oziosi (del Salerno) founded.	Moser: Vollständiger Bericht. Berkeley: Alciphron. Pope: Essay on Man.
1733			
1734	As head of University delegation, congratulates Charles of Bourbon.	Kingdom of Naples conquered by Charles of Bourbon.	Montesquieu: Grandeur et décadence des Romains. Voltaire: Lettres sur les Anglais. Berkeley: Analyst.

CHRONOLOGICAL TABLE (continued)

A.D.	VICO	NAPLES (Ruled by Bourbon kings 1734-1860)	NORTHERN ITALY AND EUROPE
1735	Appointed Royal Historiographer. Elected to Academy of Oziosi. Dedicates De aequilibrio to King Charles.	Excavations begun at Herculaneum. Reform of University by Celestino Galiani. Academy of Investiganti revived by Stefano di Stefano.	Baumgarten: De nonnullis ad poema pertinentibus. Blackwell: Life and writings of Homer. Berkeley: Querist. Linnaeus: Systema naturae.
1736	Son Gennaro begins to assume some of his teaching duties. Death of son Ignazio.	Damiano Romano: Difesa istorica delle leggi Greche venute in Roma contro . . . G. B. Vico.	Death of Le Clerc. Wolff: Theologia naturalis.
1737	Delivers annual opening address of Academy of Oziosi, of which he is now custode.	Academy of Investiganti ceases with death of Stefano di Stefano.	Ignacio de Luzán: Poética (praises Vico).
1738	Oration for marriage of King Charles with Maria-Amalia of Saxony-Poland.	Genovesi begins to frequent Vico's home.	Beaufort: L'incertitude des cinq premiers siècles de l'histoire romaine. Warburton: Divine legation of Moses. Hume: Treatise of human nature.
1739			Wolff: Ius naturae.
1740			Kant enters University of Königsberg. Accession of Frederick the Great.
1741	Succeeded in professorship by son Gennaro.		Hume: Essays. Death of Montfaucon.
1742			Jacobi born.
1743			Herder born. Rousseau in Venice.
1744	Dies on January 22-23. Scienza nuova, 3d ed.	Damiano Romano: L'origine della giurisprudenza romana contro . . . G. B. Vico.	Muratori: Annali d'Italia. Berkeley: Siris. First authorized reprinting of Galileo's Dialogo of 1632.

INDEX

Index of Personal Names

[Vico's name is excluded. Numerals of the roman fount refer to the Introduction (pp. 1–107) and the Translation (pp. 111–209) by page number; numerals of the *italic* fount, to the Notes by note number; numerals preceded by an apostrophe, to the Chronological Table by year.]